THE GLORY OF GARDENS

THE GLORY OF GARDENS

2,000 YEARS OF WRITINGS ON GARDEN DESIGN

EDITED BY **SCOTT J. TILDEN**

Abrams, New York

previous spread:
SERIYU-EN, OR GARDEN OF THE CLEAR
STREAM (James Irvine Garden)
(designed in 1979 by Takeo Uesugi)
Robert Landau/CORBIS

This book is dedicated to my mentor in gardening, Clara Gordon Hight, and to my mentor in life, Cheryl Prentiss Anderson.

This book project has been made possible in part by a grant from The Graham Foundation for Advanced Studies in the Fine Arts.

ACKNOWLEDGMENTS

First and foremost, I want to thank my wife, Cheryl Anderson, for her enthusiasm for this book project. On winter nights, we sat by the fire proofreading texts, a tiring task (100,000 words) made pleasurable by her company.

I want to express my gratitude to the professionals at Harry N. Abrams, Inc., for their unflagging support of this book project, despite my missing a deadline. The acquiring editor, Margaret Kaplan, championed the project and provided valuable counsel about organizing the material and enhancing the quality of the reader's experience. My editor, Barbara Burn, gave me the encouragement I needed to make judicious cuts in the texts and complete the book, as well as reviewing and correcting text. The designer, Henk van Assen, presents the images and words in a cohesive composition. Leslie Dutcher schooled me in the ways of copyright law and permission fees. Karina Kabigting of Corbis helped me select images from the company's excellent collection of garden photographs.

Scholars and faculty at various universities shaped my research, including Reuben Rainey, Keith N. Morgan, Robert Bruegmann, Nasser Rabbat, Melanie Simo, D. Fairchild Ruggles, Nerina Rustomji, Peter Grilli, James Wescoat, Jr., John Dixon Hunt, Glaire Anderson, Marc P. Keane, David Slawson, and Joseph Disponzio. Landscape architect Kathryn Gustafson graciously agreed to an interview. Both Ms. Gustafson and James van Sweden provided suggestions for additional designers to include in this book. Peter Walker, Shiro Nakane, and Christophe Girot wrote original essays for the book. I also want to thank the scholars, artists, garden designers, and landscape architects who provided permissions to use their writings and translations and waived their fees, including Robert Dash, Basil Guy, James van Sweden, W.M. Thackston, Rick Darke, and Fernando Caruncho. Thanks to Piet Oudolf, James van Sweden, Aaron Kiley, Robert Dash, Heidi Gildemeister, Rick Darke, and Steve Martino for use of their beautiful images. A very special thank-you to Paul Rocheleau, my frequent and favorite collaborator, and his wife, Elaine, for providing me with exquisite transparencies of American gardens.

I appreciate the help of the librarians at Harvard, Columbia, Cornell, Princeton, and Yale Universities and the LuEsther T. Mertz Library of the New York Botanical Garden. In particular I appreciate the efforts of Stephen Sinon and Marie Long at NYBG, Martha Walker and Ann Beyer at Cornell, and Susan Brady at the Yale Center for British Art.

In closing, I want to thank the permissions and rights staff of numerous publishing houses. Without their cooperation this book would not have been possible.

God Almighty first planted a Garden. And indeed it is the purest of human pleasures. It is the greatest refreshment to the spirits of man; without which buildings and palaces are but gross handiworks; and a man shall ever see that when ages grow to civility and elegancy, men come to build stately sooner than to garden finely; as if gardening were the greater perfection.

Francis Bacon (1561–1626) English philosopher, essayist, jurist, and statesman

Nowadays families of wealth and honor store up money until they accumulate tens of thousands (of taels). Yet they hide their fame and do not build (grand) residences, or if they build such homes they do not build gardens. . .I am obsessed (pi) with giving priority to the garden and relegating the house to second place. This is because a house is adequate for my body, but it is not enough for my eyes and ears. And the personal fulfillment of a garden is not just a matter of one's [own] life, but extends to sons and grandsons.

Wang Shizhen (1634–1711), Qing dynasty poet

Every emperor and ruler, when he has retired from audience, and has finished his public duties, must have a garden in which he may stroll, look around, and relax his heart. If he has a suitable place for this it will refresh his mind and regulate his emotions, but if he has not, he will become engrossed in sensual pleasures and lose his will power.

Qian Long (1711–1799), Qing dynasty emperor

I have often thought that if heaven had given me choice of my position and calling, it should have been on a rich spot on earth, well watered, and near a good market for the productions of the garden. No occupation is so delightful to me as the culture of the earth, and no culture comparable to that of the garden.

Thomas Jefferson (1743–1826), third U.S. president, botanist, and garden designer

But Ellison maintained that the richest, the truest, and most natural, if not altogether the most extensive province, had been unaccountably neglected. No definition had spoken of the landscape-gardener as of the poet; yet it seemed to my friend that the creation of the landscape-garden offered to the proper Muse the most magnificent of opportunities. Here, indeed, was the fairest field for the display of imagination in the endless combining of forms of novel beauty; the elements to enter into combination being, by a vast superiority, the most glorious which the earth could afford.

Edgar Allan Poe (1809–1849), American poet and short story writer

In none of the arts as surely as in gardening can a man of moderately poetic temperament, moderate capacity of study, moderate command of time for the purpose, produce works of a distinctive character that shall be thoroughly respectable. The effort it has already cost some millions of Americans to obtain a wretchedly small degree of success in versifying, music, acting, drawing, painting, carving, embroidery, or a hundred of the smaller decorative arts, if it had been given to study in gardening would have secured a distinguished success.

Frederick Law Olmsted (1822–1903), American landscape architect

"Eternal gardening is the price of liberty" is a motto that I should put over the gateway of my garden, if I had a gate. And yet it is not wholly true; for there is no liberty in gardening. The man who undertakes a garden is relentlessly pursued. He felicitates himself, that, when he gets it once planted, he will have a season of rest and of enjoyment in the sprouting and growing of his seeds. It is a green anticipation. He has planted a seed that will keep him awake nights; drive rest from his bones, and sleep from his pillow.

Charles Dudley Warner (1829–1900), newspaper editor and co-author with Mark Twain of *The Gilded Age*

CONTENTS

KINKAKU-JI (The Golden Pavilion)
(c. 1398)
Kyoto, Japan
Dallas and John Heaton/CORBIS

INTRODUCTION

Through all the variations, due to climate, country, history, and the natural idiosyncrasy of man, which have appeared in the evolution of the garden through successive civilizations, certain principles remain constant however much their application may change. —Sylvia Crowe

The Glory of Gardens is a sourcebook of writings on the principles of garden design by more than one hundred prominent garden designers and landscape architects. The writings cover a two-thousand-year time span and include the garden traditions of Western, Islamic, Japanese, and Chinese civilizations. My goal in creating this book is similar to that of the authors of ancient and medieval agricultural manuals and secret texts, such as the Roman scholar Varro, the Andalusian agronomist Ibn Luyun, and the Buddhist priest Zoen, who sought to share with their readers teachings of the foremost experts on garden design and horticultural practices. I chose to include the writings of other pivotal thinkers on gardens, including poets (Alexander Pope and al-Maqqari), statesmen (Thomas Jefferson and Emperor Qian Long), philosophers and scientists (Johann Wolfgang von Goethe and Michel Eugène Chevreul), and architects (Le Corbusier and Andrea Palladio).

My original motivation for collecting these garden texts stemmed from a desire to design a series of gardens at my home in northwestern Connecticut. Like English historian and garden designer Horace Walpole, I believed that "In general it is probably true, that the possessor, if he has any taste, must be the best designer of his own improvements. He sees his situation in all seasons of the year, at all times of the day. He knows where beauty will not clash with convenience, and observes in his silent walks or accidental rides a thousand hints that must escape a person who in a few days sketches out a pretty picture, but has not had leisure to examine the details and relations of every part."

I thought my initial clumsy efforts resulted not from a lack of taste but from a lack of knowledge. I began to purchase contemporary garden books. The more I read, the more I longed for a broader historical and stylistic understanding of garden design. I wanted to learn directly from the masters.

My research quickly became an end in itself, because of the fascinating nature of the subject, the eloquence of the authors, and in some cases their humor. I chose to limit my explorations to original writings by leading practitioners and thinkers of each period, because secondary sources by contemporary historians and designers are readily available. For four years, I traveled to libraries at Harvard, Columbia, Cornell, Princeton, and Yale and to the LuEsther T. Mertz Library of the New York Botanical Garden. I developed this book to share these important writings with gardeners, professionals, scholars, and students.

The focus of *The Glory of Gardens* is on one type of garden—the pleasure garden—with only secondary attention paid to vegetable gardens, orchards, memorials, public parks, corporate campuses, cemeteries, and arboretums. I disagree with John Ruskin that a "flower-garden is an ugly thing, even when best managed." I share the prejudice of Aztec rulers who favored pleasure gardens over utilitarian gardens. Spanish explorer and physician Cervantes de Salazar wrote: "In this flower garden Montezuma did not allow any vegetables or fruit to be grown, saying that it was not kingly to cultivate plants for utility or profit. He said the vegetable gardens and orchards were for slaves or merchants."

Whether Aztec or French, every great culture has developed a distinctive garden style based on those of their predecessors and on new ideas from their own society. Many designers share common ideas across cultures and time, such as remaining true to the spirit of the existing landscape while planning a garden. Seventh-century Chinese Tang-dynasty poet Yao He stated: "The important thing is the shape of the land." Eighteenth-century English poet Alexander Pope wrote in 1731: "Always consult the *genius loci*, the spirit of the place in everything." Some writers decry the human tendency to ignore the inherent qualities of the land and completely transform it. Ming-dynasty garden designer Xiao Jiucheng comments, "Of the famous scenic spots I have visited, those which have been constructed by human effort are the product of waste and hard work, while those that have accommodated (yin) what was formerly there are the product of frugality and leisure." Seventeenth-century Dutch poet Godefridus Udemans observes,

> . . . And then daring to tax God's patience, they take pains,
> As if they are short of work, to raise hills from the plains.
> To little ponds, the land is minced, most willfully
> And he's the greatest man, who spoils most skillfully!

But the differences in thinking are just as apparent. Some writers advocate a formal, geometric style, others an informal, natural style. Some suggest using exotic plants whereas others urge the planting of native flowers, shrubs, and trees. Differences also result from advances in scientific understanding of garden organisms and practices. In 1704 François Gentil maintained that "Earth-Worms are very apt to gnaw the Roots of Plants when they come at them, for which Reason one ought to suffer as few of them in a Garden as possible." In 1881 Charles Darwin argued for the high value of these animals. "Worms have played a more important part in the history of the world than most persons would at first suppose. . . . Worms prepare the ground in an excellent manner for the growth of fibrous-rooted plants and for seedlings of all kinds."

Differences also exist in cultural attitudes about teaching the fundamental principles of garden design. Zheng Yuanxun observed: "The hundred arts of the ancients have all been transmitted in books. Why is garden-making the sole exception? It is said that there are many different factors which determine a garden's appropriateness and yet there are no fixed rules. This being so, there is nothing transmittable." But what is transmittable in this book is the history of garden design theories, which change by continent and century. The authors describe garden systems, each with their own laws, axioms, and models. By steeping oneself in these texts on garden tenets and traditions, one learns not so much what to do as how to think as one develops garden plans.

My gardening and editing efforts have been equally joyful and frustrating. Sun, water, and soil limit the work of the gardener, as do the peculiarities of subject and language limit the writer or editor. This book does not include essays of arguably the two most influential garden designers of France and England. André Le Nôtre created the French formal garden style at the châteaux and parks of Vaux-le-Vicomte and Versailles. Lancelot "Capability" Brown developed the English landscape style at such estates as Stowe, Croome Court, and Chatsworth. Yet neither designer wrote extensively about his life's work or only briefly in letters. To understand Le Nôtre's system of design, you must read *La Théorie et la Pratique du Jardinage* by Antoine-Joseph Dezallier d'Argenville. Humphry Repton's *Red Books* and *Fragments on the Theory and Practice of Landscape Gardening* help today's reader understand the principles of the English landscape style.

In other cases, landscape architects have written extensively, but not about pleasure gardens. One example is America's most famous landscape architect, Frederick Law Olmsted, whose best-known design is Central Park in New York City and whose garden writings focus almost exclusively on public parks, university campuses, and large private estates. The noted Olmsted scholar Charles Beveridge kindly referred me to a single brief article by Olmsted in an 1888 edition of *Garden and Forest* magazine entitled "Plans for Small Places." Modern landscape architect Lawrence Halprin has written mostly on urban design and creativity. Excerpts from Dezallier, Repton, and Olmsted are included in *The Glory of Gardens*.

My greatest limitation, however, in putting this book together was not the peculiarities of the subject but my lack of fluency in multiple languages. Someone undertaking the task of collecting writings on garden design should at the very least be proficient in English, Arabic, Chinese, Japanese, Spanish, French, and German, or should have the financial resources to assemble an army of translators. Unfortunately, I lacked both, so I had to rely on available English translations, which I tracked down in books, journals, and through the recommendations made by university faculty. Given this constraint, a disproportionate number of designers in this book come from Western traditions, and designers from Islamic, Japanese, and Chinese traditions are underrepresented. I would have preferred an equal number of texts from each of the garden traditions, instead of such a concentration on Western designers.

Although it is hard to believe, many classics of garden design have never been translated into English. For example, scholars tell me that English translations are unavailable of the complete texts of important Islamic agricultural manuals by Ibn Wahshiya, Ibn Wafid, Abu al-Khayr, Ibn Bassal, Ibn Luyun, and Ibn al-Awwam. English translations of classic Asian texts are also few and far between. Much credit goes to Alison Hardie, Marc Keane, and David Slawson for their excellent translations of the *Yuan Ye, Sakuteiki,* and *Senzui narabi ni yagyo no zu.* Selections from these Chinese and Japanese design manuals are included in *The Glory of Gardens*.

Finally, I would have liked to include more contemporary designers, but most focus their attention on creating designs and not on writing about design. Some of the most exciting landscape architects come from non–English-speaking countries and translations are unavailable. (If readers know of translations of garden texts not included in this book, I would appreciate your letting me know through my publisher. My research continues.)

Near the end of this book project, I learned about a similar book, *Les Jardins* by Michel Baridon. The noted garden history scholar John Dixon Hunt brought this excellent book to my attention, and I highly recommend it to readers of French texts. My book differs from Mr. Baridon's in its exclusive focus on pleasure gardens, its language (English), and its larger number of designers from outside France.

In closing, I should mention that anyone visiting my home in Connecticut would be disappointed by my gardening efforts. I have spent so much time on research and on editing this book that I have had little time left for my own gardens. They are living proof that know-ledge gained and not applied counts for little. Or as eighteenth-century author Henry Home put it more eloquently in his book *Gentleman Farmer,* "Writers on agriculture, very few excepted, deliver their precepts from a study lined with books, without even pretending to experience. Principles and propositions are assumed on the authority of former writers; opinions pass current from generation to generation; and no person enquires whether they wear the livery of truth."

A note to readers. There are numerous examples of archaic spellings, non-standard punctuation, and other grammatical errors in this book. These are not errors but the result of an accurate transcription of the original text. I only made changes if the spellings made the text difficult to understand.

1

PRINCIPLES

The advice given here is no copy-book rule,

Picked up second-hand, read in books, learned at school,

But the fruit of hard labour and personal test

To which I have sacrificed pleasure and rest.

Walafrid Strabo (809–849), German Benedictine abbot, theologian, and poet

Four fundamental Maxims to be observ'd.

Art must give place to nature.

Gardens should not be made dull and gloomy, by clouding them with

Thickets and too much Cover….

Gardens should not lay too open, so that it is needless to go into them….

A Garden should always look bigger than it really is.

Jean Baptiste Alexandre Le Blond (1679–1719), French architect and garden designer

previous spread:
J. IRWIN MILLER HOUSE (designed
in 1952 by Eero Saarinen) and GARDEN
(1953, Dan Kiley)
Columbus, Indiana
Aaron Kiley

opposite:
GARDEN OF MASTER OF NETS
(1440, 1770, 1940)
Suzhou, Jiangsu Province, China
Carl and Ann Purcell/CORBIS

QI BIAOJIA
CREATING A CHINESE GARDEN (1636)

Qi Biaojia (1602–1645) was granted leave from his post with the Censorate during the reign of the Chong Zhen emperor (1635) and returned to his home in Shanyin in Zhejiang province. He documented the creation of his retirement garden in *Footnotes to Allegory Mountain* in 1636. The following text, translated by Duncan Campbell, was published in 1999.

My home is in Mei Zizhen's Village of the Superior Man, that is, along the Shanyin Road. Here I am surrounded by solitary isles such as that of Fang Gang and half bays like that once owned by Censor He Zhizhang. All that I have taken possession of myself, however, is the tiny hillock that stands besides my home, as if by virtue of a fate predestined me. Its name is "Allegory Mountain."

When I was still a little boy, my brother Jichao and my cousin Zhixiang obtained this hill in exchange for a bushel of millet. They cleared it of stone and planted it in pine, hewing the land and humping away the stones until their hands were callused and their feet blistered. I too, at that time, would pole my way here by small boat, often to play games in the mud.

More than twenty years on, the pines have grown tall and the rocks, now weathered, have acquired the patina of age. All of a sudden, my brother Jichao decided to renounce the world and took tonsure as a Buddhist monk. Zhixiang, for his part, constructed Axe-Handle Garden to serve as his retreat from officialdom. He gave over the southern slopes of the mountain in order that a pagoda be built to commemorate Master Wheat Waves, whilst the remainder of the site was left fallow, to revert to dense and overgrown vegetation. Having myself retired from office on the pretext of ill health, I happened past this place and the scenes and emotions of twenty years ago came flooding back into my mind's eye. As soon as the idea of building myself a garden had formed itself in

my mind, moreover, it seemed to acquire an urgency all of its own and there was no putting a stop to my urge. What follows, then, is a complete account of the creation of my garden.

When the project began, all I desired were four or five structures. But guests came by to pay their calls upon me there and, pointing this way and that, they declared: "Here you should site a pavilion" or "This site is perfect for a gazebo." I was unmoved by their comments, objecting in my mind that this was not at all in keeping with my own original intentions. After another turn or two through my estate, however, unconsciously, I found myself most discomforted to discover that their words had taken possession of my soul. Yes, indeed, I could not be without that pavilion there or this gazebo here. And before one stage of construction was completed, I found new ideas and novel conceptions occurring to me at every turn. Whenever I came to the end of a path or trod upon a dangerous track, I would tax my mind to come up with unexpected conceits as if heavenly inspired, to the extent that I would continue to do so even in my dreams. Thus, as my enthusiasm for the project was roused, so too did my fascination for it grow more intense. I would set off there at the crack of dawn to return only as the sun was setting. The various bothersome family affairs that I was obliged to deal with I would now do so only once the candles had been lit. Impatiently I would lie upon my pillow waiting for the dawn to shoot forth its first tongues of light whereupon I would order the serving lads to make ready my boat and set off, wishing all the time that the three *li* we had to cover to get to the site were but a single step away. I was heedless of the extreme cold or the scorching heat, the goose bumps on my flesh or the sweat that ran down my spine. Not even the most violent of storms could deter me from setting off in my boat each morning. When groping around at the head of my bed at night and finding that my cash reserve was exhausted, a sense of desolation would come over me. Yet the moment I reached the mountain again the next day and began to wander about I would worry that the rocks I had bought and the timber I had stored away were yet insufficient for the task at hand. Thus have I emptied my purse these past two years. I have fallen ill and then recovered; having recovered I have fallen ill again. This then is an account of my crazy obsession with the creation of my garden.

The garden encompasses three sides of the mountain as well as the ten or so *mu* [a measure of land area] of flat land surrounding it. Half of this area is taken up by water and rock, the other half with buildings and trees and plants. The garden contains two halls, three pavilions, four galleries, two terraces, and an equal number of belvederes, as well as three dykes. As for the various studies and studios and such like structures, each is exquisite in its own manner of seclusion or capaciousness; the adytum and the hermitages are all differently shaped, either small and constricted or wide and expansive, whilst the chambers and mountain cottages and so on are all sited on different levels of the mountain side. The bridges and gazebos, paths and peaks are dotted here and there, forming a rhythm with their wave-like contours. In general terms, therefore, what was once empty has been given solidity, that which was originally solid has been rendered empty, the gathered has been dispersed, the dispersed gathered, the precipitous leveled, and the level made precipitous. Like the skilled physician, I have prescribed potions with both restorative and purgative properties; like an able general, I have deployed my troops in formations designed both for frontal attack and for ambush; as an Old Master, my every brushstroke has brought life to my painting; and as a famous poet, my every line is tuneful....

ANDRÉ MOLLET
THE FRENCH GARDEN OF PLEASURE (1651)

A member of the dynasty of French royal gardeners, André Mollet wrote *Le Jardin de plaisir* (1651), in which he described the principles of classic French garden design. He created royal gardens in England at St. James's Palace and Wimbledon House, in Holland at Buren and Honselaarsdijk, and in Sweden. He worked with his father and brother on gardens at the Tuileries in Paris. He died around 1665. This excerpt, translator unknown, was published in England in 1670.

The Garden of Pleasure consists in Ground-works, Wildernesses, choice Trees, Palissado's, and Alleys or Walks; as also in Fountains, Grotto's, Statues, Perspectives, and other such like Ornaments; without which it cannot be perfect: Nevertheless it will be easily granted, that all these things confusedly and ill-dispos'd cause no pleasant effect; therefore we shall strive to dispose them each in its proper place, according to that which Experience hath taught us herein: To which purpose the following Designes will very much conduce.

In the first place, we say, That the Royal and Lordly House ought to be situated in an advantageous place, thereby to be supply'd with all the requisite things for its Embellishment, of which the Water has the first place, be it of Spring or otherwise; for it is with a great deal of reason that Water is said to be the Soul of Gardens, since that without it they seem always to be dying.

The second thing requisite to the decoration of Houses of Pleasure is to have the conveniency to plant before them a great Walk of double or treble rank, either of female Elms, or of Lime Trees, which are the two sorts of Trees which we esteem the fittest for this purpose; which Walk ought to be drawn by a Perpendicular Line to the Front of the House, and of a convenient and proportionable breadth to the House; and for the Basis of the said Walk, may be made a large Demy-circle, or Square; and in case the place will

CHATEAU DE VAUX-LE-VICOMTE
(designed in 1656 by Louis Le Vau) and
GARDENS (1656, André Le Nôtre)
Seine-et-Marne, France
Yann Arthus-Bertrand/CORBIS

allow it, there may be also drawn large Walks on the Right and Left of the said Front, which must be Parallel to the said House. As also at the end of the Garden another Walk in a direct Line to the great Walk, in the midst whereof there may be with conveniency a Door of Railes or Palissado's, through which, when the doors of the House are open'd, one may see from one end to the other, as far as our sight will extend. Such outward Works are most necessary to the Adorning of Houses; and as I put them here in the Front, and before the In-works; it is also by them, that one ought to begin to Plant even before the Building of the House, that the Trees may be come to half-growth when the House shall be built.

Let us come to the inward embellishments, which we commonly call Garden, which ought to be composed of Imbroider'd Ground-works, knots of Grass, Wildernesses, fine Alleys in Terraces, and flat Walks, so ordered, that they may still end at some Fountain or Statue, and at some of the extremities of these Alleys, ought to be set up some fine Perspectives painted on Cloth, that they may be removed at will, to preserve them from the injuries of the Weather. In fine, to finish our Work, the Statues ought to be erected upon their Piedestals, and the Grotto's built in the most convenient places; as also the Fountains, Spurts, Ponds, Falls of Waters, Bird-cages, and such like Ornaments, which being well order'd and placed, will give the last Perfection to the Garden of Pleasure....

But first of all is to be noted, that all Ground-works ought to be framed as near as possible may be to the House, that they may be perfectly seen from the Windows, without the obstacle which might be caused by Trees, Palissado's, or any other high Work. It is to be observed also, that the Ground-works the most remote from the eye, ought to be drawn of a larger Proportion, then those that are nearer; for it is certain, that if they be very exactly proportion'd to the distance of the site, they will thereby appear much more beautiful. And, before I go any farther, it will not be amiss to say a word or two concerning the Knots in Embroidery. They may be made in two manners, viz. with Box, or with Turff. Those of Box

are more fit for the neat and small Embroidery, because that the Box can be planted and clipped into what shape one will, and that there is less pains required in the preserving and keeping of it then that of Turff, which is to be often Mow'd and Roll'd. The Turffs are more fit for the Great works, and for Knots, then for Embroidery: yet for curiosity sake, there may be some of them made in the Garden of Pleasure, that it may want nothing of what Nature and Art can bestow on it of beauty; which is the reason we have set some down here for the satisfaction of the Curious....

After the Ground-works in Embroidery, follow the Compartiments of Turff-work, and of Flowers, which, being kept as they ought to be, will make a glorious shew; they are more proper for this Country then any other Country of the World, by reason that the Gardeners are more expert and skilful in laying and keeping of Turff then any other Country Gardiners. Nevertheless, since it may be this Book's fate to cross the Sea, we shall give some short directions to the Out landish Gardiners, how to chuse the fittest Turff for this use, as also how to keep and order it after the English manner...

There remains yet a word to say concerning the Garden-Alleys, which are the chiefest Ornaments of a Garden, and wherein *England* excelleth other Countreys, as well as by its art in Turffing; wherefore we shall give some small instructions therein, which may be of use in Forreign Countreys: which is, that, to have fair Walks, in which one may walk in all weathers with ease, there must be chosen a firm gravelly Sand, without the least mixture of any earth, except Clay, in case the gravel be too stony; and after it has been sifted somewhat grossly, let the biggest be laid in the bottom of the Walks, and that which is sifted on the top, very even, but only three or four inches higher in the middle then on the sides, just enough to drain the waters and no more; for I do not approve so great slopings which some use to give to Alleys, which are troublesome to those that walk, by their over-roundness. The Walks being thus gravelled, they must be neatly kept by Weeding and Rouling of them daily with a stone Rouler: Note by the by that the said small gravel or course sand must be laid as thick as may be, that the Worms may not pierce through; to that purpose it will not be amiss to lay all sorts of rubbish in the bottom of the said Alleys.

JOSEPH SPENCE
GENERAL GARDEN RULES (1751)

Spence (1669–1768) was a professor of poetry at Oxford University. He recorded his conversations with colleagues and friends. Particularly valuable are those about garden designs with Alexander Pope. The following letter to the Reverend Mr. Wheeler, written in 1751, summarizes Spence's precepts on gardening.

When you set me to write about gardening, you set me upon a thing that I love extremely; but as to any large tract of ground, there is no saying anything in particular without being upon the spot; and having considered it well and often. Some general rules one might mention, but after all, nine parts in ten depend upon the application. Yet I will just mention some that I followed myself.

The first and most material to consult is the Genius of the place. What is, is the great guide as to what ought to be. The making a fine plan for any place unknown is like Bays's saying "that he had made an excellent simile, if he did but know how to apply it." To study the ground thoroughly, one should not only take a view of the whole and all its parts, and consider the laying of it in general, and all its beauties and advantages or inconveniences and impediments, in particular, but also walk all around it in the line without your own bounds; to see what beauties may be added by breaking through your outline.

2dly: To fix the principal point of view for the whole plan, and any secondary points of view that may be of consequence in the disposition of the parts.

3dly: To follow Nature. Gardening is an imitation of "Beautiful Nature," and therefore should not be like works of art. Wherever art appears, the gardener has failed in his execution. Our old gardens were formed by the rule and square, with a perpetual uniformity and in a manner more fit for architecture than for pleasure-grounds. Nature never plants by the line, or in angles. I have lately seen thirty-six prints of a vast garden belonging to the present emperor of China: there is not one regular walk of trees in the whole ground; they seem to exceed our late best designers in the natural taste almost as far as those do the Dutch taste, brought over into England in King William's time. As to angles, I have such a mortal aversion to them, that was I to choose a motto for myself as a pretender to gardening, it should be, "Mutat quadrata rotundis." I should almost ever prefer serpentizing walks to straight ones, and round off the corners of groves instead of pointing them.

4ly: To assist or correct the general character of the ground, if deficient or displeasing. Thus if your ground be all dry, a winding stream should be brought into it, if possible; if not, pieces of water, with alders and weeping willows and other aquatics about them, dashed here and there, at proper distances from each other. If the ground be all flat, one should make risings and inequalities in it; very small swellings will help it much if properly placed, and natural irregular risings (or mounts) where any particular object or pleasing prospect is to be caught, etc.

5ly: To correct or conceal any particular object that is disagreeable.

6ly: To open a view to whatever is particularly agreeable.

7ly: To manage your plantations in such a manner that you may be led to some striking object, or change, unexpectedly: in which case not only the change or object, but the surprise itself is pleasing.

8ly: To conceal the bounds of your grounds everywhere, if possible. This is done by grove-works, sunk fences (the best of which is the *chevaux de fries* and what they call invisible fences, as being but little discernible to the eye. If you have sheep to keep

STOURHEAD ESTATE AND GARDENS
(designed by multiple generations of
the Hoare family beginning in 1718)
Wiltshire, England
Adam Woolfitt/CORBIS

and enliven the lawn, movable fences are the best, if any necessary, and of all such fences I should prefer what they call the Palladian rail, or wattles...

9ly: To unite the different parts of your garden gently together.

10: To contrive the outparts so, as to unite well with the country round about them.

11: To mix useful things even in the ornamental parts, and something of ornament even in the useful parts.

12: To make objects that are too near seem farther off: which is done by shewing more of the immediate ground and narrowing your view to them more and more as it recedes from you.

13: To draw distant objects nearer to you and make them seem part of your work: which is done by hiding the intermediate length of ground and planting what may fall in and unite, to the eye, with such distant objects.

14: To study variety in all things, as nothing without it can be pleasing. Inequality of ground, mixture of land and water, opposition of lights and shades, or grove and open, breaking the lines of trees, interspersing different sorts of trees in each grovette, placing trees of different greens and flowers of different colours by one another, etc. Mr. Kent always used to stake out his grovettes before they planted, and to view the stakes every way, to see that no three of them stand in a line: to which another, as necessary rule may be added: that in all smaller plantations one should never set above three or four trees of the same sort together.

15: To observe the different friendships and enmities of different colours, and to place the most friendly ones next each other.

16: In the mixing of lights and shades, to let the former have the prevalence, or, in other words, to give the whole a joyous air rather than a melancholy one. In this again the Chinese seem very much to exceed our pleasure-ground makers. They have scarce any such thing as close or thick groves in any of their near views: they fling them all on some of the hills at a distance.

All that I have laid out here so particularly (and perhaps a great deal more) is included by Mr. Pope in two lines, where in speaking of gardens he says:

He gains all Ends, who pleasingly confounds,
Surprises, varies, and conceals the bounds:

And in conversation, I have heard him include it in one single word, Variety....

ABBÉ JACQUES DE LILLE
THE GARDEN, OR THE ART OF LAYING OUT GROUNDS (1782)

For his poetry and translations, de Lille (1738–1813) won a seat in the French Academy and an appointment to the chair of poetry in the Collège de France. *The Garden,* first published in Paris in 1782 as "Les Jardins où l'art d'embellir les paysages ," called for reform of the traditional style of gardening with its straight lines, symmetry, and unnatural regularity. De Lille received inspiration from such English authors as William Mason and Alexander Pope. The excerpt below comes from the translation by Zachariah Jackson published in Dublin in 1791.

...Would you adorn the simply-charming plain,
Insult not Nature, with a gaudy train.
The talk requires a deep prophetic mind,
A genius, not a fortune unconfin'd;
Less proud, than elegant; for pomp and show,
Let simple beauties 'mid thy gardens grow.
Tis a vast picture, where in order rise
The lights and shades, to charm the wond'ring eyes.
Paint then; the flow'ry plains, their num'rous shades,

LA ROCHE COURBON CASTLE (15th century) and GARDENS (17th century)
Saint-Porchaire, France
Sandro Vannini/CORBIS

The streams of light, the mass-imbrowned glades,
The hours, the seasons as they glide away,
The circling year, the lesser-circling day,
Fring'd with embroid'ry gay the meadow's pride,
The verdure-clothed upland's sloping side,
The trees, the flow'rs, the rocks, the waters, these,
These for your colours, brush and canvas seize.
Nature is yours; then let your fertile hand
Th' obedient elements to form command.

But ere you plant, ere yet your impious spade
The sacred bosom of the earth invade,
To make your garden wear a juster face,
Know Nature, watch and imitate her grace.
Have you not oft, as 'mid the wilds you stray'd,
Struck with th' enchanting features of a glade,
Check'd short the heedless step, till rapt intense
In the fair-smiling image, ev'ry sense
Suffers a heav'nly revery of bliss?
Let your warm fancy catch a thought like this;
Transplant each striking scene; and learn from thence
To rival Nature's own magnificence.

Mark too where happy taste has touch'd the plain,
And from the choice, still learn to choose again.
Let Chantilli's fair pomp your eyes engage,
Adorn'd by heroes' hands from age to age.
Beloeil with bold magnificence endow'd,
And Chanteloup of its exil'd lord still proud,
Will charm by turns. As th' op'ning blossom fair
With timid blush proclaims that spring is near,
So Tivoli, free Nature's earliest child,
Bids France receive th' irregular and wild, . . .

Scenes such as these new beauties may bestow;
But cautious shun the rocks that lurk below.
Too often imitation wrecks our toil;
Then give not foreign graces to the soil.
First know your site, and then with pious fear
Consult the genius of the place, nor e'er
Contemn his sacred laws; yet oft our eyes
Behold a wretch, whose boldness whim supplies,
With choice unnat'ral, and absurd, confound,
Change, mix, displace the tasteless scenes around,
With union strange each beauty fair abuse,
And mar in France, Italia's lovely views.
But what the happy soil adopts with joy,
O, seize the blessing, all its pow'rs employ.

'Tis Nature deck'd in splendours all her own;
A perfect picture from no model drawn!
'Twas thus that Berghem, Poussin knew to charm;
Go, let their works divine your fancy warm!
And let your art to Nature kind restore
Each charm, which painting caught from her before.

But let us now examine well what soil
With fairest promise smiles upon your toil,
There was a time, when art with impious war
The loveliest native excellence would mar,
Would fill up vales, and raze each mountain high,
Till one insipid flatness tir'd the eye,
But now with other rage the tyrant sways,
New valleys sink, strange hills their summits raise.
Avoid extremes; vain will each labour prove,
The mountain's savage roughness to remove;
And 'mid a plain, a humble hillock plac'd
Stands a just satire on an artist's taste.

But would you wish a fair propitious site,
Which with success your labours may requite;
From the flat plain, and rugged mountain far,
Lo! yonder hill that steals into the air!
I love to view its unassuming brow
O'erlook the spreading vales that laugh below!
Nor dull nor dead appears the vacant scene,
Nor rugged interruptions intervene;
Each varying glance th'obedient heav'n commands,
Earth falls and rises, closes and expands,
From scene to scene, with fresh delight you range,
And at each step, your views, and pleasures change.

Let dull mechanics, in the cloyster'd schools,
Cramp Nature's freedom with their compass'd rules,
Their grounds with frigid symmetry confine,
And on dull paper trace the measur'd line.
You on the very borders take your stand,
The ready pencil trembling in your hand,
The landscapes, and the hills around display,
Mark how each distant object fades away,
Learn each resource, each obstacle devise,
Wonders from difficulties always rise.

The wildest waste with warmest charms may glow;
A shady robe o'er naked Nature throw;
Where'er immur'd she lies in gloomy night,
Quick let the ax admit the beaming light;
Where stagnant fens in putrid torpor sleep,
Let lakes spread wide, or fertile rivers sweep;
Thus o'er the ground your hands shall plenty show'r,
And health shall glow where sickness pin'd before;
Tho' dry the site, search, dig, explore the soil,
Where least you hope the bubbling fount may boil.
Thus when I've tortur'd long my aching brains,

And curs'd the frigid dullness of my strains,
Sudden one happy thought my Muse inspires,
And the recruited verse with ardour fires. . . .

In vain your art creates a boundless green,
Unless your taste diversify the scene.
Abhor the dullness of a measur'd frame,
In tasteless circles, or in squares more tame,
Let not dull symmetry your lawn confine;
'Tis liberty gives life to each design.
There 'mid the shades mysterious let it steal,
And in th'embracing woods its course conceal;
And here to meet the lawn, advances the groves;
Such are the simple forms that Nature loves.
To all her dictates mild with rev'rence yield;
She with rich colours dyes the laughing field.
Haste then; with flow'rs your varied garden grace;
Flow'rs give a lovelier smile to Nature's face;
Flow'rs are the models fair of brilliant art;
Ye simply-charming tributes of the heart!

PRINCE HERMANN VON PÜCKLER-MUSCAU
HINTS ON LANDSCAPE GARDENING (1834)

**Pückler-Muscau (1785–1871) brought the English landscape style
to the European continent. A German landowner and landscape
gardener, he created gardens at his own estates at Muscau and
Branitz. He also designed gardens at Babelsberg for Wilhelm I and
parks in the Weimar. Through his work *Andeutungen über Land-
schaftsgärtnerei* (1834), Pückler–Muscau influenced contemporary
garden design.**

BAGATELLE CHATEAU (designed in 1777
by François-Joseph Belange) and GARDENS
(redesigned in 1905 by J. C. N. Forestier)
Paris, France
Jean-Marc Charles/CORBIS

I may repeat here with some variation what I have said before: as the park is Nature idealized within a small compass, so the garden is an extended dwelling. Here the tastes of the owner may have free play, following his imagination and indulging even in trivialities.* Everything should be decorative, designed for comfort, and as ornamental as the means permit. Let the lawns appear as a velvet carpet embroidered with flowers; gather together the rarest and the most beautiful exotic plants, curious animals, multi-colored birds** (provided that Nature or art will enable them to thrive); polished benches, refreshing fountains, the cool shades of dense avenues, order and fancy; in short, everything in turn to evoke the richest and most varied effects, just as one furnishes every salon in the interior of a house in a different style. Thus, one may continue the suite of rooms on a greater scale under the open sky, whose blue vault, with ever-renewed cloud canopy, takes the place of the painted ceiling, and in which sun and moon are the perpetual illumination. To draw up rules for such details is more in the province of the decorative gardener, still more of the individual taste of the master, and perhaps most of all should be left to the delicate taste and delightful fancy of women. Hence, as regards this point I shall only make some general remarks.

It is essential that the confines of each garden, in which I always include the "pleasure-ground," for the sake of security should have an enclosure which separates it from the park.

If the locality allows of a high terrace, or a continuous ha-ha, this would, in most cases, be the best enclosure for a "pleasure-garden," and regular lines that are not concealed, but quite visibly mark the difference, are here to be recommended; for a garden is the occasion for very obvious art, and must therefore appear as such. While this barrier keeps out of the gardens the cattle or the deer grazing in the park, or visibly divides from them the meadows intended only for hay, the eye dwells with pleasure, first, upon the rich colors of the foreground, with its wealth of flowers and the emerald carpets of carefully kept lawns, and beyond, upon the open landscape with its imposing trees or the waving grasses

sown with wild flowers, where the mowers swing their glittering scythes in the sun or repose at noon in the fragrant hay. This contrast between free Nature and artistic cultivation, visibly separated and yet melting into one harmonious picture, is doubly soothing to the feelings.

It depends on the locality whether all the different gardens (and the more there are the more pleasing effect of variety they produce) shall be enclosed in one large space, most fittingly near the dwelling-house, or whether they shall be scattered about the park. I have pursued a middle course, extending the "pleasure-ground" all around the castle, and not, as is generally done in England, only on one side; the flower gardens approach close to the windows, a conservatory opening from the salon forming a connecting link; then at a little distance, as a plot by itself, but still within the circumference of the "pleasure-ground," the orangerie, the winter garden, the conservatories, and the vegetable gardens; but the orchards, the vineyard, and the nurseries I have distributed, at a distance from the castle, through the park; moreover, I have laid out several smaller gardens, in different styles, around the other principal buildings of the park, which I will describe more in detail farther on.

Although all these gardens are decorated here and there by scattered flower beds, the great mass and variety of flowers are reserved for the flower gardens proper. I repeat here that the selection and distribution of the flowers must be left to the individual taste of the owner, though I will say in passing that flowers of the same kind in large masses generally make a far more impressive effect then a mixture of many different kinds in the same bed. Yet the *nuances* are so various, and there is so much to be considered in the designing, that only years of practice and experience will give the best. The light cast upon the flowers by the surrounding objects is a prime consideration. A rose in shadow and a rose in light yield quite different colors; much more the blue flowers. But especially striking is the effect brought about by the contrast of dark shade with bright sunlight on full white flowers mixed with others of brilliant color. Generally speaking, it is advisable to break strong-tinted flowers with white, in order to make the former stand out in stronger relief.

A winter garden, as the name implies, must be confined to evergreen plants, and in our cold climate it is very difficult to grow any variety. Orangeries and hothouses belong to them; also statues and fountains, which, even when the water freezes, do not lose their picturesque character. Regular arrangements after ancient models, or French taste growing therefrom yield the best results, and if the effect of turf is desired, then creeping evergreen plants or the bright green dwarf bilberry and cranberry plants may be utilized. I can only touch slightly on these points, partly on account of the numerous details which lie out of the scope of this work, and partly because further remarks will be forthcoming in my description of the park at Muscau.

I close this chapter, therefore, with the remark that kitchen and fruit gardens, although essentially for use, can be made pleasing to the eye by the happy arrangement of the beds of the first, and in the second by the training of fruit trees *en espalier* or by the trellising of them on walls ... by convenient paths, and by the utmost cleanliness and order, so that one may here enjoy the warm sunlight in the spring, or later in the year pluck the ripest fruit. In England, where everything is made to serve the utmost convenience, strawberries are planted in terraces near the paths, to be reached without troublesome stooping. And raised paths are made under the fruit trees, so that cherries and apples grow on the level of the stroller. Several lengths of wall are built in the middle of the kitchen garden, affording not only a protected sunny side, but also a shady side, and all kinds of fruit trees are skillfully trained on them. English fruit, even in the open, gets too little sunlight, and the ripest are still, as in the time of the Duc de Langeais, the *cooked* apples.***

*   Of course there may be things that are obvious absurdities. In a garden in Vienna, for instance, I saw a house in the shape of a tub in which sits an immense Diogenes of cardboard, who seems to have just extinguished his light

in deference to the spectator; or elsewhere a bench, where a person who sits down upon it is drenched, after a few minutes, with a squirt of water, and other like impertinences.

**   But there must be no superfluity, nor any trace of dirt or odors, and if this cannot be so managed, then the menagerie should be removed; for curiosities which can be admired only with the handkerchief at the nose are undesirable in a place which should be devoted only to the comfortable enjoyment of beauty.

***   The well-known saying was, "Qu'en Angleterre il n'y avait de poli que l'acier et ne fruits murs que les pommes cuites" (There is in England nothing polished but steel, and no ripe fruit but the baked apple.).

HENRY FRANCIS DU PONT (WILLIAM H. FREDERICK JR.)
CANONS OF DESIGN (1995)

Du Pont (1880–1969) assembled one of America's foremost decorative art collections and created beautiful gardens at his home, Winterthur, in Delaware. His gardens evolved over seventy years, as he experimented with landscape design and individual plant species collected from throughout the world. William H. Frederick Jr., a noted landscape architect in his own right, describes du Pont's design guidelines in this excerpt from *The Winterthur Garden,* edited by Denise Magnani.

If we are to learn about design from this garden [Winterthur], it is important to understand the guidelines to which H. F. du Pont adhered. From witnesses, correspondence, written notes, and orders for plants, we know a great deal about the process by which he achieved his results; yet, nowhere does he actually spell out any principles of design. Because I have loved and worked with similar landforms for forty-two years and because I share du

Pont's passions for both the great cornucopia of plants available for our gardens and the potential of color and choreography as design tools, it has been natural for me to make the following subjective deductions.

1. *Respect the site; do not impose your will on it.* Du Pont loved the native woodlands and agricultural scene. He capitalized on what was there rather than making major changes.

2. *Incorporate the garden into the existing landscape. The garden is not a separate entity.* Du Pont created vistas from the house and garden to the agricultural and woodland scenes, allowed the existing landscape to flow into the garden, and maintained open spaces in the garden that echo open spaces in the agricultural landscape.

3. *Contrast richly, heavily planted areas with open space.* With this technique, du Pont gave the viewer's eye a restful change of pace between intensive experiences.

4. *The garden is a social experience. It should be easily accessible and tempting to visitors on foot.* Du Pont made every effort to draw visitors farther and farther into the depths of the garden.

5. *The style of planting design should be largely naturalistic— free flowing as in nature—except where strong rectilinear Renaissance design serves a special purpose.* The most obvious examples of the latter are in areas associated with the architecture of the house, such as the Reflecting Pool garden. Du Pont applied this principle to the Sundial Garden as well, which is situated at a point farthest from the house and roughly halfway in the circulatory path through the garden areas. This garden area serves the useful purpose of being an anchor area of psychological security in what might otherwise appear to be an expanse of amorphous naturalism.

6. *The driving force in the development of the garden should be colorful horticultural displays of hardy woody and herbaceous plants rather than sculpture, water displays, or other architectural elements.* Du Pont was a plant lover and took great interest in the enormous cornucopia of garden plants available and becoming available, including natives, alien introductions, and those newly created by plant breeders.

7. *Develop a theme for each area of the garden and build the planting design of the area to enhance that theme.* Du Pont based themes sometimes on a particular genus, sometimes on a specific season of bloom, and sometimes on color. Azaleas, quince, peonies, and primroses provide examples of a genus used as a theme. Oak Hill, the March Bank, the Sundial Garden, and the Sycamore Area have seasonal themes. The Winterhazel Walk and the Greensward follow color themes. In each case, once H. F. du Pont chose a theme, he was highly disciplined in sticking to it and not cluttering the picture with unrelated plants or ideas.

8. *Base site selection of each area on the requirements of the plants involved.* This often happened by trial—the test plantings of azaleas in the portion of the woodland opened up by the chestnut blight is a case in point—or serendipity. An example of the latter is the *Anemone apennina,* which was originally heavily planted on the March Bank and failed to thrive there; it subsequently appeared in Azalea Woods, where the plants were allowed room to spread and put on a breathtaking display.

9. *After selecting a site and theme plants, add other plants that bloom at the same time to strengthen the feature; also add a few plants that bloom earlier and later where it seems appropriate to choreograph a modulated entrance and exit.* Winterhazel (*Corylopsis* in variety) and Korean rhododendron (*Rhododendron mucronulatum*) are the principal performers on the Winterhazel Walk. H. F. du Pont added *Helleborus foetidus* and green shades of *H. orientalis* to pick up the green in the green-yellow winterhazel blossoms. He also added pink and maroon shades of *H. orientalis,* the lavender *Corydalis bulbosa* and *Lathyrus vernus,* and the mauve-flowered *Primula abschasica* to pick up the warm lavender of the Korean rhododendron. The main season of bloom on the Greensward centers around the pink *R. mucronulatum* 'Cornell Pink'. The picture starts unfolding, however, a week or two earlier with forms of *Viburnum farreri* and continues

later with the pink of royal azaleas (*R. schlippenbachii*) and R. 'Miss Susie'.

10. *Plants, especially woody plants, should be spaced so that they are uncrowded and can show off their natural form.* This is clearly exemplified by several rearrangements that du Pont made. In the case of azaleas in Azalea Woods and quince on the Quince Walk, crowded, mature plants were dug up and replanted farther apart so the natural form of each plant would be visible in the years to come.

11. *Plant as though making broad, bold brush strokes of single colors on a canvas.* Du Pont used large numbers of a single plant for the major colors in each composition. Snowdrops (*Galanthus*), *Crocus tomasinianus,* and *Chionodoxa lucilliae* are used by the thousands on the March Bank. Pink pearl azaleas (*Rhododendron* [Kurume] 'Pink Pearl') number in excess of fifty in Azalea Woods. Du Pont's color and textural combinations were successful because of this courageous approach.

12. *In each color scheme look for the one small touch that can be added to enliven the picture.* This often involved du Pont's adding a few plants of an unexpected, even nonharmonious hue. Examples include the orange azaleas in the basically pink Azalea Woods, chartreuse *Viburnum* with *Chaenomeles* on the Quince Walk, and tangerine *Primula* in the Quarry Garden.

MARC P. KEANE
DESIGN PRINCIPLES (1996)

A licensed landscape architect and garden designer, Keane studied design and practiced in Japan. He has lectured in the Department of Environmental Design at Kyoto University of Art and Design and practiced garden design in Japan. He was also the Lawrence Halprin Fellow at Cornell University and Research Associate of the Institute of Medieval Japanese Studies, Columbia University. This excerpt is taken from his book *Japanese Garden Design*.

LEARNING FROM NATURE

The gardens of Japan are works of art that use nature as a material of creation. The first and foremost design principle, therefore, is to learn from nature. On the other hand, a complementary principle would be, do not copy nature—interpret it. Both of these principles are as old as gardening is in Japan and can even be found included in the overall principles of gardening detailed in the *Sakuteiki*:

> *Recall the vistas of various famous places, select what attracts you and add your own interpretation. It is best to use this as a theme to design the whole of the garden while adding just the right amount of changes....*

PERSONAL EXPRESSION IN TRADITION

The *Sakuteiki* expounds the following principle:

> *Keep close to heart the works of past masters and, giving due respect to the opinions of the client, imbue the garden with your own taste.*

... Ninety percent of all "designs" are "givens": aspects that are determined by the nature of the materials, the site, and climate—just to mention a few of the predominant constraints. "Given" aspects of design must simply be obeyed; water does not flow uphill, rocks fall over if not set well, and plants die when

JOJUIN GARDEN AT KIYOMIZUDERA
TEMPLE (early Edo period, 1600–1868)
Kyoto, Japan
Catherine Karnow/CORBIS

planted in the wrong place. These prerequisite factors have become incorporated into a body of knowledge that designers now call tradition. Any design must obey these factors or invite failure. Incorporating tradition does not, however, mean visionless replication of past forms. The proper sense of incorporating traditions was expressed succinctly by the seventeenth-century poet Matsuo Basho:

> Do not seek to emulate the old masters.
> Seek what they sought....

ENCLOSURE AND ENTRY

Enclosure necessitates entries; it is quite common for the garden designer to introduce gates that connect the garden to the outside world as well as gates within the garden which divide it into a series of layered spaces. A good example of these divisions is seen in the stroll gardens of the Edo-period daimyo estates, within which are designed a series of changing scenic views that are revealed in succession as one moves along the garden path. Occasionally, scenes are divided by physical, wooden gates—more likely the transition is marked by a grove of trees the stroller passes through, a bend or rise in the path, or some other ephemeral "gate."...

VOID AND ACCENT

Another important design technique related to spatial development within gardens is the design of expressive spatial voids called *ma*, a tiny word that has complex meanings as various as space and time.... Garden designers create ma in a variety of ways: as a physical space experienced when moving through the garden; a visual space in a contemplation garden that is only entered with the mind; or a time/space—a pause that is created in movement through the garden to enhance one's appreciation of it. In religious terms *ma* is used to represent the concept of *mu,* nothingness, a central posit of Zen Buddhism. Aesthetically, designers use ma to establish *yohaku-no-bi,* the beauty of paucity that was so important to the arts of the middle ages.

BALANCE

Balance is, along with ma, one of the most important design techniques that will lend a Japanese feeling to a garden. Balance in Japanese garden design can be described as being asymmetric, off-centered, and based on triads.... In the case of a contemplation garden in which the view is framed by an opening in the architecture, the garden is designed so that it will not be balanced symmetrically. Instead, the designer presents the viewer with a pleasing arrangement of forms of which no single one is absolutely dominant. Even though there is usually a hierarchy of forms, the eye is not meant to stop at the zenith but instead is always drawn back to a source to begin meandering again.... In the garden, for instance, straight paths are used sparingly, thus avoiding a centered, axial relationship. Even if paths are made straight, however, the axis of the path will be designed so that the line of sight of a person walking the path dead-ends in a wall or hedge, or includes an askew view of some element of the garden like a gate or teahouse. Without symmetry or central focal points, the Japanese garden designer achieves visual stability through the use of triads or triangular shapes.... The most obvious example of the use of triads in the garden is the way the designer arranges rocks in groups, and the way those groups relate to one another....

PLANES AND VOLUMES

Another aspect of balance used by garden designers is the relationship between two-dimensional, planar elements and those that are three-dimensional or volumetric.... Nowhere is this more clearly realized than in the design of *kare-san-sui* gardens in which rocks and tightly clipped evergreens are used as foils against the stark surface of the raked sand, and the walls or hedges that enclose the garden. The reduction of the elements in kare-san-sui to their most simplified state—planes and volumes—is not unlike the sentiments of cubist art, and explains, in part, why these ancient gardens appear to be so "modern."

SYMBOLOGY

... Religious symbology in the garden is very common and incorporates both Shinto and Buddhist images—for instance, the triad of boulders used to create an image of Buddha and his attendants.... The most common symbols of felicity are the images of the island/mountain Horai (where the Immortals were said to live) and the associated tortoise and crane islands.... Garden designers also employ symbology in order to re-create an extensive landscape scene within the confines of a small garden.... In this way mountain ranges become a group of upright boulders and the ocean is found in a sheet of white sand; one pine can represent the wind-swept bluffs along the ocean and a cluster of trimmed camellias depict the depth of a hidden valley....

BORROWED SCENERY

Borrowed scenery, *shakkei,* is a technique for enlarging the visual scale of the garden beyond its actual physical boundaries by incorporating a distant view as an integral part of the garden.... When designing a shakkei garden, the background already exists as a distant mountain, a waterfall, or even a large manmade object such as the sweeping roof of a temple. The middle and foreground are left to the garden designer to create....

MITATE

Mitate (pronounced me-tah-teh) is a design technique originally associated with the tea garden. Freely translated as "seeing anew," mitate is the process of finding a new use for an old object—objects themselves are called *mitate-mono.* Some of the best examples of mitate-mono are the stone lavers (*chozubachi*) found in the tea garden which guests use to purify their hands and mouth before entering the tea room. Many chozubachi are made from stones that were originally used for another purpose—a section of a multi-roofed stone stupa, a bridge pier, or the base of an old lantern....

THE PATH

... For the garden designer, paths have a more important role than merely a design element. Through careful design of the paths, the gardener controls not only the cadence of motion through a garden but what is seen as well.... Take for instance the design of a stepping-stone path in a tea garden. Walking across uneven stepping stones (*tobi-ishi*), the guest is forced by the precariousness of the footing, to look down and focus on the path. The designer has effectively stopped the guest from looking about at that time, but after a short run of stepping stones, the designer will invariably place a larger stone, perhaps at the junction of a second path or before the *tsukubai.* The larger surface of the stone allows the guest to stop comfortably, raise his head and look around at the garden. The designer has carefully chosen this spot for its view....

2

SITE

One ought not to build in valleys enclosed between mountains; because edifices in valleys are there hid, and are deprived of seeing at a distance, and of being seen. These are without dignity and grandure, and also entirely contrary to health.

Andrea Palladio (1508–1580), Italian Renaissance architect

To build, to plant, whatever you intend,
To rear the Column, or the Arch to bend,
To swell the Terras, or to sink the Grot;
In all, let Nature *never be forgot.*
Consult the Genius *of the* Place *in all,*

Alexander Pope (1688–1744), English poet

The taste of all the architects I have ever known leads them, for the sake of "prospect," to put up buildings on hill-tops. The error is obvious. Grandeur in any of its moods, but especially in that of extent, startles, excites—and then finally fatigues, depresses. For the occasional scene nothing can be better—for the constant view nothing worse.

Edgar Allan Poe (1809–1849), American poet and short story writer

previous spread:
CASTELLO DI BROLIO (10th century)
and GARDEN (1850)
Chianti, Italy
Vince Streano/CORBIS

opposite:
CLINIQUE ST. PAUL (12th century)
St. Rémy de Provence, France
William Manning/CORBIS

PIETRO DE' CRESCENZI
ON MAKING GARDENS (1305)

An Italian nobleman, Crescenzi (1230–1305) wrote a treatise on gardens and agriculture *Liber ruralium commodorum*, published in Bologna in 1305. In it he describes garden design of the Middle Ages with references to classical authors Cato and Varro. The excerpt below is from the translation by Johanna Bauman, first published in 2002.

ON SMALL GARDENS OF HERBS

Certain gardens may be made only of plants, others of trees, and yet others of both. When consisting only of plants they require fine and compact soil, so that they may yield fine and delicate plants that greatly please the sight. Therefore, the place which is prepared for such a garden should first be freed of weeds, which is difficult to do, unless first, after the space has been cleared of roots, it is well leveled and then the space is thoroughly soaked with scalding water, so that the remaining roots and seeds lying hidden in the ground will be altogether incapable of sprouting. And then the whole plot should be filled with a fine turf of thin grass, and the turfs themselves completely compressed with wooden mallets and the blades of grass trodden underfoot, until hardly any of them are visible. Then it [the grass] will burst forth gradually like hair and cover the surface like a green cloth.

The site of the garden should be of such a measure as may suit those plants that are expected to exist in it. Along the edge of the garden should be planted fragrant herbs of all kinds, such as rue, sage, basil, marjoram, mint, and the like, and also flowers of every type, such as violet, lily, rose, gladiola, and the like. Between these plants and the level turf raise and form (another) turf in the fashion of a seat, flowering and pleasant. Plant trees or train vines on the turf against the heat of the sun; the turf will have a pleasant and cool shade from their leaves, in the manner of an overhang.

Shade more than fruit is sought from those trees, and therefore they should not be dug or manured, activities that might harm the turf.

But care must be taken that the trees are not exceedingly thick or too many in number, which, by removing air, damage health; and this is because a garden needs free air and excessive shade breeds impurities. Furthermore, the trees should not be noxious, such as nut trees and some others, but sweet, fragrant in flower and pleasant in shade, such as vines, pears, apples, pomegranates, laurels, cypresses, and the like. Behind the turf there should be a great number and variety of medicinal and aromatic herbs, since they not only delight by their odor, but their flowers also refresh the sense of sight by their variety. Disperse rue among them in many places, because of its beautiful green color and because its bitterness drives poisonous animals from the garden.

There should be no trees in the middle of the turf, but this level place should rather enjoy free and pure air, since that air is healthier, and also since spiders' webs stretched from one branch to another would block the way and contaminate the faces of those passing through, as would be the case if the garden or the turf had trees planted in the middle of it. And, if possible, a very pure spring should be diverted into the middle of the garden, because its purity produces much pleasantness. The garden should be open to the north and east because of the health and purity of these winds. It should be closed in the direction of the opposing winds, namely the south and west, on account of their violence, impurity, and unhealthy quality. Although the northeast wind may hinder fruit, it marvelously preserves the spirits and ensures health. For delight and not fruit is sought in the garden.

ON LARGE AND MODERATE GARDENS OF PERSONS OF MODERATE MEANS

Let the space of the earth set aside for the garden be measured according to the means and rank of persons of moderate means, namely two or three or four or more *iugera* (.675 acre) or *bubulcae*.

The space should be surrounded with ditches and hedges of thorns and roses, and, moreover, in warm places a hedge of pomegranates should be made and in cold places of nuts or plums and quinces. Again, plough the space and make it flat on all sides with a rake or with hoes; afterwards, mark out the entire space where trees are to be planted with a cord. Plant lines of pears and apples in it, and, in warm places, lines of palms and lemons. Or plant lines of mulberries, cherries, plums, and lines of such noble trees as figs, nuts, almonds, quinces, and pomegranates, each one clearly in its own line or row according to type.

The lines or rows should be spaced twenty feet apart, more oor less, or forty feet or more, according to the will of the master. The large trees should be spaced in a line twenty feet from each other and the small trees should be spaced ten feet from each other. Noble vines of different types that provide delight and utility may be planted between the trees. Hoe the lines of trees so that the trees and vines grow stronger, and treat the intervals as meadows and weed them often. Mow the meadows of the garden twice a year, so that they may remain beautiful. Trees should be planted and shaped, as was stated above in Book V, in rows of each kind. Again, pergolas formed in the manner of a house or a tent should be made in the most suitable part [of the garden].

ON GARDENS OF KINGS AND OTHER ILLUSTRIOUS AND WEALTHY LORDS

Because such persons by reason of their riches and power are able to satisfy their own will in all earthly things and almost nothing is wanted by them, except the labor of setting workers to task, they should know they are able to make gardens having many delights in this manner. They should, therefore, choose a flat place, not marshy or screened from the flow of good winds, in which there is a spring flowing through the place. And the spot should be twenty *iugera* or more, according to the will of the master. Suitably high walls should surround it, and in the northern part it should be

planted with a grove of various trees, in which wild creatures placed in the garden may flee and hide.

In the southern part there should be built a handsome palace, in which the king or queen may linger when they wish to escape from heavy thoughts and to renew the spirit by means of joys and solaces. For from this area it (the palace) will create shade for the garden in the hot season and its windows facing onto the temperate garden will enjoy a view unhindered by the heat of the sun. An enclosure for animals, which is discussed above, should be made in another part of the garden; in this *vivarium* should be made a fish pond in which various types of fish are raised; and hares, stags, roebucks, rabbits, and similar non-predatory beasts should be put in it.

And above certain bushes placed near the palace, a kind of house should be made that has a roof and walls densely woven from thick boughs, into which are placed pheasants, partridges, nightingales, blackbirds, goldfinches, linnets, and all other kinds of singing birds. In the garden there should be rows of trees spaced far apart from the palace to the distant grove, so that the animals placed in the garden may be seen easily from the palace.

In this garden there should also be a palace with walks and bowers made from nothing but the trunks of trees, in which the king and queen can meet with the barons and lords when it is not the rainy season. And a palace of this type can be made easily in such a manner: the whole space of the walks and bowers should be measured out and demarcated and, if it pleases, fruit trees that grow easily, such as cherries and apples, should be planted in place of walls; or, what is better, willows or elms or birch trees should be planted there, and their growth should be controlled for several years, both by grafting and by stakes, poles, and ties, so that walls and a roof might be formed from them.

LEON BATTISTA ALBERTI
SELECTING THE IDEAL SITE (1450)

The son of an exiled Florentine, Alberti (1404–1472) was inspired by the art of antiquity in Rome and developed a theory of beauty based on the mathematical proportions of classical buildings. When he moved to Florence in 1334, his principles were confirmed by the work of Brunelleschi. His most important architectural writings are *De pictura* (1435) and *De re aedificatoria* (1450). This excerpt comes from the latter book, which remained the classic treatise on architecture from the sixteenth century to the eighteenth and was published in a new translation by Joseph Rykwert, Neil Leach, and Robert Tavernor in 1988.

As for the locality, the ancients put much effort into ensuring that it should contain (as far as possible) nothing harmful and that it should be supplied with every convenience. Above all, they took the greatest care to avoid a climate that might be disagreeable or unwholesome; it was a very prudent precaution, even an indispensable one. For while there is no doubt that any defect of land or water could be remedied by skill and ingenuity, no device of the mind or exertion of the hand may ever improve climate appreciably, or so it is said. Certainly the air that we breathe and that plays such a vital role in maintaining and preserving life (as we can ourselves observe), when really pure may have an extraordinarily beneficial effect on health. . . .

It is no bad thing, then, to consider the quality and angle of the sun to which a locality is exposed, so that there is no excess of sunlight or shade. . . . Personally, I prefer gentle breezes to winds, though I would consider winds, however fierce and blustery, less irksome than a stagnant and heavy atmosphere. Water that does not move, Ovid tells us, absorbs badness. . . . For this reason it is advisable to avoid any location in whose neighborhood anything noxious is given off, such as offensive smells or unclean vapor

rising from marshes, and in particular from polluted waters and ditches. . . .

South-facing coastlines are not recommended, primarily because the reflected rays of the sun afflict them with two suns, in effect; one burns down from the sky, the other up out of the water. Such places are subjected to sharp changes in temperature, as the chilling shades of the night draw in at sunset. Some are even of the opinion that at sunset the overall effect of the sun, both direct and reflected off the water, sea, or mountains, is at its most harmful, since a place that has already been heated by the sun all day is made sweltering by the additional heat produced by the reflection. If on top of all these effects you are also exposed to oppressive winds, what could be more harmful or intolerable? Morning breezes too have been rightly reproved, as they bring with them raw vapors as they rise. . . .

Let the site therefore have a dignified and agreeable appearance, and a location neither lowly nor sunk in a hollow, but elevated and commanding, where the air is pleasant and forever enlivened by some breath of wind. . . .

When selecting the locality, it is not enough to consider only those indications which are obvious and plain to see, but the less evident should also be noted, and every factor taken into account. . . . Nor is it inappropriate to take inanimate objects into consideration when looking for indications of the climate and winds: we may deduce from neighboring buildings, for example, that if they are rough and rotting, it is a sign of some adverse outside influence. If trees should all lean in one particular direction, as though by common consent, or have broken branches, clearly they have suffered the violence of the wind. Similarly, when the upper surfaces of tough stones, whether local or imported, are unusually eroded, they betray sharp changes in temperature between hot and cold. Above all, any region beset by these storms and temperature changes should be avoided: exposure to extremes of hot and cold weakens and impairs the structure and composition of the body and its parts, and may lead to disease and premature old age; indeed

the main reason why a city lying at the foot of mountains that face west is considered especially unhealthy is that it is particularly exposed to sudden nocturnal exhalations and the chilling darkness....

... In the countryside there are fewer restrictions, and the rich are readier to invest money. But let us first rehearse briefly a few general comments on the design of villas: an adverse climate and porous soil are to be avoided; building should be undertaken right in the countryside, at the foot of mountains, in a well-watered and sunny spot, in a healthy region, and in a healthy part of that region. It is thought that a severe and unhealthy climate may be caused not only by disadvantages outlined in book 1, but also by thick woods—especially those containing trees with bitter leaves— in that the air will putrefy if reached neither by sun nor by wind; another cause may be sterile or unhealthy soil, where all you will harvest will be timber.

JEAN-BAPTISTE DE LA QUINTINYE
OF THE EXPOSURE OF GARDENS (1690)

One of the greatest agriculturalists of the seventeenth century, Quintinye (1624–1688) visited England in 1670 and was encouraged by Charles II to stay on as superintendent of the royal gardens. He chose instead to return to France, where he became director of fruit gardens and potagers for Louis XIV. His masterpiece *Instruction pour les jardins fruitiers et potagers* was posthumously published at Paris in 1690 and is still considered the best early work on planning and growing a kitchen garden. The book was translated by the garden designer John Evelyn in 1693 as *The Compleat Gard'ner; or, directions for cultivating and right ordering of fruit-gardens and kitchen gardens,* from which the following excerpt is taken. This was one of the first French garden books to be translated into English.

OF THE EXPOSURES OF GARDENS, AS WELL IN GENERAL AS IN PARTICULAR; WITH THE EXPLICATION OF WHAT MAY BE GOOD AND ILL IN EVERY ONE OF THEM

It is not enough for a Garden to have a good Ground, and to be well situated, it must also be well expos'd; and a small rising not being well expos'd, can not be call'd an advantageous Situation.... Generally speaking, this Exposition of the South is free from the Northern Winds, which by their usual coldness are always cruel and fatal to all manners of Gardens, which is the reason it is generally chosen before that of the East; but yet it is most certain that in light Grounds, the last being favour'd by Night Dews, and the first gentle and mild Rays of the Rising Sun, is incomparable for Maturity, Size and Taste, as well as for the Preservation of Trees and Legumes, etc. and especially because over and above all this, it defends us from the North West Winds; that Wind rises between the West and North, and as it regularly blows in the Spring, it is commonly attended by white Frosts, which are very destructive to the Blossoms and Fruits of Trees, whereon it lights, which is the reason that People easily bear with that Eastern Exposition even in strong Earths, but still I do certainly believe it best for light Earth....

OF THE THIRD CONDITION WHICH REQUIRES IN OUR GARDENS THE CONVENIENCE OF WATERINGS

Nothing can be more certain, and more universally granted, than that it is impossible to have fine and good Gardens, especially Kitchen Gardens, without being able for a considerable part of the Year to secure them from their Mortal Enemy, which is Drought; the Spring and Summer are subject to great heats and scorchings....

From whence it naturally follows, that Water is absolutely Necessary in Gardens, and that plentifully too, in order to perform the Necessary Waterings they require in due time; for indeed what can be made of any Ground without Water, it will remain altogether useless for Productions, and disagreeable to sight; therefore the best way is to pitch upon Situations that have the Convenience

of Water; and whoever does not make that one of his first Considerations, deserves blame, or pity.

The most common, and at the same time most wretch'd recourse for Waterings is that of Wells: It is true that they are necessary, when no better can be had, but at least they should be chosen shallow, for certainly it is to be fear'd, that the Waterings will be very Inconsiderable, and consequently of little use, when the Water is difficult to be drawn up; the advantage of Pumps, though often deceitful, may be look'd upon as something in that Case; but the disburthening of some Springs or Conduits, a Neighboring Canal, or a small Pond well stor'd, and well kept with Pipes and Tubs distributed into several Squares, are, as it were, the Soul of Vegetation; without it all is dead, or languishes in Gardens, though the Gard'ner be not faulty; but with it the whole Garden must needs be Vigorous, and abounding in every Season of the Year, which will redound to the Honour of him who has the Management of it, whereas it will utterly Disgrace such as have nothing to plead for an Excuse.

OF THE FOURTH CONDITION, WHICH REQUIRES THE GARDEN TO BE PARTLY UPON A LEVEL, IN ALL THE SURFACE OF IT

It is very difficult, nay very rare to meet with Situations that are so equal in all their Extent, as not to have any Rise or Fall on any side; but yet it is not impossible: I do not think it very necessary to look for any to be as smooth as Water, but yet it is a happiness when such are met with; great Inequalities are certainly troublesome for Gardens. The Inundations or Overflowings which happen after long Rains, cause cruel Disorders in them, and cut out a World of Work to repair them; moderate Inequalities do no great harm, but rather good, especially in a dry Earth, when inclining to a Wall expos'd to the East, that part, as we have already said, being seldom soak'd by the Waters that fall from the Skies; they light most upon the Exposure of the West; and thus a fall guiding the Waters towards that East part, is very favourable....

OF THE LAST CONDITION, WHICH REQUIRES THAT BOTH THE FRUIT AND KITCHEN-GARDEN SHOULD NOT BE FAR DISTANT FROM THE HOUSE, AND THAT THE COMING TO IT SHOULD BE EASIE AND CONVENIENT.

I am not ignorant that the Countrey affords large and moderate Houses, of which the first may be accompany'd with several Gardens, and the other satisfy'd with one only. As to those which may have several Gardens, it is proper that those that are design'd for Flowers and Shrubs, I mean the Parterres, should face the principal Aspect of the House, since nothing can be more agreeable than to see at all times on that Side the charming variety of a Succession of Flowers whatever they be; they are so many different Scenes, or Decorations upon a Stage, of which the Figure never alters, they afford perpetual matter to delight the Eye, and charm us with their Sweets; but whereas generally those Parterres are as publick, and as open to every body as the very Court of the House, it is not fit to put anything into them, the loss of whereof might discompose us.

PRINCE CHARLES-JOSEPH DE LIGNE
CREATING A FINE VIEW (1781)

A Belgian nobleman, Ligne (1735–1814) influenced garden design through his writings and counseled Marie-Antoinette on the Petit Trianon, the Duc de Chartres on the Parc Monceau, and the Baron de Monville on the Desert de Retz. He wrote about garden design and his garden travels in *Coup d'œil sur Belœil et sur une grande partie de jardins d'Europe* (1781). The excerpt is from the 1991 translation of modern scholar Basil Guy.

In the advice that I distribute without being asked (for the worst little author, or maker of gardens, thinks that he at least has no need of any), I always say: "It is by doing, reflecting, walking about, and noting down that you will see what persons with fitful notions cannot see. Let your eye never weary of wandering over the beauties of Nature, and you will learn from her how to combine them." I have looked long at open fields, and I have learned that the red of poppies, the blue of cornflowers, the yellow of turnips make the best of palettes; unite them with the tender green of flax, the honeygrass, the mottled buckwheat, the pale gold of wheat, the vivid green of barley, and many other species that I do not yet know and you will have an enchanting effect. To me, not liking walls and satisfied with hedges and canals, this picture is one joy more in a country home....

Sometimes people ask, What is a fine view? You get used to it; it is a joy forever. If you are continually going to the window, I must say that is because you never tire of the wonderful spectacle of Nature. It helps to expand the mind, which is limited, because of the sense of sight—or so it seems to me. The ocean on which our eyes can never come to rest, whether because of its uniform flatness or because of the agitation of the waves, does not give the same impression as a fine decorative skyline. A view over the earth is forever varied by effects of light. Storms and the rising or setting of the sun change, or restlessly renew, the same tableaux. What would you rather do: build so that you can enjoy perspectives over beautiful surroundings or create a garden? If the latter, it is much better that it be hidden, so that contemplation becomes a substitute for that other pleasure. Let this garden be only for meditation. Let it be small and enclosed by a low, lightweight grille. You need only one large tree in the middle and, beside it, a small but broad waterfall, two feet high with a bench over it. There should be an open greening room and a closed one, somewhat farther along, likewise hidden, containing a parrot or perhaps a monkey with a large perch near a round bed of flowers, amid which there should be a round basin with a six-foot fountain jet at the center. In all this garden should take up no more than an acre, since all the surroundings are gardens, thanks to my clearing—or to fate—which has set me as an example on two mountains that together gratify me to the full....

I do not want people to plant but rather to uproot. Axe in hand, a ladder on the shoulder, let them go into a forest. Let them stop where they find the most ancient oaks and flowing springs of limpid water, now swift, now still, now broad as a river, now contained and bubbling as a brook, majestic if dammed, threatening if merely thwarted. Let these people on their ladder try to discern mountains (if there be any nearby), cliffs, or smiling vales where the eye comes to rest on the verdure of the fields. Then let them open a clearing on to vistas with a mill, a bell tower, a torrent, a turret, and superb coppices amid a handsome greensward. Let the axe continue to clear a place for a dwelling in appropriate style. And to be more certain of the pretty contours of the paths, of grassy saloons, of the location of flower beds, bridges, follies, and sad or happy scenes, let your pencil correct all simple, uncomplicated forms on the plan....

If niggardly Nature has hidden her treasures from you, you need only hire a woodsman for the work I recommend. Let it be neither limited, nor sad, nor gloomy—as it frequently is in gardens in the modern style when the end of a lawn is marked off by plantings. From the house I should like to be able to see halfway up a very gentle slope at least beyond the framework of the trees, for all these lake-shaped grassy vales filled with large and small clumps of trees, with a white roadway across or around them, resemble one another, and though they may be agreeable to behold, are annoying to inhabit.

I would not be disappointed were it possible to catch a glimpse of some great capital from the house. "There," I'd say, sitting at the foot of some old oak, "is the concert of foibles and vices. There on a parade ground you may notice the minatory air of peacetime heroes nervous, perhaps, about their performance in plays that every day they will have to rehearse." Or again, I'd say, "Those foolish people there are hastening to waste their time at shows that they must know by heart. And others, more dangerous, are running after ambition and ready to intrigue against someone in high places. There you see lovers going to profess to several women what they

do not believe, perhaps incapable of proving what they claim. And there you see spiteful people, husbands on the alert, wives in arms, out to make amorous conquests." The more I recognize such agitation, the more I enjoy my peace and quiet.

It is impossible to see over the top of the woods or to procure intermittently an opening in some interesting and distant object, I would almost prefer to have a goosefoot formed by three long straight lines starting at any façade of the castle. And so as to be in the shade immediately on leaving the building, I insist on having the forest behind the house. Without the goosefoot, we are once more cooped up in the mistakes of a French garden; and without the forest, we are no less tanned by the sun in going across a lawn than at Versailles.

CHRISTIAN CAY LORENZ HIRSCHFELD
EXAMINING THE SITE (1779–85)

A German scholar and gardener, C.C.L. Hirschfeld (1742–1792) was a professor at Kiel University and also director of a fruit tree nursery. He wrote an important five-volume treatise entitled *Theorie der Gartenkunst* between 1779 and 1785. This excerpt is from the translation by modern scholar Linda B. Parshall published in 2001 as *Theory of Garden Art.*

1. The site of a garden is, so to speak, the canvas on which the garden artist paints. Therefore I will begin by examining this space.

The following is really self-evident; no region should be chosen that has unhealthy air; that is poisoned by rotting marshes and nearby morasses; that lies entirely in a depression or consists of nothing but arid, sandy soil; that can only be improved with considerable effort and expense; that can have no open vistas or is surrounded by wretched moors and dying vegetation. The need for health, comfort, and pleasure is so obvious that no one with human feeling can deny it. . . .

2. There are several reasons to choose a site that is naturally beautiful. It inspires the genius of the garden artist, who then works beneath the gaze of delightful nature, his model and competitor. It also lessens effort and costs by providing materials such as ground, trees, bushes, and water more generously. It heightens the effect of the garden's interior through the impressions made by the surrounding vistas. . . .

But vistas should not be completely open at all points, not observable in their full grandeur from every part of the garden, because they would interfere with the effects of the different garden scenes when these are meant to be on display. Views into the distance should thus be sometimes closed, sometimes opened; they should be amended according to one perspective or another, so each view's own effect is not only heightened and multiplied but brought into harmony with the garden's other scenes. No garden artist should ever disregard this essential rule. Where soft melancholy, contemplation, and peace dominate, where the eye is to be entertained by observing the present scene alone, a cheerful vista would be misplaced. . . .

3. The scale of the site helps determine the inner layout and arrangements of all the scenes. The larger the circumference, the more is expected of the garden artist's genius. Any area destined to be a garden must be extensive enough so the scenes do not pile up but follow each other gradually, so the emotions are not confused but are brought forth little by little in a harmonious, progressive sequence.

A site that is too narrow, even if it is long, is difficult to shape into a successful garden. Whenever possible it should be extensive on all sides.

4. A site consisting of nothing but a level is not very suitable for a garden, because it is too uniform, and manmade alterations are too expensive. It is better to choose a region that, although not entirely without levels, since these are always useful, also boasts

natural rises, hollows, and considerable variety. Such a site is not just inherently variable, it can also enhance the variety and effect of the garden scenes that will be placed there. It is wise to accept whatever advantages nature offers in perfecting a garden's design.

Flowers, shrubs, trees, water, and grazing herds are suitable means to relieve the uniformity of a plain. But a mountainous or hilly landscape is naturally more changeable and animated. . . .

5. First and foremost, one must study the natural character of any region one wants to shape into a garden, in order to become familiar with it and to make the best possible use of it. This rule is seldom observed. So many common gardeners have their plans and sketches finished before they even know where a garden should be sited. So many architectural theorists design gardens without paying the slightest attention to variations in the ground that must be seen and evaluated before any drawing is ventured. From this comes the habit of looking only at paper and never at the land, from this the infinite uniformity that has spread its sad appearance throughout European gardens, because it has never occurred to anyone to seek advice from the very best instructor: the genius of the ground.

It cannot be overemphasized that nature should be followed; but she should not be spoiled by wasted effort and expense nor deformed by misguided attempts at improvement. Also, no garden plan should imitate just one pleasing model; rather, each case must be considered according to the particular disposition of the region where the garden is to be constructed. This way is truer to nature; various gardens will be beautiful, without any being exact copies. . . .

6. It is a garden artist's duty to correct or conceal the intrinsic defects of his site—defects that nature can readily ignore in her larger efforts—yet he must do so without excessive fastidiousness. . . . He does not remember that small shortcomings can coexist with beauty, and that when they are removed, naturalness, always pleasing, loses something as well.

7. One cannot be reminded enough to avoid unnecessary destruction of the natural objects found at garden sites. Many people believe that before they can begin planting, they must remove everything nature has allowed to grow; yet experience shows that they would achieve their goals much earlier and more happily if they assisted nature through more moderate changes and additions. Meanwhile, when the new plantings fail to thrive or are slow to attain a certain perfection, these people tire of the new design, or change it from time to time until so much is altered that the project is beyond help.

Something that at first glance appears superfluous or even adverse can, after closer reflection, be deftly woven into the plan. It is a sort of crime when a tree that has taken half a century to achieve its lovely growth is cut down for the sake of a trifle. . . .

Do not misinterpret these remarks. If something noticeably disturbs an agreeable view or simply creates opposition, go ahead and cut it down; any garden artist who introduces plantings is also set the task of removing anything disruptive to his plan for beautification. But do not ruin anything without need. There is a familiar anecdote about how the duc d'Antin had an entire, beautiful woodland razed just to cater to one of Louis XIV's momentary whims, and this deserves recalling so as to put similar royal flatterers to shame. . . .

8. This much can generally be maintained: borders should not be forced into specific, measured forms such as squares; they should not have noticeable or precise edges; they are more agreeable if they merge gradually into the open landscape, without a clear boundary marked by a wall or ditch. In this way a garden looks not only more natural but also more spacious. The sight of the end of a pleasant spot irritates us, as does the idea that there we have to turn back again. But an extended vista and the discovery of new objects in the distance satisfy a need of our imagination in a tangible way. . . .

The most agreeable borders of a garden are still a wood, a meadow, or especially a lake. Each is constantly pleasing, not only because of its inherent qualities, but also because it occupies and entertains the eye, inviting it to linger. In contrast, we flee from the end of a garden bordered by a dark pond, a peat bog, or a barren moor.

JOSIAH CONDER
ASPECT AND PROSPECT (1893)

An English architect, Conder (1852–1920) went to Japan in 1877 to become the first architecture instructor in the Engineering Department of the Imperial University. In addition to designing Western-style buildings in Japan, he became an avid student of Japanese arts. He wrote *Landscape Gardening in Japan* in 1893, based on his readings of the works by garden masters listed in his footnote.

Before referring in detail to the models followed in the arrangement of different kinds of gardens, it is interesting to note instructions laid down by various writers* as to garden composition in general. . . .

Before proceeding with the garden construction, a complete survey and thorough examination of the site and of its surroundings are required. Its size, peculiarities of shape, levels, and drainage must all be considered. If the area be a bare and level one, the designer has considerable license, provided that he keeps in mind the aspect, neighbouring prospects, and the character of garden best calculated to suit his client. Guided by these limitations, he will consult his sketches, and perhaps make frequent visits to existing gardens, to assist him in originating a design. This he will subject to thorough reconsideration in every detail. If, however, the locality selected possesses certain natural facilities, such as fine clumps of trees, natural hills, a stream, or a cascade, the artist's controlling motive will be to work these features cleverly into his design. In

the same way, a neighbouring view may be skillfully taken advantage of, the garden being so arranged that it appears, when regarded from the foreground, as a part of the general composition.

Aspect must be considered as well as prospect. An open view to the south or south-east is a great natural advantage, as is also an elevated wooded bank or a grove of high trees to the north or west. In Japan, a southern aspect is always sought for the principal rooms of dwellings. The summer breezes mostly blow from this direction, and the altitude of the sun when in this quarter prevents its glare penetrating the eave-shaded chambers. Next in favour is the eastern aspect, because it receives the pleasant and comparatively harmless morning sunshine. The north is, of course, the coldest and most cheerless quarter, but the west is even more disliked, on account of the fierce glare of the low afternoon sunshine which enters every opening. Moreover, the bitterest and bleakest winds of winter blow from the north and west. In the neighbourhood of Tokio, however, the world-famed mountain Fujisan is to be seen towards the west, for which reason it is customary to seek a partially open prospect in this direction, some important room in the dwelling having a small round window to afford a view of this peerless peak. Rules governing the aspect of apartments must necessarily control, to a great extent, the whole garden composition. The principal living and reception rooms of a residence form the central point of view from which the artificial landscape is regarded. Within the compass of the grounds may be several distinct views, each seen to greatest advantage from certain secondary stations, but the united composition as a whole must be best commanded from the dwelling itself. From here, also, should be obtained the finest prospect of some central object in the distance which dominates the landscape.

If a garden be constructed in a place where fine trees already stand, others of the same species should be planted beyond them, so that they may appear to blend into the composition. The same method should be followed with regard to any existing rocks or boulders of a picturesque appearance; they should be retained, and

RITSURIN PARK (Edo period, 1600–1868)
Takamatsu, Japan
CORBIS

reinforced by additional stones harmonising with them in character, and arranged so as to unite them to the general landscape. In taking advantage of an outside view to impart the idea of expanse, it is recommended to plant within the grounds trees of the same kind as those seen in the distance, their heights being gradually raised or lowered so as to lead the eye by degrees to the scale of the background.

Somewhat conflicting instructions are laid down as to the portion of a landscape garden which should first be worked upon, some writers holding that the foreground takes precedence, and others contending that the background should receive primary attention. All agree, however, that the mid-distance is of less importance, and may be finished last. The best method is probably that recommended by one authority of roughing out almost simultaneously, and elaborating alternately, step by step, both the foreground and the distance; for though it is generally considered that that background ranks first in importance, its true value is best secured by accommodating it to the scale and character of the nearer portions of the garden.

As mentioned previously, Sen-no-Rikiu is said to have taken a system of composition by which larger trees were planted in the front parks of the grounds, and lower ones in the background, thus assisting the effect of perspective distance—an advantage particularly desirable in small gardens. On the same principle he maintained that more distant hillocks should be made lower than the nearer ones, and the level of artificial water higher in the background than in the foreground. This method is known by the name of the "Distance-lowering Style" (Saki-sagari), as distinct from the "Distance-raising Style" (Saki-agari), attributed to another artist—Furuta Oribe. The latter treatment consisted in placing the taller trees and more elevated hills behind, and gradually lowering the heights of objects towards the front of the garden.

*   Hishigawa Kichibei, Kitamura Enkin, Akisato Ritoken, Abe Rekisai, Choseisha, Gokiogoku Kakuo, Yokoi Tokifuyu, Honda Kinkichiro, and Takatsu Chugoro.

KATHRYN GUSTAFSON
THE IMPORTANCE OF SITE (2004)

The American landscape architect and artist Kathryn Gustafson (born 1951) studied landscape architecture in Paris. Her recent work includes Westergasfabriek Culture Park in Amsterdam, the National Botanic Garden of Wales, the Diana, Princess of Wales, Memorial Fountain in London, and the Garden of Forgiveness in Beirut. Her recent American commissions include Lurie Garden in Chicago and plans for the Museum of Fine Arts, Boston. This essay was based on an interview with the editor of this book.

The first visit to the site is a primordial experience for the designer. I need to sit down quietly and observe the landscape. The land has many messages to convey, if you simply take your time—watch and listen. In addition to the natural and climatic aspects of the site, there are also cultural and historical messages. The designer must conduct extensive research to understand past uses of the site and their meanings.

Ultimately the most important determinant of the design for a site is its program and its eventual uses. The site could serve as a freeway, garden, playground, or memorial. Each one of these programs shapes decisions on the development of each part of the site. The optimal design is one informed by communications with the client as well as the natural, cultural, and historical messages of the site.

Success is measured by the degree in which design and site merge in a self-evident and harmonious way. The space needs to have a conceptual force. It should have emotional and intellectual impact on the people passing through it. People respond to and appropriate spaces that they feel connected to. This connection and pride in place leads the public to take care of these spaces. Equally important, the space attracts care and concern of people if it meets a diversity of needs and desires. A park needs to have

previous spread:
JAY PRITZKER PAVILION (design begun
1999 by Frank Gehry) and THE LURIE
GARDEN (lead designer Gustafson Guthrie
Nichol Ltd, begun 2000)
Chicago, Illinois
Gustafson Guthrie Nichol Ltd

opposite:
THE LURIE GARDEN (lead designer
Gustafson Guthrie Nichol Ltd, begun 2000)
Chicago, Illinois
Gustafson Guthrie Nichol Ltd

places where one can find sun or shade; places of rest; places of excitement; and places for intimate conversations and large gatherings.

Let me provide an example of how the above multi-variants shape the design of a site. The Seattle office of Gustafson Guthrie Nichol (GGN Ltd) worked on the creation of the 2.5-acre Lurie Garden for Chicago's Millennium Park, which opened in July of 2004. The park stretches between the Chicago Art Institute and the Pritzker Bandshell by Frank Gehry. The park is a transition fabric between the city and Grant Park, an integration of culture and landscape.

The design takes its conceptual basis from the history of Chicago and the site itself. Chicago is called the "City of Big Shoulders," so the park has a big-shoulder hedge that is fifteen feet high and fifteen feet deep. It protects an inner sanctuary of two gardens: the Dark Plate and the Light Plate. The Seam runs between these two gardens and is the point where Chicago pulled itself out of the water and marshes after the Great Fire of 1871 and then rebuilt itself above the water and land. The Dark Plate represents the ecological natural past, and the Light Plate represents the present and foresight of the population, their courage and energy to embrace the future. The Dark Plate's hardscape and softscape are very textured with dappled light. It is not a marsh in any sense, but is dense with light and shadows. A white cloud that encloses and frames the space is achieved with flowering cherry trees.

The Light Plate simulates an open prairie: full of sun and colors. It has 240 varieties of perennials changing throughout the seasons. Helping us on this project was Piet Oudolf, a Dutchman who is one of the best plantsmen in the world. The first time I saw one of his planting mixtures I said, "That looks like Italian food to me. It's full of colors and textures and exoticism." It was an amazing meal visually.

The Hedge is a mixture of evergreen and deciduous plants. The clipped beech and hornbeam will provide spring and fall color, and the many different evergreen plants give the hedge a marbled coloration. Le Nôtre at Versailles prefigured all the hedges with wood trellises and barriers, so that Louis XIV and his guests could visualize the garden in the future. The Lurie Garden has a large armature, which defines the form the hedge will take when it matures and will also serve as a pruning guide for maintenance purposes.

The Seam that is the border between the Light and Dark Plates has a limestone wall, a water feature, and a boardwalk. The water feature is designed to make the water lap against the wall and produce a sound very much like that of nearby Lake Michigan. A lake's sound is different from an ocean when it laps under piers and along the shore. We tried to echo the sound of the lake in the water feature.

In the landforms of the Light Plate and Dark Plate, we were inspired by the rolling hills of the Midwest. The topography is reflected in the ground planes of the Garden, which are formed to give that feeling of rolling, which I find quite beautiful.

The lighting for the Garden is very diverse and subtle to accentuate the qualities of the landscape features. The Dark Plate is about texture. All its light poles rise above the trees, and their lights shine through to cast shadows of branches on the ground. In the Light Plate, there are projectors that illuminate the entire plain.

There are also hedges in the Extrusion Plaza. They emerge out of the paving in that walkway. They are about Chicago's steel and extruded metal industry as well as the rail lines through the site.

The Lurie Garden demonstrates how the site's program with its natural, cultural, and historical aspects shape the final design. But even if the visitor is unaware of Chicago's ecological, economic, and social heritage, the garden can be simply enjoyed as a site for pure pleasure, decompression, and discovery. That's what a garden is for.

3

PLAN

Square forms are the most practical in gardens, be they perfect or oblong … they contain the straight lines that make allées *long and beautiful, and give them a pleasing perspective. But I do not believe that, with all the beauty such straight lines afford, we should neglect to mix in round and curved forms, or to place oblique forms among the square ones, in order to achieve variety that nature demands.*

Jacques Boyceau de la Baraudiere (died c. 1633), French garden designer and writer

You see nothing laid out in a line, nothing made level. The carpenter's line never entered this place. Nature plants nothing by the line.

Jean-Jacques Rousseau (1712–1778), French philosopher and novelist

In France they do not exactly comprehend our ideas on Gardening and Placemaking which when rightly understood will supply all the elegance and all the comforts which Mankind wants in the Country.… To produce these effects there wants a good plan, good execution, a perfect knowledge of the country and objects in it, whether natural or artificial, and infinite delicacy in the planting, etc.

Lancelot "Capability" Brown (1716–1783), English landscape architect

The landscape architect, or the architect, or the gardener should make his plan as an instruction for something that will grow into being.… After that he takes this plan and throws it in the fireplace and doesn't keep it as a record, because the next garden he makes must be completely different, because the garden is very, very private and belongs to an individual.

Louis I. Kahn (1901–1974), American architect

previous spread:
HAMPTON COURT PALACE (16th century)
and GARDEN (17th century)
East Molesey, England
Ted Spiegel/CORBIS

opposite:
GENERALIFE GARDENS AT THE
ALHAMBRA (1237–1492)
Granada, Spain
Paul Almasy/CORBIS

IBN LUYUN
PLANNING FUNDAMENTALS (c. 1349)

The poet Ibn Luyun (1282–1349) wrote *Kitab ibda al-malatha wa-inha al-rajaha fi usul sina at al-filaha* (Book on the principles of beauty and the purpose of learning which treats the fundamentals of art and agriculture) in Almeria, Spain. Later known as the "Andalusian Georgics," this book in verse draws on writings of Islamic, Greek, and Roman agricultural texts to guide gardeners. This excerpt is from a translation by James Dickie that was first published in 1976.

With regard to houses set amidst gardens an elevated site is to be recommended, both for reasons of vigilance and of layout;

and let them have a southern aspect, with the entrance at one side, and on an upper level the cistern and well,

or instead of a well have a watercourse where the water runs underneath the shade.

And if the house have two doors, greater will be the security it enjoys and easier the repose of its occupant.

Then next to the reservoir plant shrubs whose leaves do not fall and which (therefore) rejoice the site;

and, somewhat further off, arrange flowers of different kinds, and, further off still, evergreen trees,

and around the perimeter climbing vines, and in the centre of the whole enclosure a sufficiency of vines;

and under climbing vines let there be paths which surround the garden to serve as margin.

And amongst the fruit trees include the (common) grapevine similar to a slim woman, or wood-producing trees;

afterward arrange the virgin soil for planting whatever you wish should prosper.

In the background let there be trees like the fig or any other which does no harm;

and plant any fruit tree which grows big in a confining basin so that its mature growth

may serve as a protection against the north wind without preventing the sun from reaching (the plants).

In the centre of the garden let there be a pavilion in which to sit, and with vistas on all sides,

But of such a form that no one approaching could overhear the conversation within and whereunto none could approach undetected.

Clinging to it let there be (rambler) roses and myrtle, likewise all manner of plants with which a garden is adorned.

And this last should be longer than it is wide in order that the beholder's gaze may expand in its contemplation.

VINCENZO GIUSTINIANI
INSTRUCTIONS TO A BUILDER AND GARDENER (c. 1615–20)

Giustiniani (1564–1637) was a Genoese nobleman, banker, patron and collector of the arts, traveler, and garden designer. Between 1615 and 1620, he wrote a letter to the lawyer Teodoro Amideni to provide counsel on the siting, planning, designing, and construction of a private house and garden. Peter Armour translated the letter and excerpt below.

One must be especially careful in choosing a site. . . . In particular, one should avoid a site which would expose it to harmful winds, or a position which would cause many difficulties in construction work, such as a marshy region, or a mountainside, or the bottom of a valley through which a swift stream runs, or a place liable to erosion or landslides from a mountain or terrain which is unstable, clayey, with pinched, sharp, and unreliable soil. One should avoid a site which is very uneven, rocky, and hard, where leveling would

VILLA ROTUNDA (designed c. 1566 by
Andrea Palladio)
Vicenza, Italy
Yann Arthus-Bertrand/CORBIS

require excessive expenditure in proportion to the rest of the work. One should choose a site which is high rather than low, so that the building will stand out; it should be exposed to healthy winds and protected from harmful ones; and it should be easily reached without discomfort to the owner or to those who live on his lands or in neighbouring places.

If, however, there is no freedom of choice regarding the site and one has to decide to build on a particular spot, all I can say is that one must adapt to the inevitable and try to resolve the difficulties which present themselves in order to complete the project with the best possible results, under the conditions described above, avoiding risks and providing for safety as best as one can with the least expense. . . .

All that remains now is for me to say a few things briefly about gardens and a way of forming and ornamenting them based on the little experience I acquired by designing my garden in Bassano from the very beginning, laying it out on an uneven and very irregular site, as I have mentioned, and in remodeling those I own in Rome, when I transformed them from untidy vineyards into ornate gardens set out with as much order as I could.

I say, therefore, as I have also indicated above, that one must first lay down the size and method of the work from the beginning, but with great vision, anticipating being able in due course to enlarge it without changing the initial order and form, for dismantling and then rebuilding is not only a waste of money but also earns one discredit, and the resulting piece of work is disordered, patched up, and confused. One should ensure that the open piazzas, theatres, and walks are as long and spacious as possible; the worst defect is for them to be cramped or narrow. They should be straight, level, and set at right angles, as far as the site allows, and the site can be changed and adapted slightly so that it does not spoil the general symmetry of the plan. Care should be taken to plant groves, trees on espaliers, and other trees and shrubs which are appropriate to the climate and the soil, and some which keep their

leaves in winter too; otherwise, one will always be back at the beginning, patching up and replacing withered plants with new ones, and never see the garden in the form desired in the first place. It is not a good idea, therefore, to go in for intricate designs of close-cut lawns and flowers which need meticulous care to protect them from the four extremes of weather; they are very costly and also irksome because of the continual patching up and failures. It will be quite enough to lay out some small areas in this way, especially near fountains; they will serve to give variety and a sort of ornamentation in miniature to the whole garden. Greater attention must be paid to its more solid and durable ornamentation, namely, large groves with a natural, wild look; groves of trees which always keep their foliage, planted with order, at angles, and in directions which give them matching alignment from every viewpoint, following a line carefully marked out with twine; and also "web-groves" (*ragnaie*) which are very common in Tuscany, not just for their appearance but also for the scope they give for various methods of bird-snaring, and which should consist of suitable trees and have some small supply of running water. The garden should also have covered avenues in which one can walk in the heat of summer. These are very common in France, where I have seen some very beautiful examples, and they are called allées.

One must be very careful to ensure that the espaliers last well, and if the climate is chilly and subject to ground-frosts, snow, and hail, one must choose trees which can usually withstand these conditions, such as junipers, boxwoods, noble laurels, arbutus, and perhaps the common laurel and the laurustinus. Because of the greater risks if the site is hot and dry, one will need ready supplies of water, and in this case one can choose Seville oranges, citrons, lemons, and other similar trees of quality.

One should in fact strive to create the most durable garden possible, one which will not force the owner to be constantly busy attending to it, preoccupied in protecting it daily from damage, and making good any losses. All this would be a form of torture rather than pleasure.

My final point is that, if the garden is a large one, or at least bigger than average, with a variety of avenues, open piazzas, and porticoes at the ends of the avenues, it will be necessary to give as specific a name as possible to everything, according to its qualities, ornamentation, shape, position, or other token. This is so that, when talking about the garden, everyone understands perfectly which part is meant; otherwise, there will always be confusion. As an example, I shall give you the names of some parts of my garden in Bassano, which you have seen and examined: the garden of the squares above the grotto of the dwarf-trees; the main avenue to the web-groves, the covered walks, the gallery, the avenue of the pear-trees, the avenue of the roses; the theatre of Navona; the piazza of the Rocca; Mount Parnassus; the avenue of Aesculapius; the barrel grove; the avenue of the fish-pond; the hillock; the square piazza; the avenue of the hillside; the avenue of the river-banks; the avenue of the stream; the avenue of the hazel-nuts; the fir-grove; the round piazza; and so on. I list these names in order to refresh your memory of the delight you showed when you saw all these places. I shall not deal with fruit-trees and vines because these belong to vineyards rather than to gardens, although gardens should not be entirely without them and should have some planted in specially selected, sunny positions; they should be of good varieties and give pleasure to the owners. To add that gardens must have running water which flows from the highest source and as plentifully as possible seems to me to be superfluous, for there is no one, however dull-witted and foolish, who does not acknowledge the effects of beauty, utility, nobility, and grandeur which it creates for the owner and for all who see it, to their great satisfaction and delight.

JI CHENG
LAYOUT (c. 1631–34)

Born in 1582 in China's Jiangsu Province, Ji Cheng was a prominent Ming-dynasty landscape and rock artist. His designs included gardens south of the Chiangjiang (formerly Yangtze River). He wrote *Yuan Ye* (The Craft of Gardens) between 1631 and 1634. It is believed to be one of the first general manuals on landscape gardening in the Chinese tradition. This except was taken from the translation by Alison Hardie, published in 1988.

LAYOUT

The most important element in the layout of gardens is the siting of the principal buildings. The primary consideration is the view, and it is all the better if the buildings can also face south. If there are some tall trees around, then keep one or two of them growing in the courtyards. When you build walls you must spread them widely and preserve plenty of open space within them, so that you can arrange and lay out the place exactly as you wish. Once you have picked a site for the main buildings, you can use the remaining space for the construction of pavilions and terraces. Their form should follow what is appropriate, and you should cultivate the plants around them very carefully.

ON GARDENS

Generally, in the construction of gardens, whether in the countryside or on the outskirts of a city, a secluded location is the best. In clearing woodland one should select and prune the tangled undergrowth; where a fine piece of natural scenery occurs one should make the most of it. Where there is a mountain torrent one may cultivate orchids and angelica together. Paths should be lined with the "three auspicious things" whose property it is to symbolize eternity. The surrounding wall should be concealed under creepers, and rooftops should emerge here and there above the tops of the trees. If you climb a tower on a hill-top to gaze into the distance, nothing but beauty will meet your eye; if you seek a secluded spot among banks of bamboo, intoxication will flood your heart. The pillars of your verandah should be tall and widely spaced; your windows and doors should give an unimpeded view.

The view should include a watery expanse of many acres and contain the changing brilliance of the four seasons. The shadow of phoenix trees should cover the ground, the shade of pagoda trees pattern the walls. Willows should be set along the embankments, plum trees around the buildings; reeds should be planted among the bamboos. A long channel should be dug out for the stream. With hillsides as tapestries and mountains as screens, set up a thousand feet of emerald slopes; though man-made, they will look like something naturally created. Shadowy temples should appear through round windows, like a painting by the Younger Li. Lofty summits should be heaped up from rocks cut to look as if they were painted with slash strokes, uneven like the half-cliffs of Dachi. If you can have a Buddhist monastery as your neighbour, the chanting of Sanskrit will come to your ears; if distant mountain ranges can be included in the view, their fresh beauty is there for you to absorb. With the grey-violet of vaporous morning or pale evening mist, the cry of cranes will drift to your pillow. Among the white duckweed and red polygonum, flocks of gulls will gather beside your jetty. To see the mountains, ride on a bamboo litter; to visit the river, lean on an oaken staff. Slantwise soar the parapets, crosswise strides the long rainbow bridge. You need not envy Wang Wei's Wangchuan; Jilun's Golden Valley will count for nothing. Is Xiaoxia the only bay worthy of the name? There are more open spaces here than Cangchun. . . .

SITUATION

In laying the foundations of a garden you should not feel any restriction as to the direction it faces; the shape of the ground will have its natural highs and lows. There should be something to arouse interest as you pass through the gate; you should follow the natural lie of the land to obtain interesting views, whether the garden lies beside wooded hills or abuts on a stream or pool. To make good use of unusual features adjacent to the city you must keep far from major thoroughfares. To find outstanding sites in the local villages, you should avail yourself of the uneven height of deep woods. If you place your garden in a country village you can gaze into the distance; if it is in a market town it will be more convenient to reach from your home. If you are constructing the garden from scratch, then it will be easy to lay out the foundations, but for immediate effect you can do no more than plant some willows and transplant bamboo. There is more skill involved in redesigning an old garden, although you have the natural advantages of ancient trees and profusely growing flowers.

Some gardens are naturally rectangular, some rounded, others linear, others curving. If the garden is lengthy and curving it should take the form of a circular jade. If it is straight and wide it should suggest spreading clouds. If it is high and square you should make use of pavilions and terraces. If it is low and concave you can dig out pools and ponds. When you are taking geomantic readings to locate the garden, it is advantageous to have an area of water, and when starting to work on the main plan, you should go straight to the water source. You should dredge the course of the stream and find out where the water comes from or flows to. . . .

If the garden is to be adorned with scenery belonging to another landowner, providing there is a single thread of connection between them, then it is not really separate, and it is quite appropriate to "borrow" the view. If it faces on to a neighbor's flowers, however small a glimpse of them is to be had, they can be called into play and one can enjoy an unlimited springtime. If you build a bridge across water which would otherwise form a barrier you can then construct a separate cottage worthy of a painting. If you pile up rocks to make a surrounding wall, you can have something comparable to a mountain retreat.

If there are trees which have stood for many years that would get in the way of the eaves or walls of your building, you should set

HUMBLE ADMINISTRATORS GARDEN
(designed c. 1509 by Wang Xianchen)
Suzhou, China
John T. Young/CORBIS

the foundations back a bit, or else lop off a few branches to avoid the roof, for it is comparatively easy to construct carved beams and soaring pillars, but it takes a long time to grow pagoda trees old enough to give real shade and bamboo groves like a mass of green jade.

To sum up, if one chooses an appropriate site, the construction of the garden will follow naturally. . . .

SITES BESIDE A MANSION HOUSE

If there is the merest fraction of land beside or behind your mansion, you can construct a garden there; not only is it convenient for enjoying your leisure moments in, but it can also be regarded as an excellent cordon for protecting the house. Excavate a pool and dig out a moat, arrange rocks and build up a mountain, construct a gate to welcome arriving visitors, and keep a path open to connect it to the nearest building. With bamboo growing elegantly and trees flourishing, with shady willows and bright flowers, an area of five *mu* is not a restriction; in fact you can rival Lord Wen's Garden of Solitary Delight. Throughout the four seasons never let the flowers fade, and you will be able to wander through them together with your pageboy Little Jade.

During the days of blossoming mornings and nights of moonlit dusks, when your household is serving you with wine, you may reveal the treasures concealed in your seraglio; when guests gather together for a poetry contest, you can make them drink a forfeit of three ladles of wine as in "The Golden Valley." With people chanting stanzas all around you, it will be like a little paradise. You will constantly have your couch strewn with lutes and books, and never be without the wraith-like stems of bamboo.

If you build your hut by a mountain torrent, it seems you are sure to find peace and quiet. But if you bring the mountains to your home, what need is there to search for remote places? Your mansion will inherit the lofty style of the poet Xie Tiao, and the hill-tops will be pierced with the echoing whistle of the hermit Sun Deng.

When looking for plum blossoms you can do without Meng Haoran's donkey. And when you boil water from snow you will be accompanied by a concubine as lovely as Tao Yi's. You can entrust your purified body to the Dark and the Yellow, and then you need not consider your attitude towards other people.

You would never think that a garden which will last a thousand years could be made by the hand of man, who lasts but a hundred. The pleasure and relaxation of it are enough in themselves, but more, the garden will protect your mansion and keep it free from disturbance.

ANTOINE-JOSEPH DEZALLIER D'ARGENVILLE
OF THE DISPOSITION OF GARDENS (1709)

A French naturalist, engraver, and writer on art, Dezallier (1680–1765) published *La Théorie et la pratique du jardinage* (The Theory and Practice of Gardening) in 1709. The work elucidates the garden design principles of Le Nôtre and his school. The selection below is based on the John James translation of 1712.

To make a complete Disposition and Distribution of a general Plan, Respect must be had to the Situation of the Ground: For the greatest Skill in the right ordering of a Garden is, thoroughly to understand, and consider the natural Advantages and Defects of the Place; to make use of the one, and to redress the other: Situations differing in every Garden.

The Variety and Diversity of the Composition contributes no less to complete a Garden, than the most discreet and well-contriv'd Distribution; since, in the Opinion of every one, the

VERSAILLES CHATEAU (designed in 1661
by Louis Le Vau) and GARDENS (1662,
André Le Nôtre)
Versailles, France
Adam Woolfitt/CORBIS

Gardens that afford the greatest Variety, are the most valuable and magnificent.

'Tis, therefore, the great Business of an Architect, or Designer of Gardens, when he contrives a handsome Plan, with his utmost Art and good Œconomy to improve the natural Advantages, and to redress the Imperfections, Shelvings, and Inequalities of the Ground. With these Precautions he should guide and restrain the Impetuosity of his Genius, never swerving from Reason, but constantly submitting, and conforming himself to that which suits best with the Natural Situation of the Place. . . .

These that follow are somewhat near the general Rules one ought to observe in the Disposition and Distribution of Gardens.

There should always be a Descent from the Building to the Garden, of three Steps at least; this renders the Fabrick more dry and wholesome; and from the Head of these steps you have a general View of the Garden, or of great Part of it, which yields a most agreeable Prospect.

A PARTERRE is the first thing that should present itself to Sight, and possess the Ground next the Fabrick, whether in Front, or on the Sides; as well as on Account of the Opening it affords the Building, as for the Beauty and Splendor wherewith it constantly entertains the Eye, when seen from every Window of the House. The Sides of a Parterre should be furnished with such Works as may improve and set it off; for this being low, and flat, necessarily requires something raised, as Groves and Palisades are. But, herein, Regard should be had to the Situation of the Place; and it should be observed, before you plant, whether the Prospect that Way be agreeable; for then the Sides of the Parterre should be kept entirely open, making use of Quarters of Grass, and other flat Works, to make the best of the View, and taking Care not to shut it up with Groves, unless they are planted in Quincunce, or opened with low Hedge-Rows, which hinder not the Eye from piercing through the Trees, and discovering the Beauties of the Prospect on every Side.

If there be no Vista, but on the contrary, you have a Mountain, Hill, Forest, or Wood, that by their Vicinity deprive you of that Pleasure, or some Village too near adjoining, the Houses of which make no agreeable Sight; you may then edge the Parterre with Palisades and Groves, to hide those ill-favour'd Objects; for by this Means you lose nothing, nor have anything to regret in Time to come.

Would it not be a great Grievance, to be obliged, some Years after planting, to grub up a Wood, or to cut it down to a certain height, because 'twas ill placed at first, and takes away the Prospect, which is the most valuable Thing about a Country-Seat?

GROVES make the Chief of a Garden, and are a great Ornament to all the other Parts; so that one can never plant too many of them, provided the Places design'd them take not up those of the Kitchen and Fruit-Gardens, which are Things very useful and necessary for a great House, and which should be constantly placed near the Bass-Courts.

To accompany Parterres, we make choice of those Designs of Wood-work that are most delicate, as Groves opened in Compartiments, Quincunces, Verdant-halls, with Bowling-greens, Arbour-work, and Fountains in the middle. These small Groves are so much the more agreeable near a House, in that you presently find Shade, without going far to seek it; besides, they communicate a Coolness to the Apartments, which is very much courted in hot Weather.

It would be of use to plant some small Groves of Evergreens, that you might have the Pleasure of seeing a Wood always verdant in the very coolest Seasons. They would look very well when seen from the Building; and I earnestly recommend the Planting of some Squares of them in a handsome Garden, to make a Diversity from the other Wood; which, having lost its Leaves, appears quite naked all the Winter.

The head of a Parterre is normally adorned with Basons, or Water-works; and beyond, with a circular line of Palisades, or

Wood-work, cut into a Goose-foot, which leads into the great Walks; and the Space between the Basons and the Palisade is fill'd with small pieces of Embroidery, of Grass-work, set out with Yews, Cases, and Flower-pots.

In Gardens that have Terraces, whether Side-ways or in Front of the Building, where there is a delightful Prospect, as you cannot shut up the Head of the Parterre by a circular Palisade, you must, to continue the View, lay several Compartments of a Parterre together, such as Embroidery, Green-Plots, after the *English* Manner, or Cut-work, which should be divided at convenient Distances by Cross-walks, taking care that the Parterre of Embroidery be always next to the Building, as being the richest and most magnificent.

The Principal Walk should be made in Front of the Building, and another large one to cross it at right Angles, provided they be double, and very wide. At the End of these Walks, the Walls may be pierced with Grills, or have Openings with Ditches at the Foot of them, to continue the View.

If you have any Part of your Ground naturally low and marshy, that you would not be at the Expense of filling up, you may employ it in Bowling-greens, Water-works, and even in Groves, raising the Alleys only to the Level of those that are near them, and that lead thither.

After you have laid out the great Walks and chief Lines, and have dispos'd the Parterres and Works about the Sides and Head of them, as is most suitable to the Ground, you may furnish the rest of the Garden above with many different Designs, as tall Groves, Quincunces, Close-Walks, Galleries, and Halls of Verdure, Green-Arbours, Labyrinths, Bowling-greens, and Amphitheatres, adorned with Fountains, Canals, Figures, etc. Which works distinguish a Garden very much from what is common, and contribute not a little to render it magnificent....

You should observe, in placing and distributing the several parts of the Gardens, always to oppose them one to another: For Example; A Wood to a Parterre, or a Bowling-green; and not to put all the Parterres on one Side, and all the Wood on other; nor to set a Bowling-green against a Bason, which would be one Gap against another: This must be constantly avoided, by setting the Full against the Void; and Flat-works against the Raised, to make a Contrariety.

And this Diversity should be kept not only in the general Design of a Garden, but likewise in each distinct Piece; as, if two Groves are upon the Side of a Parterre, tho' their outward Form and Dimensions are equal, you should not, for that reason, repeat the same Design in both, but make them different within. For it would be very disagreeable to find the same Thing on both Sides; and, when a Man has seen one, to have nothing to invite his Curiosity to see the other; which makes a Garden, so repeated, justly reckon'd no more than half a Design. This Fault was formerly very common; but is not so of late, every one being now convinced, that the greatest Beauty of Gardens is Variety. The several Parts of each Piece should also be diversified, as, if a Bason be circular, the Walk that surrounds it should be Octangular; and so of Bowling-greens, and Grass-Plots, that are in the midst of Groves....

In the Business of Designs, you should studiously avoid the Manner that is mean and pitiful, and always aim at that which is great and noble; not making little Cabinets and Mazes, Basons like Bowl-dishes, and Alleys so narrow, that two persons can scarce go abreast in them: 'Twere infinitely better to have but two or three Things, somewhat large, than a dozen small ones, which are no more than very Trifles.

Before the Design of a Garden be put into Execution, you should consider what it will be in 20 or 30 Years to come, when the Trees are spread, and the Palisades grown up: For, very often, a Design, which looks handsome and of good Proportion when it is first planted, in Process of Time becomes so small and ridiculous, that one is obliged to alter it, or to destroy it entirely, and plant another in the room of it....

THOMAS D. CHURCH
THE DOMINANT IDEA (1955)

Pioneer of the California Style, Church (1902–1978) utilized in his garden designs asymmetrical plans, raised beds, seat walls, paving, and broad timber decks. His best-known commission, the El Novillero garden at Sonoma, California (1947–49), has become an icon of twentieth-century landscape architecture. Church described his view of garden design in his first book, *Gardens Are for People* (1955), from which the following essay is an excerpt.

It is important that the garden be built around a dominant idea. Do one thing well and let all others be subordinate in scale to this idea. If it be a central grass plot surrounded by a flower border do not clutter the area with miscellaneous planting and garden ornament which will distract the eye and diminish the dramatic effect of the scale of the original conception. Do not be afraid of large paved surfaces on terraces and entrance courts. The scale of these areas and the simplicity of their unbroken lines are an important consideration in the pleasant relation of the garden to the house. Hard, uncompromising lines in the garden can be softened, to almost any extent desired, by planting. Once it is realized that this softening should be done by planting rather than by altering the dominant lines of the floor plan of the garden, you are on your way to a successful garden layout.

We all know completely natural gardens which are the envy of everyone who sees them—steep wooden slopes, or the banks of a stream, or a rocky hillside turned into an enchanting garden. If they are truly enchanting, it will be found that they dominate their surroundings, including the house (unless the garden is far enough away from the house not to count). Their charm will be found to lie in their suitability to their site and not in blindly following the conventions of informal gardening.

No definite style of garden from the past answers all the needs of today's small garden. Many gardens from the past help us to understand the underlying principles of building gardens for maximum enjoyment. There were the smart town gardens of Pompeii; the courtyard gardens of Spain; the walled flower gardens of Queen Elizabeth and Henry VIII. They all contributed to our knowledge of scale and livability as applied to the areas surrounding the house. This is a new era in garden making, because while many things have entered our life to make the problem complex, our ideas and requirements tend toward simplicity of solution....

Even the term "Garden" has changed its meaning. A garden used to have a horticultural meaning—a place where plants were grown to be displayed for mass effects or to be examined individually. It was a place to walk through, to sit in briefly while you contemplated the wonders of nature before you returned to the civilized safety of indoors. It was generally designed to provide a long vista from some dramatic spot within the house, such as the entry hall, the front steps, or a bay window. It was a place to be looked at rather than a place to be lived in.

The new kind of garden is still supposed to be looked at. But that is no longer its only function. It is designed primarily for living, as an adjunct to the functions of the house. How well it provides for the many types of living that can be carried on outdoors is the new standard by which we judge a garden.

This change in our ideas of what a garden is supposed to do for us was brought about by the force of several circumstances: the shrinking of the size of our houses due to high building costs, the disappearance of gardeners, the coming of power tools, and the increased use of glass. As the house grew smaller, many functions that used to go on inside the house were forced into less expensive space. Smaller rooms set up the need for bigger windows and whole walls of glass—to dissipate the feeling of claustrophobia. So presently it became inevitable that the garden should attach itself

EL NOVILLERO GARDEN (designed
in 1947, 1953 by Thomas Church)
Sonoma, California
Marc Treib

to the house, not only in use but structurally and visually. The garden had to go to work for us, solving our living problems while it also pleased our eyes and our emotional and psychological needs.

So a new trend was born—out of human necessities. No arbitrary whims or designer's caprices created this new kind of garden. It evolved naturally and inevitably from people's requirements. And out of the solutions to these requirements has come a whole new visual aesthetic, contributed to by many landscape designers in many parts of the country. Though this new kind of garden design was born out of the problems of new houses, it has lately been applied to the old as well. For it helps us get more usefulness from our property and gives a new usefulness to old houses.

Peace and ease are the dominant characteristics of the new garden—peace and beauty for the eye and ease of maintenance for the owner. Fewer and simpler lines are being used in the garden, and fewer and simpler materials. All is calculated to give complete restfulness to the eye. If the eye sees too many things, it is confused and the sense of peace is obliterated.

Simplification of lines does not mean eliminating outdoor structure. The closer house and garden are, in use and appearance, the more they begin to interlock visually. More and more the lines and materials of the house are carried outdoors and into the landscape. . . .

To succeed in making a logical and intelligent plan which will produce the maximum in terms of use and beauty, one must have simplicity of layout, integrity in the use of plant and structural materials, and a sure sense of proportion and pleasing form. Whether your design is "formal" or "informal," curved or straight, symmetrical or free, or a combination of all, the important thing is that you end up with a functional plan and an artistic composition. It must have good proportion and proper scale and plants that have been chosen wisely and cared for affectionately.

Rhythm and movement are essential. You expect them in the pictures you hang on your wall, in the music you listen to, in the poetry you read. In the garden it's the wind in the foliage and the dog running across the lawn. It's the line of the terrace and the repetition of richly textured foliage. The eye is a restless organ.

Symmetry can have motion. It's unimaginative formality that can become static. The eye prefers to move around a garden on lines that are provocative, never lose their interest, never end in dead corners, occasionally provide excitement or surprise, and always leave you interested and contented.

Someone may say, "I don't want it formal, laid out on an axis." The truth is your garden is never without at least one axis and probably has two or three. All compositions, however free, are built around them. The great designers of natural gardens may seem to have thrown away their T-squares, but the axis is just as strong as in the mirror pool of the Taj Mahal. It's just less obvious.

The axis becomes visual rather than mechanical and needn't be at right angles to the eye. The eye is tolerant. It may be influenced by a view, nudged by a tree, encouraged by a meadow, or seduced by a brook. Don't fret if your garden is never quite perfect. Absolute perfection, like complete consistency, can be dull. . . .

Yesterday's houses were high off the ground, needing a buffer of lilacs to relate them to the garden. Today they are low and friendly, sitting at ground level. The foundation has disappeared, but the habit of planting to hide it still remains.

Too much enthusiasm in planting at the base of a house can do a garden in quicker than anything else. It is a shame to veil any house in shrubbery when the house itself is well designed. To heavily fringe such a house with foundation planting is to deny its architectural entity and to negate the strength it gives to the garden composition. The relationship between the house and garden is maintained and emphasized by light, air, and visual space flowing freely from one to the other.

. . . .

DAN KILEY
CREATING LANDSCAPE SEQUENCES (1999)

Kiley (1912–2004) received his academic training at Harvard University. Along with James Rose, Garrett Eckbo, and Thomas Church, he rejected the formal Beaux Arts style, although he continued to employ classical elements in his modern compositions. Kiley designed parks and gardens for public and commercial buildings, such as the Oakland Museum and the Ford Foundation. This excerpt is from *Dan Kiley: The Complete Works of America's Master Landscape Architect* by Dan Kiley and Jane Amidon.

. . . .

I suddenly saw that lines, *allées* and orchards/bosques of trees, *tapis verts* and clipped hedges, canals, pools and fountains could be tools to build landscapes of clarity and infinity, just like a walk in the woods. I did not see then, and to this day do not see, a problem with using classic elements in modern compositions, for this is not about style of decoration but about articulation of space. The thing that is modern is space. You can't touch it; it is elusive but felt. I realized that the goal was to produce the art of necessity, to avoid caprice and ambiguity. To this end, as Goethe put it, ". . .Classic is the sound and Romantic is the sick. The Classic unfolds, the Romantic adds. . . ."

From that point onward, I experimented with the translation of various classic elements into a modern spatial sensibility, with the intention of creating landscape sequences to meet the daily needs of American families. I found that structural clarity and dynamism applied to corporate and public settings as well with powerful results. . . .

Each time you walk in nature, it is a fresh and original experience. Whether you squeeze through a small opening amongst maple trees, or pick your way across a rushing stream, or climb a hill to discover an open meadow, everything is always moving and changing spatially—towards the infinite. It's a continuing kind of

pull. Instead of copying the end-result of an underlaying process, I try to tap into the essence of Nature: the process is evolution; things are moving and growing in a related, organic way; that's what is exciting, this sense of space and release and movement. As Ralph Waldo Emerson put it, "Nature who abhors mannerisms has set her heart on breaking up all style and tricks." Instead, one must go right to the heart and source: the interplay of forms and volumes that, when arranged dynamically, release a continuum that connects outwards. Should not the role of design be to reconnect human beings with their space on their land?

The design we're looking for is always in the nature of the problem itself, it's something to be revealed and discovered. You might say that you are searching for the design latent in all conditions. That's how it all starts, really: I am excited first to get a diagram. If the diagram isn't right, no matter how much you "design," you can never solve the problem. . . . It is intrinsic; it's all there, waiting for you to release it. A site is almost never a big, blank slate waiting for your creative genius; it is a set of conditions and problems for which one seeks the highest solution. . . .

I feel that my current work is reaching a new level of integration and fluid order. We are reaching for a reduction and amplification of elements, relationships, and materials to achieve the purest connection to outer orders. My intent is to achieve the efficiency of form that leads to harmonic balance, the result of tapping into the source of life out of which Nature operates. Emerson knew this truth when he wrote, "It is the very elegance, integration, and proportioned harmony between opposing tensions that make our world a manifestation of ordered beauty. Nature is economical and embodies its organic harmonies in the fit and graceful patterns. Nature takes the shortest route and is a fertile balance of tensions."

When one of my sons was young, he would tag along behind the older generation and ask, "When are things going to be real?" This question stirs me even today, as it grasps at the core of life: there is never a point when one can stop and say, "Now I am done; this is the way it is and will be." To maintain a connection to the

ever-changing, growing network that is life, we must always be moving, ready to see and respond and evolve. Design is truly a process of discovery. It is an exciting dialogue that draws upon all of one's knowledge, intuitions, values, and inspirations. Luis Barrágan once said that "beauty speaks like an oracle, and man has always heeded its message in an infinite number of ways . . . a garden must combine the poetic and the mysterious with serenity and joy." It is the mystic and the beautiful that we seek to attain through revealing our place in the order of Nature. . . .

Frederick Law Olmsted posited that above all else, a design must be apt. Appropriate. It must respond to the orientation, the topography, the plant materials, the hydrology, and the built elements of a site, as well as to the locational codes, budget, and needs of the client. In the most basic sense, these aspects are interrelated, and their cumulative influences result in the notion of context. This is one of the few points on which I agree heartily with Olmsted, and it is one that guides my work every day. A designer must study and understand the idiosyncrasies of a given project, for that is where initial inspirations and indications come from. Design is not about preconceived ideas, and it does not spring from the air— it is a studied reaction to a set of given conditions. Then, intuition kicks in and brings fluidity and magic to the scheme. . . .

In this period, my partners and I became well versed in systems of order and scale, still using classic tools (lines or grids of trees, planes of grass and water, repetition, and rhythm) to form newly organic geometries. The geometries are often irregular but always balanced. Above all, geometries—usually expressed first as a pavement pattern on the ground plane, then seen in the modulation of plant beds and water elements, and finally confirmed with tree placements—instill a unity that relates directly to building and context. Spatial volumes that accommodate programmatic elements—blocks of trees, rows of hedge or ground cover, water walls and fountains—are integrated into the underlaying, unifying order in a harmonic manner. . . .

The best part of design is that there are no rules. One can do something different each time, start fresh (but with added depth of experience) on each problem, see the site with open, clear eyes that allow the highest solution to come forward. Design is truly a process of discovery. It is an exciting dialogue that draws upon all of one's knowledge, intuitions, values, and inspirations. To be good, the designer has to trust his or her instinct and go out on a limb to propose the best scheme, even though nothing like it has been done before.

JAMES VAN SWEDEN
ELEMENTS OF DESIGN (1997)

James van Sweden, born in 1935, earned a Bachelor of Architecture degree from the University of Michigan in 1960. He then studied landscape architecture at the University at Delft in the Netherlands and served as assistant town planner for the city of Amsterdam. Upon returning to the United States in 1963, he became a partner in charge of urban design and landscape architecture for Marcou, O'Leary and Associates in Washington, D.C., where he practiced until he formed a partnership with Wolfgang Oehme in 1977. This passage appeared in *Gardening with Nature: How James van Sweden and Wolfgang Oehme Plant Slopes, Meadows, Outdoor Rooms, and Garden Screens* (1997).

Wolfgang and I apply a few rules of thumb in beginning to draw a planting scheme. First we consider the site's natural framework. Following the Japanese tradition, we search for surrounding views to feature as "borrowed scenery": distant hills, a body of water, or even major trees on a neighbor's property. Next we take note of interesting features in the natural topography, such as the site's orientation to sunlight, breezes, and the quality of light at various times of day. Then we test the soil and carefully study the garden's climatic zone.

We begin our planting schemes by drawing in major design features, such as trees, shrubs, and large ornamental grasses. Large trees give the garden an overhead canopy. Smaller trees, shrubs, and grasses, placed singly and in groups, give structure to the garden, provide focal points, and frame views. Smaller plants soften walls, subdivide spaces, create transitions, and establish boundaries. We depend on the sculptural qualities of the plants to create patterns of tension, balance, and rhythm that pull the visitor visually and physically through the garden.

Next we fill in the ground plane with herbaceous perennials. These are the plants that create our lush and undulating "ground cover."... Taller specimens within these broad masses subdivide the planting into different layers that then move in all directions. While the overall size of these plant masses may change as they develop, the size of specific perennials and their relative proportion to each other will not change. We rarely include annuals in the planting areas, recommending instead that they be planted in containers to give color throughout the summer season.... Everyone loves color, so we use plants that are beautiful in flower. However, the full color range of leaves and dried seed heads from early spring through winter is just as important to us....

To connect the garden with its surroundings we place plants in broad, sweeping masses. At the same time, we design our gardens to be enjoyed at close range. These are spaces to be lived in, not just looked at, so we design comfortable places within the garden from which it can be enjoyed. From the house, a terrace, or a bench, our gardens radiate out with increasing simplicity until the distant view dissolves into a vast meadow.... This technique pulls the garden together and integrates it with its surroundings. It works in varying degrees at every scale....

Let me now share with you some basic tenets of garden design I have arrived at over the years that will help you achieve these objectives. Wolfgang and I rely on design tools such as those listed below when we start to lay out a garden....

- Establish a garden style. In addition to personal preference and lifestyle, factors that may influence your selection of a style include the architecture of the house and existing garden features that you want to keep. Remember that geometric shapes, straight lines, right angles, and strong axes are more formal in appearance, whereas curvilinear lines, free-form groupings, asymmetric patterns, and soft edges are more relaxed and informal.

- Think of your plan in three dimensions. Try to envision the plants' height and mass as you sketch them, and keep in mind that plants grow; your sketches should represent them in their mature state. If your garden space is flat, use plant masses of varying heights to give it three-dimensional interest.

- Play with spatial perception. You can expand or compress your perception of space through plant groupings, tree canopies, reflections on water surfaces, light and shade contrasts, and framing of distant views. Remember that linear patterns leading away from the eye stretch the space and make it look longer and narrower, whereas cross patterns foreshorten the space. Similarly, soft planting edges that blend with foliage on adjacent properties create an illusion of greater space.

WEEKEND RETREAT AND GARDEN
(designed in 1993 by James van Sweden)
Western shore, Chesapeake Bay, Maryland
James van Sweden

- Take advantage of existing slopes. An upward-sloping garden has the drama of a raked stage, whereas a downward sloping garden does not reveal its mysteries until visitors walk through it and then look back from below. Plants with deep fibrous roots such as *Rhus aromatica, Campsis radicans, Ceratostigma plumbaginoides, Hypericum calycinum, Carex muskingumensis* (palm sedge), and *Sesleria autumnalis* (autumn moor grass) are best for steep slopes. Heavy mulching may be necessary until the plants are established.

- Set up a progression of views. If you are fortunate enough to have a pleasing distant view, make it part of your garden. Think in terms of foreground, background, and even middle ground. Exaggerate a favorite view by framing it with plants or a structure such as an arbor.

- Never compete with natural beauty. If your garden is surrounded by dramatic natural scenery, keep your planting scheme simple. Use fewer varieties and larger masses; select textures and colors that are sympathetic with the background.

- Don't show everything at once; let your garden unfold as a series of discoveries. Even in a small garden, a meandering path that disappears behind plantings or a low wall entices visitors to investigate what lies beyond.

- If part of your garden is used for entertaining, consider the "outdoor room" concept. Your outdoor room can have "walls" (either plants or built features), a "carpet" (lawn or pavers), and a "ceiling" (tree canopy or vine-covered arbor).

- Reclaim the front yard for yourself. Be selfish with your view by placing the taller plant masses toward the street. Avoid "foundation" planting.

- Use patterns of sun and shade as part of your design. For example, it's always a delight when walking through a shady part of the garden to come upon an unexpected spot of brilliant sunlight.

- Use lawn and paved surfaces advisedly and only for specific purposes. Wolfgang and I limit lawn to functional roles: as an informal circulation system, as a good surface for yard games and children's play, and as a "carpet" for outdoor rooms.

4

STRUCTURE

The famous Le Nôtre, who lived in the last age, contributed to the destruction of nature by subjecting everything to the compass: the only ingenuity required, was measuring with a ruler, and drawing lines like the cross-bars of a window: then followed the plantation according to the rules of symmetry; the ground was laid smooth at great expense, the trees were mutilated and tortured in all ways, water shut up within four walls, the view confined by massy hedges, and the prospect from the house limited to a flat parterre, cut into squares like a chess board, where the glittering sand and gravel of all colors, only dazzled and fatigued the eyes; so that the nearest way to get out of this dull scene, soon became the most frequented path.

René-Louis de Girardin (1735–1808), French nobleman, garden designer, and writer

I repeat that man, by reason of his very nature, practices order; that his actions and his thoughts are dictated by the straight line and the right angle, that the straight line is instinctive in him and that his mind apprehends it as a lofty objective.

Le Corbusier (1887–1965), French architect

In these [Renaissance gardens] the authority of man was made visible by the imposition of a simple Euclidean geometry upon the landscape, and this is seen to increase within the period. Man imposes his simple, entertaining illusion of order, accomplished with great art, upon an unknowing and uncaring nature.

Ian McHarg (1921–2001), American landscape architect, professor, and writer

There are only two attitudes toward nature. One confronts it or accepts it. The former finds in nature but the rawest of materials to do with as one will—a form is imposed upon chaos. The latter discovers in chaos a new kind of naturalness—and to naturalize nature is to accept it.

Teiji Ito (1922–), Japanese garden writer

previous spread:
600 ANTON FOUNTAIN (designed in
1991 by Peter Walker)
Costa Mesa, California
Pamela Palmer

opposite:
THE LINGERING GARDEN (C. 1522)
Suzhou, China
Michael Freeman/CORBIS

SIMA GUANG

THE GARDEN OF SOLITARY DELIGHT (AFTER 1073)

Born in Xiaxian, Shanxi, Sima Guang (1019–1086) was a Song-dynasty writer, historian, and minister. Also known as Ssu-ma Kuang, he rose rapidly in office and ultimately reached the position of minister of state. In 1070 he resigned and devoted himself to the completion of his masterwork, a history of China known as the *Zizhi tongjian* (Comprehensive Mirror for Aid in Government). Sima Guang wrote of his life after retirement and the creation of his garden; this excerpt is from the translation by Alison Hardie published in 1988.

Mencius said: "To delight in pleasure by oneself is not as good as taking pleasure together with the multititude; and to take pleasure with the few is not as good as taking pleasure together with the multitude." This is the pleasure of princes and nobles and cannot be attained by the poor and lowly. Confucius said: "To eat rice and vegetables and drink water, and then pillow one's head on one's arm: it is here that pleasure lies"; and Master Yan: "A bowlful to eat and a ladleful to drink: this is a pleasure that need not be foregone." This is the pleasure of saints and sages and cannot be attained by the ignorant. Now when the tailor-bird nests in the wood, it occupies no more than one branch, and when the tapir drinks from the river, it takes no more than will fill its belly; each takes its allotted portion and is content, and this is what I, the Old Pedant, delight in also.

In the fourth year of the Xining period [A.D. 1071] I first made my home in Luoyang, and in the sixth year [1073] I bought twenty *mu* of land by the north gate of the Zunxian District to make a garden. I built a hall in the middle, in which I placed five thousand volumes from my library, and named it "Hall for Reading Books." South of the hall was a group of rooms, and I directed a watercourse to flow northwards and pass below the buildings. In the centre I made a marsh, three feet wide and deep, and I separated the water

into five streams running into the marsh in the form of a tiger's claws. From the north side of the marsh the water flowed underground and came out by the north steps, from where it cascaded into the courtyard like an elephant's trunk. From here it was divided into two channels and flowed round the four corners of the courtyard, meeting again in the north-west corner, from where it flowed away. This area was named "The Gallery for Playing with Water."

North of the hall was a marsh with an island in the middle, and on the island I planted bamboo in a ring like a jade circlet, thirty feet around, and I bound the tops together like a fisherman's hut, and called it "Retreat for Catching Fish." North of the marsh was a building lying crosswise, with six columns and with extremely thick walls to ward off the heat of the sun. You could open a door to get out to the east, while along the north and south sides were set large windows to catch the cool breezes. In front of and behind it were planted many beautiful bamboos to make a cool place in the summer heat, and it was named "The Studio for Planting Bamboos." To the east of the marsh I divided the ground into one hundred and twenty plots and planted all sorts of herbs, labeling them with their names. To the north of this plot I planted bamboo in a square pattern like a chess-board, ten feet across; I bent over the tops of the bamboos and joined them together to make a house. I also planted bamboo in front of this, enclosing a path like a portico, and covered it all with climbing herbs, and on all four sides I planted medicinal trees, making a fence; I named it "The Herbal Nursery." To the south of the nursery I placed six railings, two each supporting peonies, tree-peonies, and mixed flowers; I only planted two plants of each type, just enough to become familiar with their appearance and no more. To the north of these railings was a pavilion which I named "The Pavilion for Watering the Flowers." The city of Luoyang is not far from the mountains, but owing to the dense and flourishing growth of the woods, it is seldom possible to see the mountains; therefore I constructed a terrace in the middle of the garden, and put up a building on top of it in order to get a view of Wan'an, Xuanyuan and even as far as Taishi mountains, and I named this "The Terrace for Looking at the Mountains."

I spent most of my time in the study reading my books. I found teachers among the wise men superior to me, and friends among the mass of worthy folk. We speculated on the origins of benevolence and virtue, and explored the laws of ritual and music. From before the beginning of creation, and stretching beyond the limits of the four directions—the principles of all things corporeal and incorporeal were all present to our gaze. My weakness was that my learning was inadequate, but on the other hand I asked nothing of anyone and needed nothing from the external world. When mind and body were both weary, I could cast my rod and catch fish, or gather herbs in my skirt, or open the channels to irrigate my plants, or wield an axe to chop down bamboo, then bathe my hands in warm water, and climb to a high place and gaze as far as my eyes could see, wandering freely exactly as I wished. The bright moon would appear at the appointed time, the fresh breeze would arrive of its own volition. There was nothing to drag me along and nothing to impede me; my ears, eyes, lungs and guts were all under my own control, alone and uninhibited. I don't know what other pleasure there is between heaven and earth that can take the place of this. So I named the whole place "The Garden of Solitary Delight." Some people criticized me, saying: "I have heard it said that the gentleman must share his pleasure with others, but now you find satisfaction in solitude, and do not extend your pleasure to others; this is unacceptable." I excused myself, saying: "I am just an old fool; how can I be compared with a gentleman? I am afraid the pleasure I get on my own is not sufficient; how could I extend it to others? Moreover, what I take pleasure in is poor, mean, low and uncivilized, in fact everything that the world rejects; even if I were to shove it at people, they would still not accept it, so how could I force it on them? If there were anyone willing to share this pleasure, I would bow down and present it to him; I would never dare to keep it to myself!"

ATTRIBUTED TO ZOEN
STRUCTURAL ELEMENTS (c. 1466)

The two oldest extant Japanese garden manuals to have been translated into English are *Sakuteiki* (Notes on Garden Making, c. 1050) and *Senzui narabi ni yagyo no zu* (Illustrations for Designing Mountain, Water, and Hillside Field Landscapes, 1466). The basis for the text of the latter is a Kyoto temple scroll that bears the name of the priest Zoen as its compiler, although the attribution of the text is dubious. David Slawson published his translation of this text in his book *Secret Teachings in the Art of Japanese Gardens: Design Principles, Aesthetic Values.*

IF YOU HAVE NOT RECEIVED THE ORAL TRANSMISSIONS, YOU MUST NOT MAKE GARDENS

[1]   Here I shall abstract some instructive points from the records and drawings of Tung-fang Shuo's residence. First, when laying out the plains, the mountains and peaks, and the waterfalls and rivers of a garden, you must regard rocks and trees as the structural elements. Hence you must consider fully the relationships of Mutual Destruction and Mutual Production in respect to the Five Colors of rocks. Since the ten thousand stream valleys are nearly always bordered by mountains, you must make two mountains, one on the left and one on the right. The *yang* mountain must be very high, the *yin* mountain somewhat lower. Locate the *yang* mountain opposite the residence at the place where you feel it would stand out the most. If you plan to have a waterfall, it must be articulated with the stream valley design; depending upon the site, however, there are also times when you must adapt the design of the waterfall to the existing topography. Mountains, water, and rocks are like the three legs of a tripod—if even one is missing, there can be no garden.

[2] …When the water is made to flow from the northeast, water-related misfortunes will be carried away. You should bear this in mind when you make the stream valley of the garden. For the stream valley, you must first of all construct the two mountains, *yin* and *yang*. Make the *yang* mountain very high, and the *yin* mountain somewhat lower. Then there is the matter of the waterfall and river. Since the Green Dragon is on the left and the White Tiger is on the Right—the result of siting the house so that it faces south as is standard—you should make the waterfall flow down from the northeast toward the southwest. The water may also be made to flow down from the northwest, in which case it is known as the Water of the Spirit Kings. This is the water of Wisdom of the myriad felicitous spirits—or Spirit Kings—especially Benzai Ten. A flat-topped rock called the Rock of the Spirit Kings is set in the northwest. But because it is forbidden for this rock to be below the level of the feet, it must not be set there if the land drops off from the edge of the veranda of the house, and so forth and so on. Under no circumstances must the waterfall and river be directed from the southeast. This is called "reverse current" and is what people are referring to when they speak of "water that flows the wrong way." You must not willfully reverse the specified course of a large river to suit the site. The term "reverse current" is applied to this. …

[10] In the planting of trees and herbs, you make their natural habits your model. You will not go astray so long as you bear in mind the principle of planting trees from deep mountains in the deep mountains of the garden, trees from hills and fields in the hills and fields, herbs and trees from freshwater shores on the freshwater shores, and herbs from the seashore on the seashore. For the landscape garden mirrors nature. And thus it is said that in each and all we must return to the two words, natural habitat. …

[13] In setting rocks and planting trees, you should never use any that are exotic or showy, nor should you plant trees with dead or drooping branches in the area right in front of the bamboo blinds where the master, the eldest son, and the other family members reside. Respect the area the occupants live in and use such materials only in the other areas as befits the more striking topographical features found there. …

[17] There is an expression, "ten thousand trees in a single glance." If asked what this means, I would reply that you must plant the trees in a garden so that all are visible without exception in just one glimpse. No matter how fine a tree you plant up close to the eaves, it must not conceal the smaller trees in the distance. …

[22] In the landscape garden, you must regard rocks and trees as the structural elements. When obtaining either trees or rocks, you must keep uppermost in mind the three forces—horizontal, diagonal, and vertical. Do not position a rock in such a way that it has a sharp point sticking out in the direction of the position from which the master customarily faces the garden, no matter how fascinating the scenic effect. You must prune out, with consideration for the overall effect, any superfluous branches of trees and herbs growing too close together, one above the other, and sticking out in the direction of the master's position, even though they may have a scenic effect. If the branches are too sparse at the tips, it is unsightly. At the same time, there must be as few branches as possible. It is said there is a reason for this.

ABDUL-HAMID LAHAWRI
ARRANGEMENT OF A KASHMIR GARDEN (1657-58)

In 1639 the fifth Mughal emperor, Shah Jahan, commissioned the poet Abdul-Hamid Lahawri (died 1654) to document his reign in the illuminated manuscript *Padshahnamah* (Chronicle of the King of the World), considered one of the masterpieces of Mughal art. At that time, Shah Jahan was struggling with insurrections and building the Taj Mahal for his beloved wife, Mumtaz Mahal, who had died giving birth to their fourteenth child. The text below, which describes Shah Jahan's Kashmir gardens, is an excerpt of that manuscript, translated from Persian by W. M. Thackston.

Excursions to most of the pleasure places of this paradisiacal land (Kashmir) are by boat, and since the excess water from Lake Dal has been made into a large canal joining the river Bahat (Jhelum), one can come and go between Dal and the Bahat by boat. From the city at the bottom of the lake to the village of Kuhna Pul, which is about sixteen imperial *kos,* and up to Bara Mola, which is twelve *kos,* people go by boat. Gardens and orchards filled with fruits and herbs delight the eye and heart.

The best of all these is the Farahbakhsh Garden, which was laid out by royal command, as a sample of eternal paradise, and its fruits are reminders of the delights of the next world. Its Shâh Nahr canal and avenue are specimens of Salsabîl and Kawthar, and its lofty pavilions are equal to the flawless palaces of paradise. The founder of these edifices is His Majesty Sahib-Qiran II (Shahjahan).

From one end to the other of this garden is an avenue thirty yards in width, and during his felicitous days as prince both sides of the avenue were, by his royal command, planted with plane trees and poplars at a distance of ten yards apart. From the date of founding until now, which has been fourteen years, through his kind attention, year by year the fecundity and fertility has increased.

Formerly this garden was known as Shalamar, but now that it has been newly decorated and limitlessly indulged by the advent of the incomparable palm of the garden of the caliphate, and the plants and trees have reached perfect maturity and lushness through his alchemical favor it has been named Farahbakhsh.

By royal decree a beautiful bathhouse, adjacent to this garden, to the north, has been constructed. The aforementioned canal, which is ten yards wide and has been named Shâh Nahr by His Imperial Majesty, enters the avenue from behind the garden and flows through the middle of it. It passes through the edifice in the midst of the garden and, going down a waterchute, spills, below the aforementioned edifice, into a pool that is thirty yards by thirty yards, with a *chabutara* (terrace) in the middle and eight jets. It also passes through a pavilion at the beginning of the garden and, going down another waterchute, enters a lower pool that has nine jets and is thirty (yards) by thirty. Spilling down three more waterchutes, it passes along the avenue opposite the garden and joins Lake Dal. The width of the Shâh Nahr in this avenue, which is also thirty yards wide, is ten yards. Boats can enter from Lake Dal at the aforementioned avenue and reach near the pavilion at the beginning of the garden.

At the end of the avenue at the end of the Shâh Nahr where it joins Lake Dal His Majesty selected the pavilion that overlooks Lake Dal in one direction and the avenue in the other and through the middle of which boats come and go and ordered that two *ayvâns* (iwans) facing the Shâh Nahr be built opposite each other. On two sides of the pool in front of the pavilion at the entrance to the garden two residences were built and behind that a place for the servants of the harem. The poplar that the Emperor planted in the Shâh Nahr with his own blessed hand during his days as prince and the two plane trees that stand opposite each other at the two entrances of the Shâh Nahr, at the foot of which (trees) a *chabutara* has been built and the surface planted in clover, have imparted yet another splendor to the ever-increasing beauty of this paradisiacal garden so that, in fact, the beauty of this garden is more than can be written....

MUGHAL GARDEN (17th century)
Kashmir
Craig Lowell/CORBIS

This meadow of eternal spring possesses all sorts of fruit, most of which are grown in a cold climate. Among them is the *shâhâlû,* which is also called cherry. For bigness and sweetness they are better than the cherries of Kabul. The apples also are colorful and big. The pears are so delicate and juicy that they cannot be taken as far as Bhanpur. The melons, if not blighted, are as good as the best Kabul melons. Watermelons are extremely large and sweet. There are all sorts of grapes, but they are so watery they are not sweet. The peaches are as nice and delicate as Kabul peaches. All sorts of apricots are abundant, but the mirzai and safedcha of Kabul are much better than the apricots of here. The seedless berries are plentiful, but the seedless berries of Kabul are better than those of Kashmir. The pomegranates are inferior. The almonds are abundant. The pistachio trees, although present, are few. Nowhere are there so many walnuts as this place, so much so that throughout the province walnut oil is used in lamps. The largest types of fruit displayed to His Majesty have been a one-mithcal cherry, a fifty-seven-mithcal apple, a ninety-five-mithcal quince, and a nineteen-mithcal apricot. Medicinal fruits and herbs are too many to be described.

REGINALD BLOMFIELD
THE FORMAL METHOD (1892)

The English architect and author Reginald Blomfield (1856–1942) advocated a formal style of gardens, opposing the more natural style proposed by William Robinson. His commissions include Godington Park and Athelhampton Gardens. In 1892 Blomfield wrote *The Formal Garden in England,* illustrated by his collaborator in garden design, F. Inigo Thomas. A section of the book appears below.

The Formal System of Gardening has suffered from a question-begging name. It has been labeled "Formal" by its ill-wishers; and though, in a way, the term expresses the orderly result at which the system aims, the implied reproach is disingenuous. . . . It will be well to clear the ground by a statement of the principles and standpoint of the Formal School as compared with Landscape Gardening.

The question at issue is a very simple one. Is the garden to be considered in relation to the house, and as an integral part of a design which depends for its success on the combined effect of house and garden; or is the house to be ignored in dealing with the garden? The latter is the position of the landscape gardener in actual fact. There is some affectation in his treatises of recognizing the relationship between the two, but his actual practice shows that this admission is only borrowed from the formal school to save appearances, and is out of court in a method which systematically dispenses with any kind of system whatever.

The formal treatment of gardens ought, perhaps, to be called the architectural treatment of gardens, for it consists in the extension of the principles of design which govern the house to the grounds which surround it. Architects are often abused for ignoring the surroundings of their buildings in towns, and under conditions which make it impossible for them to do otherwise; but if the reproach has force, and it certainly has, it applies with greater justice to those who control both the house and its surroundings, and yet deliberately set the two at variance. The object of formal gardening is to bring the two into harmony, to make the house grow out of its surroundings, and to prevent its being an excrescence on the face of nature. The building cannot resemble anything in nature, unless you are content with a mud-hut and cover it with grass. Architecture in any shape has certain definite characteristics which it cannot get rid of; but, on the other hand, you can lay out the grounds, and alter the levels, and plant hedges and trees exactly as you please; in a word, you can so control and modify the grounds as to bring nature into harmony with the house, if you cannot

bring the house into harmony with nature. The harmony arrived at is not any trick of imitation, but an affair of a dominant idea which stamps its impress on house and grounds alike.

Starting, then, with the house as our datum, we have to consider it as a visible object, what sort of thing it is that we are actually looking at. A house, or any other building, considered simply as a visible object, presents to the eye certain masses arranged in definite planes and proportions, and certain colors distributed in definite quality and quantity. It is regular; it presents straight lines and geometric curves. Any but the most ill-considered efforts in building—anything with any title to the name of architecture—implies premeditated form in accordance with certain limits and necessities. However picturesque the result, however bravely some chimney breaks the sky-line, or some gable contradicts another, all architecture implies restraint, and if not symmetry, at least balance. There is order everywhere and there is no escaping it. . . .

Something, then, of the quality of the house must be found in the grounds. The house will have its regular approach and its court-yard—rectangular, round, or oval—its terrace, its paths straight and wide, its broad masses of unbroken grass, its trimmed hedges and alleys, its flower-beds bounded by the strong definite lines of box-edgings and the like—all will show the quality of order and restraint; the motive of the house suggests itself in the terrace and the gazebo, and recurs, like the theme in a coda, as you pass between the piers of the garden gate. . . .

Thus, the substantial difference between the two views of gardening is this. The formal school insists upon design; the house and the grounds should be designed together and in relation to each other; no attempt should be made to conceal the design of the garden, there being no reason for doing so, but the bounding lines, whether it is the garden wall or the lines of paths and parterres, should be shown frankly and unreservedly, and the garden will be treated specifically as an enclosed space to be laid out exactly as the designer pleases. The landscape gardener, on the other hand, turns his back upon architecture at the earliest opportunity and devotes his energies to making the garden suggest natural scenery, to giving a false impression as to its size by sedulously concealing all boundary lines, and to modifying the scenery beyond the garden itself, by planting or cutting down trees, as may be necessary to what he calls his picture. In matters of taste there is no arguing with a man. Probably people with a feeling for design and order will prefer the formal garden, while the landscape system, as it requires no knowledge of design, appeals to the average person who "knows what he likes," if he does not know anything else.

EDITH WHARTON
COMPOSITION OF ITALIAN GARDENS (1904)

The American writer Edith Wharton (1862–1937), an enthusiastic gardener, delighted in the splendor of the Italian countryside. She joined forces with the illustrator Maxfield Parrish and created the book *Italian Villas and Their Gardens* (1904), which covers eighty gardens and sixty garden architects. Wharton explains how the great houses and their grounds create a sense of enduring enchantment.

Though it is an exaggeration to say that there are no flowers in Italian gardens, yet to enjoy and appreciate the Italian garden-craft one must always bear in mind that it is independent of floriculture.

The Italian garden does not exist for its flowers; its flowers exist for it: they are a late and infrequent adjunct to its beauties, a parenthetical grace counting only as one more touch in the general effect of enchantment. This is no doubt partly explained by the difficulty of cultivating any but spring flowers in so hot and dry a climate, and the result has been a wonderful development of the more permanent effects to be obtained from the three other factors in garden-composition—marble, water, and perennial verdure—and the achievement, by their skillful blending, of a charm independent of the seasons.

It is hard to explain to the modern garden-lover, whose whole conception of the charm of gardens is formed of successive pictures of flower-loveliness, how this effect of enchantment can be produced by anything so dull and monotonous as a mere combination of clipped green and stone-work. . . .

Some of those who have fallen under the spell are inclined to ascribe the Italian garden-magic to the effect of time; but, wonder-working as this undoubtedly is, it leaves many beauties unaccounted for. To seek the answer one must go deeper: the garden must be studied in relation to the house, and both in relation to the landscape. The garden of the Middle Ages, the garden one sees in old missal illuminations and in early woodcuts, was a mere patch of ground within the castle precincts, where "simples" were grown around a central well-head and fruit was espaliered against the walls. But in the rapid flowering of the Italian civilization the castle walls were soon thrown down, and the garden expanded, taking in the fish-pond, the bowling-green, the rose-arbour and the clipped walk. The Italian country house, especially in the centre and south of Italy, was almost always built on a hillside, and one day the architect looked forth from the terrace of his villa, and saw that, in his survey of the garden, the enclosing landscape was naturally included: the two formed a part of the same composition.

The recognition of this fact was the first step in the development of the great garden-art of the Renaissance: the next was the architect's discovery of the means by which nature and art might be fused in his picture. He had now three problems to deal with: his garden must be adapted to the architectural lines of the house it adjoined; it must be adapted to the requirements of the inmates of the house, in the sense of providing shady walks, sunny bowling-greens, parterres, and orchards, all conveniently accessible;

and lastly it must be adapted to the landscape around it. At no time and in no country has this triple problem been so successfully dealt with as in the treatment of the Italian country house from the beginning of the sixteenth to the end of the eighteenth century; and in the blending of the different elements, the subtle transition from the fixed and formal lines of art to the shifting and irregular lines of nature, and lastly in the essential convenience and liveableness of the garden, lies the fundamental secret of the old garden-magic.

However much other factors may contribute to the total impression of charm, yet by eliminating them one after another, by *thinking away* the flowers, the sunlight, the rich tinting of time, one finds that, underlying all these, there is the deeper harmony of design which is independent of any adventitious effects. This does not imply that a plan of an Italian garden is as beautiful as the garden itself. The more permanent materials of which the latter is made—the stonework, the evergreen foliage, the effects of rushing or motionless water, above all the lines of the natural scenery—all form a part of the artist's design. But these things are as beautiful at one season as at another; and even these are but the accessories of the fundamental plan. The inherent beauty of the garden lies in the grouping of its parts—in the converging lines of the long ilex-walks, the alternation of sunny open spaces with cool woodland shade, the proportion between terrace and bowling-green, or between the height of a wall and the width of a path. None of these details was negligible to the landscape architect of the Renaissance: he considered the distribution of shade and sunlight, of straight lines of masonry and rippled lines of foliage, as carefully as he weighed the relation of his whole composition to the scene about it.

Then, again, any one who studies the old Italian gardens will be struck with the way in which the architect broadened and simplified his plan if it faced a grandiose landscape. Intricacy of detail, complicated groupings of terraces, fountains, labyrinths, and por-

PERENNIAL GARDENS (designed by
Piet Oudolf)
Piet Oudolf

ticoes, are found in sites where there is no great sweep of landscape attuning the eye to larger impressions. The farther north one goes, the less grand the landscape becomes and the more elaborate the garden. The great pleasure-grounds overlooking the Roman Campagna are laid out on severe and majestic lines: the parts are few; the total effect is one of breadth and simplicity.

It is because, in the modern revival of gardening, so little attention has been paid to these first principles of the art that the garden-lover should not content himself with a vague enjoyment of old Italian gardens, but should try to extract from them principles which may be applied at home. He should observe, for instance, that the old Italian garden was meant to be lived in—a use to which, at least in America, the modern garden is seldom put. He should note that, to this end, the grounds were as carefully and conveniently planned as the house, with broad paths (in which two or more could go abreast) leading from one division to another; with shade easily accessible from the house, as well as a sunny sheltered walk for winter; and with effective transitions from the dusk of wooded alleys to open flowery spaces or to the level sward of the bowling-green. He should remember that the terraces and formal gardens adjoined the house, that the ilex or laurel walks beyond were clipped into shape to effect a transition between the straight lines of masonry and the untrimmed growth of the woodland to which they led, and that each step away from architecture was a nearer approach to nature.

RICHARD HANSEN AND FRIEDRICH STAHL
FRAMEWORK IN PERENNIAL GARDENS (1981)

As a research fellow and professor, Hansen (born 1912) began in 1947 to apply the scientific study of plant sociology to the trial gardens of Weihenstephan in Germany. He developed the idea of planning borders as integrated, largely self-sustaining communities rather than as collections of individual plants. In the process, he wrote, with Friedrich Stahl (born 1918), the principal reference work on the new German style, *Die Stauden und ihre Lebensbereiche* (1981), published in Britain and the United States as *Perennials and Their Garden Habitats*, translated by Richard Ward.

TREES AND SHRUBS: THE FRAMEWORK OF A PLANTING
Perennials need the support of structural and architectural garden elements in order to be fully effective. It is therefore important to consider any appropriate trees and shrubs before laying out a perennial planting. Trees and shrubs provide the permanent framework of a garden, remaining effective in winter when other plants are dormant underground. Moreover, they can often provide shelter from the wind and improvement of the microclimate in front of a draughty wall or hedge.

This complementary use of herbaceous and woody plants often reflects their characteristic occurrence in the wild, particularly in a planting of wild perennials. Of course, a flowering border can be a beautiful sight with or without trees and shrubs. In winter, however, when the yellowing stems of perennials have been tidied away and snow lies on the ground, it is the woody species, together with some equally persistent grasses, that come into their own, freed from the competition of their more colourful companions and periodically transformed by the countless tiny crystals of a hoar frost.

A constantly flowering border is almost unthinkable without shrubs. One possibility is to set a planting of summer- and autumn-flowering perennials in front of a free-growing hedge of spring-flowering shrubs, with perhaps a few bulbs to add to the early display. Alternatively, it may be perennials that predominate in spring, followed by roses and other late shrubs in summer. Even those plants that serve primarily as structural elements should also be considered in the light of their possible contribution to the flowering sequence.

A well-laid-out garden does not flower a little bit everywhere and all the time, but is composed of thoughtfully arranged plant groupings with a harmonious and complementary succession of flowering highlights. Trees and shrubs form the persistent framework for these groupings. It is therefore natural that they should be the first plants to be selected and put into position.

STRUCTURE AND RHYTHM IN A PLANTING

Just as most perennial plantings require a persistent framework of trees and shrubs, they also need a secondary structure of dominant herbaceous plants to give them life and impact. These can be characterized as "theme plants." Among border perennials they are distinguished by their striking habit, exceptional flower colour and abundance of bloom. These help them to stand out from among a mass of other perennials, and they do much to determine the flowering climax of a whole border.

The principle is just as applicable to a planting of wild perennials. Here, too, one should first place the dominant, character-giving perennials before ordering the spaces between with plants of a quieter nature.

Theme plants form the basis of any herbaceous planting, particularly where border perennials are concerned. Arranged rhythmically throughout a planting, they are the ordering principle that binds everything into a unified whole. Their repetition should not be allowed to become a rigid pattern of equally sized groups and intervals. Powerful species can be set in an irregular sequence of one to three individuals, weaker ones in groups of three to five. Different cultivars may be used to bring variety to the theme

plants. Delphiniums can be planted in a range of different blues and purples; border phloxes in various tones between white and red. The assortment is large enough to give plenty of room for experiment.

Deliberate ordering is essential to the creation of a well-balanced border planting. The arbitrary arrangement of a great many randomly chosen perennials can never lead to satisfactory results. It produces only a disordered and expressionless jumble of forms, colours and flowers, mostly lacking in any sort of harmony. Of course, we are all free to plant whatever takes our fancy. However, our collector's instinct and pride of possession, love of flowers and passion for novelty and change, often result in plantings composed of a large number of single specimens and small groups, not unlike the systematic beds of a botanic garden. Such an overloaded and densely planted arrangement promotes excessive competition between plants and a high demand for maintenance, exhausting to both soil and gardener.

As the result of many years' breeding and selection, border perennials have become so imbued with our culture that we are now constrained too use them in a clearly structured, rhythmic and controlled style that reflects a human rather than a natural order, and so complements their artificiality.

How should one proceed? In spite of the limitations imposed by the conditions of any particular site, there are all sorts of possibilities in the design of a border planting, and it is important that there should be a clearly defined intention in laying out the plants. Perennial plantings do not belong to the primary structure-giving features of a garden but must be harmoniously worked into the existing spatial framework. One of the first considerations is therefore the shape of the plantings, including the height of its various constituents.

We can rightly reject the popular method of assigning the front third of the border to low plants, the middle to middle-sized, and the back to tall ones. If this scheme is carried out evenly along the entire length of the border then the effect is boring and seldom beautiful. It only becomes interesting when the individual zones vary in their width; when the low plants are sometimes extended towards the back of the planting and sometimes confined to a narrow strip at the front, allowing the medium and tall plants to move backwards and forwards in corresponding fashion and so preparing the way for surprising details and different visual effects.

Another possibility is to place taller perennials either singly or in small groups among a carpet of lower plants. The effect of such a planting relies heavily on the contrast between the tall and low-growing plants, and this can be accentuated by a careful choice of colours and flowering season. It should be noted that the selection of plants, particularly among the tall species, must be severely limited to avoid spoiling the effect with a chaotic mixture of different forms and colours. Coordinating themes, whether of flowering season, flower colour or habit of growth, must be especially well conceived and clearly brought to expression.

GROUPING (SOCIABILITY) WITHIN A PLANTING

As we have seen, the unified appearance of a border planting depends on the repetition of differently sized groups of various perennials. On the whole, these will include a few tall species, rather more middle-sized and many low ones. A planting of wild perennials, on the other hand, has its composition determined by the texture and shape of the individual plants and not by any formal consideration of height. Nevertheless, it remains important to group the various species according to their inherent sociability, always taking nature as a guide. An arbitrary distribution can severely limit the long-term viability of a planting.

PIET OUDOLF, WITH NOËL KINGSBURY
PLANTING PALETTES (1999)

Born in Holland in 1944, Oudolf is the founder of New Wave planting. His designs feature blocks of perennials with a rich variety of species chosen on the basis of foliage, inflorescence shape, overall texture, color, and interest throughout the seasons. Oudolf has created gardens in Holland, Germany, and England, and he partnered with Kathryn Gustafson's design team on the development of the monumental Millennium Park in Chicago. Oudolf also designed gardens at Battery Park in New York City to honor victims of the September 11 attacks. His thoughts on planting schemes below originate from the book *Designing with Plants,* which he co-authored with Noël Kingsbury.

PLANTING PALETTES

In the same way that a painter works with a palette of coloured pigments, so the garden designer can select what plants to use from a palette of plants. Traditionally, a plant's colour was its most important characteristic, but in this book [*Designing with Plants*] plants will be examined in a different light for other qualities: firstly, for the shapes of their flower- and seedheads; then for their leaf shape and texture; and only then for colour.

Structure is the most important component in a successful planting; colour is important too, but it is a secondary consideration. If the forms and shapes of plants in a border work well together, and you choose plants that still resemble their wild ancestors, it is difficult to imagine an unharmonious colour combination arising. One reason for this is the proportion between the flowers and foliage of wild plants. Garden plants often have flowers that are large relative to the rest of the plant; so good proportions are lost and there is less green to buffer strong colours....

From when it first emerges from the ground in spring to when its rain-lashed and frost-scoured remains collapse sometime over

PERENNIAL GARDENS (designed by
Piet Oudolf)
Piet Oudolf

the winter, a perennial has a form that is intrinsic and unique to itself. The sensitive gardener will observe that there are many more stages in the life of a perennial that are deserving of study and appreciation than simply the flowers—buds, unfurling leaves, seedheads, autumn foliage, winter's skeletal remains—although the dominant feature of most perennials remains the flowers and how they are arranged in a head—what botanists call the inflorescence.

The first part of this examination of the planting palette will look closely at these flowerheads and the characteristic forms that they take, forms that are often apparent even some time before the flowers actually emerge from their buds and forms that are, in many cases, strong sculptural features in the garden well after the flowers themselves have died and turned to seed. Often the core of the flower will expand and stiffen to form the seedhead, which will thus retain the essential shape of a flower, and will remain as a reminder of it, long after the flower itself has died.

Flowerheads come in a variety of forms, all of which have been adapted by nature to attract pollinating insects to the flowers, or, in the case of the grasses, to distribute the pollen on the wind. It is these forms that give flowering plants so much of their character, beyond the superficial layers of colour, and thus it is not surprising that plantings based on these forms will have a far greater durability and sense of balance than those which are planned purely around colour.

Botanists have various names which they use to classify the characteristic shapes of flowerheads (raceme, panicle, umbel, etc.), but these often do not relate to their aesthetics, or how they work in the garden. Here flower shapes are grouped into rough categories according to their appearance. Sometimes there is confusion caused by our calling something a "flower" when in fact it is a multiplicity of flowers making up a single solid head, as in a daisy. These so-called "compound" flowerheads are particularly well adapted for insects, enabling them to browse large numbers of flowers for nectar without having to move any distance at all.

Foliage lasts longer than flowers, and has its own range of colours, shapes, and textures, which the gardener would do well to pay plenty of attention to. Attractive and well-combined foliage is like a background to whatever performance the flowers put on— quite essential, in other words.

SPIRES

Spires thrust our vision skywards, reminding us of other realms, connecting heaven and earth. Spire-shaped flowerheads add lift to the garden, severing its bonds to the earth. Spires contrast dramatically with other flowerheads and introduce a note of clarity amid other less clearly defined flower shapes or a mass of foliage. The form of a spire makes it a dominant visual element in any planting but they never look quite right on their own; a clump or loose gathering of spires is always more satisfactory....

BUTTONS AND GLOBES

Buttons and balls are defined points, concentrated clusters of flowers tightly packed. They stand out against soft shapes like plumes or against veils of fine stems. In the summer they are often points of concentrated colour. In the winter they are often the only clear points in a planting, standing out against the soft and ill-defined decay of everything else as dark spots. In winter the number of buttons is increased, as certain other flowers, daisies in particular, lose their petals to be left with the round central head....

PLUMES

Plumes are a soft form, intermediate between spires and umbels. They too are composed of a myriad of tiny individual flowers, but arranged in a looser, fluffier, often more transparent way. Being somewhat intermediate they act to connect the shape of spires and unbrels in the upper reaches of the border. Their vague fluffy quality is particularly effective *en masse,* evoking in particular the flowering of many marsh plants, like reeds and meadowsweet. The way that some plumes tend to be unidirectional is a particularly

attractive feature, as all the breeze will direct all the plumes in a planting to point the same way, for example the seedheads of the miscanthus grass....

UMBELS

Umbels are the familiar upturned bowl shapes of many common wildflowers and "weeds." These are the flowers of wild, unkempt places, many of them not regarded as garden flowers. But once we have set aside the shibboleth that a plant has to be colourful to be allowed into the garden, we can begin to appreciate the beauty of these flowers. Umbels are, in a way, the opposite to spires, their gently rounded shapes counterbalancing the energy of the sky-seeking spires. Composed of hundreds, or even thousands, of minute individual flowers, they often have a soft and gentle look....

DAISIES

Daisies remind us of the sun, not just because of their shape but also because they are so often found in sunny places: meadows, fields, and prairies. Plants with daisy flowers tend to flower from midsummer onwards too, which makes them even more strongly associated with the sun and the heat. There is something undeniably optimistic about them. Daisies are like even more concentrated versions of umbels, masses of tiny flowers so closely packed together that they are usually taken to be a single flower, but with the outer flowers having ray-like petals, creating the characteristic daisy appearance....

SCREENS AND CURTAINS

Plants do not always have solid shapes; some form a network of stems, leaves, and flowers that allow you to see right through them. Think of how you can see through the flower stems of grass. Transparent plants are mostly air, and their loose growth creates another perspective as you look through them to the plants growing behind. The very narrowest spire shapes may be transparent, especially when used *en masse,* or the branching stems

of umbellifers. Conventional planting, with its massed ranks of planting, misses out on this special quality.

FERNANDO CARUNCHO
GEOMETRY AND THE GARDEN (2000)

The gardens and landscapes designed by Fernando Caruncho (born 1957) are based on ancient principles and elements of garden art: geometry and symmetry; stone and water; bay, box, cypress, and olive. Caruncho's designs emerge from the great garden traditions of Spain, where he was born and educated and undertook his first commissions. Caruncho has created public and private gardens throughout Spain and in Florida, Tokyo, and the south of France. His reflections below appeared in an interview, "Dialogue with a Gardener," from *Mirrors of Paradise: The Gardens of Fernando Caruncho.*

When I realized, through my work on ancient philosophy, that geometry was a formula of wisdom for ancient man, I became totally intrigued by the subject. I began to study geometry, and I came to realize that, of all the things that have been handed down to us from ancient times, geometry has remained unchanged and has been endlessly repeated. Since the Neolithic Age, man has tirelessly repeated the same patterns on everything from pottery to weaving. So geometry was man's original means of expression, even before it was formulated as a science....

It came originally from Assyrian Babylonia where it was used to measure the distance between the stars. These calculations were part of the art of navigation. Geometry was also a necessity in ancient Egypt. It was a means of measuring and anticipating the flooding of the Nile.

CAMP S'ARCH (designed in 1999
by Fernando Caruncho)
Menorca
Jerry Harpur

CASA FORMENTOR (designed in 1999
by Fernando Caruncho)
Palma de Mallorca
Jerry Harpur

Where can we find a straight line in nature? Nowhere, because it does not exist. It was invented by man, and it was man who combined different points to create a shape and then developed it further to create meaning. Who can see angles in the stars, ellipses in the heavenly bodies, and solstices in the sun? Who is able to express and explain all these things through geometry and arithmetic? Only this rational animal called man.

From time immemorial geometry has been the rational and civilized way to express knowledge. It has been a status language, the language of those who, together with the priests and the kings, were in contact with the gods. It was a magisterial formula used by wise men to figure out enigmas. What are the Tibetan mandalas, the Babylonian ziggurats, the Egyptian pyramids, or the Gothic cathedrals but geometric expressions that relate the spirit of man to space? The gardener, like the sailor or the builder, has always needed to know about geometry, since without it he cannot measure the space in which he will design his dreams. . . . .

Geometry is the grammar of shape. When I began applying it in my gardens, I realized that the golden section occurred repeatedly within each design, without any calculation on my part. This happened again and again, as if it were something that came automatically to me. I realized that I was illuminating living, geometric shapes within the garden. . . .

When one looks at a garden that doesn't have pure, geometric lines and recognizable shapes such as circles, ellipses, or squares, it is easy to think that it has no geometry. This is not true. Any good garden or landscape can be inspired by geometry, even if its true lines are concealed by the irregular outlines of organic shapes. The straight line reminds us of the presence of man, while the curve represents a return to idyllic nature.

All these things point in one direction: the geometry of the landscape doesn't necessarily create a garden, and neither does an irregular, organic shape. It is only when the geometric elements in a formal garden or the organic shapes in the landscape garden begin to relate to one another that there is a vibration of light, a soul, a garden. . . .

I began to add the other ingredients that were soon to become fundamental to me: proportion, scale, and volume. Proportion refers not only to measurements, but also to the relationship between the three physical components of the garden: mineral, water, and vegetable. The mineral element encompasses the architecture of the house and any walls, stairs, or pathways in the garden. Water refers to everything from the little water jet that rises in the basin of a fountain to the extensive planes and mirrors of water in pools and ponds. The vegetable category extends from the ivy in the heart of a parterre to the landscape surrounding the garden.

The proportions of the three elements—mineral, water, and vegetable—are dictated by geometry. Light, the most sublime and mysterious of all the phenomena found in a garden, will emanate from their combination. Where it strikes the garden, light will be reflected by the mineral, absorbed by the vegetable, and reflected again by vibration on the water of a pool.

All these elements will combine to produce an expanding and contracting movement inside the lightbox that is the garden. It is the vibration of light that injects life into the heart of the garden. To my mind, this is the most important element in the garden. There may be trees and walls and ponds, but it won't be a garden if there is no vibration. It is the expansion and contraction of light in the garden that gives it life. . . .

Light makes the difference between a garden and a green space. A garden designed without thought for the movement of light can be nice, bright, pleasant, and even beautiful. However it will always lack the special, magical quality that can be brought to it only by light. This is the quality that gardens such as the Alhambra, Boboli, or Vaux-le-Vicomte offer. As soon as you enter them, the air and the light will tell you that you are in a garden. All these places are in the great tradition of the Western, geometrical garden. Within their boundaries, the knowledge of the Western world has been reborn under the influence of the East.

following spread:
MIROKUNOSATO, MODERN CHINESE
ART MUSEUM GARDEN (designed in 1988
by Shiro Nakane)
Numakuma Town, Japan
Shiro Nakane

NIJYUGO-BOSATSU JIGEN NO NIWA
(Garden of 25 Bodhisattvas) (designed
in 1997 by Shiro Nakane) at SANZEN-IN
TEMPLE
Kyoto, Japan
Shiro Nakane

Light is the invisible incarnation, the great source of intuitive knowledge. As Descartes said, light is necessary for the perception of both the obvious and the obscure things that are clarified by it. The obsession with trying to control light came from the East. The quicksilver pool built by the Omeyad princes at Medina Azahara near Cordoba in tenth-century Spain was placed in front of a massive vault built from cedar wood and lined with mother of pearl. The vault represented the seven skies, and these were reflected in the marvelous mercury light.

The fascination with light was passed from the East to the West, where it reached its peak during the Age of Enlightenment, when philosophers such as Spinoza made dramatic discoveries and Goethe refuted Hume's theories about light and color.

It was the same obsession with light that drove Le Nôtre to persuade the king to create the big water expanse at Versailles, and Fouquet to build the wonderful Vaux-le-Vicomte. Anyone passing through one of these gardens is aware of the light that surrounds him, imperceptibly transmitting a natural light into his mind. This light wells up from the timeless residue of childhood knowledge. It is the great miracle of the garden. When you walk in a great garden it is as if time has stopped—and it is true, you are in a time warp. The same thing happens when you pause in front of Velázquez's *La Meninas* in the Prado or a Vermeer in the Rijksmuseum. The light pervades everything.

SHIRO NAKANE
STRUCTURE IN THE JAPANESE GARDEN (2004)

Born in Kyoto in 1950, Nakane received his early training from his father, the noted Japanese garden designer Kinsaku Nakane. Shiro is president of Nakane & Associates, which restores and creates Japanese gardens in Japan and throughout the world. He lectures widely and has served as a director on the Japanese Institute of Japanese Gardens and the Japan Garden Society. He wrote this essay for *The Glory of Gardens*.

The Japanese garden is an interpretation of the ideal natural landscape as perceived by the Japanese in the cultural, social, and environmental mirror of their times. Although the types and combinations of plants within the garden reflect the surrounding indigenous vegetation, they, like society, change slightly from year to year.

Western visitors to Japanese gardens often comment that except for an occasional azalea or camellia, there are few flowering plants. But as the picture scrolls show, the Japanese have possessed a tradition to live symbiotically with nature, and their gardens and surrounding nature included exactly the same vegetation and landscape. Such a manner of living symbiotically with nature, enjoying the changes of four seasons, and making them a part of daily life can be easily seen in the seasonal enjoyment of Japanese, such like *haruno-asobi* (spring picnic), *senzai-bori* (transplanting of wild plants), *mushi-kari* (catching chirping insects), and *momiji-gari* (excursion for viewing autumn leaves). The original Japanese garden was the composition or creation of an idealized "artificial" natural landscape, which was consistent with the natural dispensation and rationality and, at the same time, was beautiful and desirable for humans.

As advanced Chinese culture spread throughout Japan, Japan's luxuriant primeval laurel forest was felled, and the Japanese garden

started to echo the natural course of plant succession. When flowering plants took hold on newly cleared lands, they began to appear in gardens as well. But as fields slowly reverted to forest again, pine thickets inspired new designs, and today, with the increasing number of naturally occurring evergreens, the Japanese people forget that flowering plants ever played a major role in their gardens.

Building a garden is like painting on a three-dimensional canvas. Rocks are one of the most important elements. They are arranged according to the laws of perspective, in well-balanced compositions based upon the triangle. But the master Japanese gardener learns his craft through natural observation, not theoretical study. As in a painting, literalism and abstraction play a part in the Japanese garden; we judge each in terms of both composition and technique.

Westerners often admire the pine trees in Japanese gardens. But though they can read about the time-consuming and highly painstaking care these trees require, and can eventually come to understand the relationship between the trees and garden, when Westerners start to think about building their own Japanese gardens, they remember just the beautifully shaped pines. They forget the difficulty of maintenance and the difference in climate, as well as the fact that few Westerners have cultivated the degree of patience characteristic of the Japanese. I am often reminded of cheerleaders' pompons when I see shaped pines in Japanese gardens in the United States and Europe.

An examination of new landscape creations referred to as "Japanese gardens," especially those created overseas, reveals that in virtually every case the most characteristically conspicuous objects are *matsu* (pine trees), *ishidoro* (stone lanterns), and *tsukubai* (compositions of washbasin). Moreover, once these objects have been arranged within a garden, the landscaper frequently appears to cherish the illusion of perfect assurance that this arrangement alone constitutes a Japanese garden.

Indeed, pine trees, stone lanterns, and washbasins have played important roles as elements of traditional design of Japanese gardens. However, they no more make up the essence of the Japanese garden than chrysanthemums, Mount Fuji, and geisha girls represent Japanese culture.

Having originated in certain small islands in a far eastern corner of the Asian continent, Japanese gardens are indeed a plastic art of a very local geographical character. Nevertheless, the apparent admiration and esteem enjoyed by Japanese gardens throughout the world is presumably attributable to the recognition of its universal artistic merits, which transcend all racial, religious, and cultural differences.

The appreciation of this Japanese garden as simply an artistic classic is indeed possible. However, a classic always remains a classic, and the continuation of a classic theme without essential modification presumably ends in mere imitation.

Contemporary reinvigoration of this classic art requires new developments appropriate for today. However, as prerequisites for modern developments of this kind, the significance and background of traditional Japanese garden forms and design features must first of all be thoroughly understood, then culled and selected in accordance to necessary modern criteria, and supplemented by the appropriate addition of new elements.

For example, the Buddhistic and Taoistic philosophy that constitutes the background of design features such as Shumisen (Mount Sumeru) and Horaito (the Isle of the Immortals) may not necessarily be in demand among contemporary humans. Nevertheless, even if this philosophical background of certain specific types of design features is discarded, the formative beauty of *ishigumi* (rock arrangement) represented, for example, by Shumisen and Horaito structures would undoubtedly continue to appeal to the aesthetic sensibilities of modern humans.

This ingenious, formative beauty constitutes one of the reasons for the continuing high esteem enjoyed by historical Japanese gardens even during the present age. Accordingly, a study of the artistic character of these superb traditional forms and their application to contemporary plastic arts, either Eastern or Western, would undoubtedly result in an effective new development along required lines.

Upon examining the design features and botanical cultivation of Japanese gardens, one notices the astonishing extent to which these have conformed to changes in the environment. Research into the classic aspects of Japanese gardens could conceivably shed light on the urgent challenge to modern society presented by environmental consideration and attempts to coexist with nature.

Japanese gardens, with their history of 1,400 years and the traditional design features that have persisted in this sphere, are of profound historical interest as regards investigation of the Japanese classics. In addition, they provide training with respect to the techniques of natural and subtle balancing or harmonization in the formative arts and elucidate the challenges of ensuring harmony with nature and developing methods for their control and application. These important aspects of the art, which transcend a mere appreciation of the garden, appear to contain answers to the vital questions at hand.

What impresses me in the process of investigating and restoring rock arrangements at classic gardens is the abundance of the predecessors' wisdom and ability to maintain them for hundreds of years.

On the other hand, we landscape architects today very much depend on convenient current materials, such as concrete and vinyl, and these may be too easy compared to working with rocks. In addition to these, we are fortunate enough to have heavy machines like cranes but, unfortunately, we not only have been neglectful of the traditional techniques of our predecessors but we have also lost most of them.

However, concrete, one of the current essential materials that enables us to make contemporary landscape construction, is said to last only fifty to one hundred years. If this is true, we landscape architects must abandon our pride, as artists did before us, and leave artistic creation behind until it becomes classic.

According to such self-examination, when I arrange rocks, I have started to use a minimal amount of concrete, and only in places, such as waterfalls and cascades, where we must control water. So long as we use the traditional techniques that make the rocks support each other, we can maintain rock arrangements at the edge of the shore for hundreds more years. After all, the natural world creates outstandingly beautiful landscapes without any artificial materials, and these last for a very long time.

As for the planting, I usually try to plant as many available native wild herbs as possible, and I expect some of these species among them, those that can accommodate themselves to the site, to grow gregariously in the future.

"Reproduction of natural environment" and "coexistence with nature" are not so difficult. The traditional techniques and attitude of the Japanese were originally based on coexisting with nature, saving resources, and decreasing waste materials.

I hope the essential beauty of the Japanese garden will give you an enlightened appreciation of the Japanese garden that will enable you to incorporate its elements into your own garden designs, creating something like the best of the Japanese gardens, something that springs from your unique sense of the natural world.

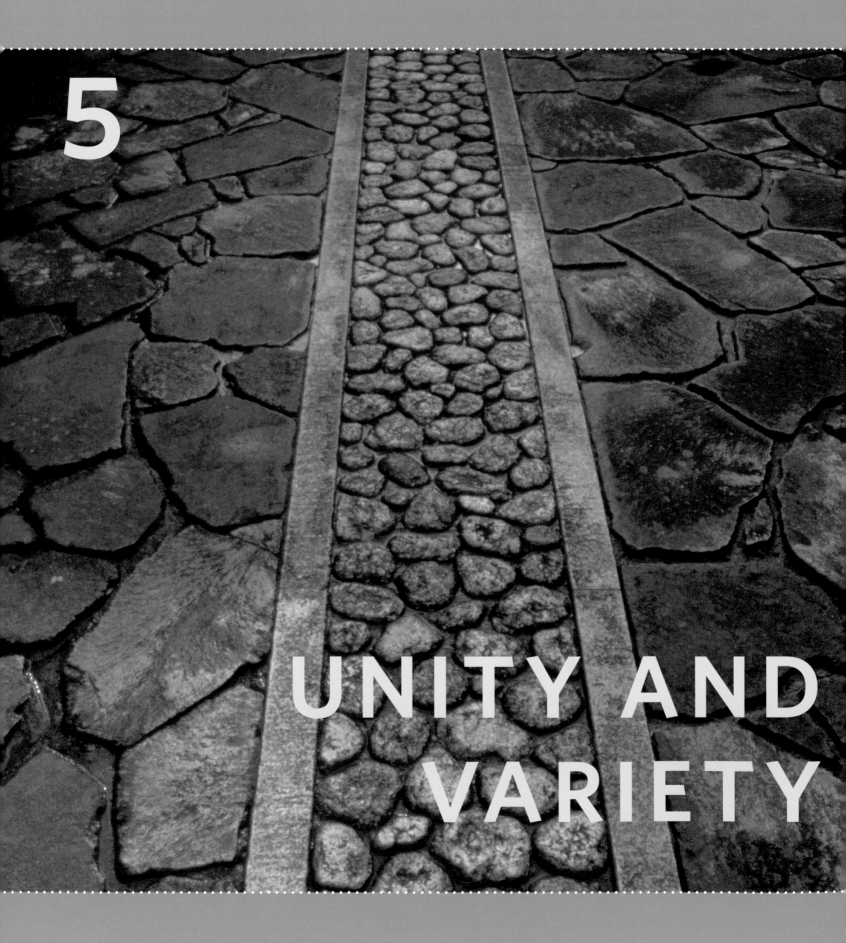

5

UNITY AND
VARIETY

Order gives due measure to the members of a work considered separately, and symmetrical agreement to the proportions of the whole.... Arrangement includes the putting of things in their proper places and the elegance of effect which is due to adjustments appropriate to the character of the work.

Marcus Vitruvius Pollio (1st century BCE), Roman architect and engineer

Thus they [Renaissance garden-makers] learnt the value of striking contrast; of sudden and thrilling surprise; of close confinement as a prelude to boundless freedom; of scorching sun as a prelude to welcome shade or cooling river; of monotony, even of ugliness, set for a foil to enchanting beauty, as a discord is used in music....

Sir George Sitwell (1860-1943), English garden writer

In the creation of a garden, the architect invites the partnership of the Kingdom of Nature. In a beautiful garden, the majesty of Nature is ever present, but Nature reduced to human proportions and thus transformed into the most efficient haven against the aggressiveness of contemporary life.

Luis Barragan (1902-1988), Mexican architect

RENÉ-LOUIS DE GIRARDIN
OF THE WHOLE (1777)

A French nobleman, Girardin (1735–1808) traveled to England and throughout the Continent to study gardens. He gained fame for the garden designs he implemented at his estate at Ermenonville. Jean Jacques Rousseau spent the last two months of his life at Ermenonville and was buried there. Girardin drafted a widely regarded treatise on picturesque beauty and gardens in 1777. The excerpt below appears in Daniel Malthus's translation in 1783 of Girardin's *De la Composition des paysages, ou, des moyens d'embellir la nature autour des habitations, en y joignant l'agréable à l'utile.*

OF THE WHOLE

Beautiful nature, and a picture, can have but one principle, since one is the original, and the other the copy. Now this principle is, that the whole should be comprehended in one complete design, and that all the parts should correspond. Discordance in the perspective, or in the assemblage of colours, can no more be endured in a view than it can upon canvas.

The essential part, is to begin by forming the great outline, and the landscapes for the dwelling, on those sides where the *principal views* are directed; I say the principal views, because if you have a pleasing landscape only on one side, the strait avenue which shuts out the country, the iron rails like the grate of a convent, and the arid paved court, will by the comparison become more insupportable. As the house is the point of residence, it is there that you have most leisure to look at the surrounding objects; and during the time of refreshment, and in the intervals of conversation, the eye naturally wanders over the country. "Nature," (says a man whose every word is a sentiment) "nature flies from frequented places; it is at the tops of high mountains, in the depth of forests, and in desert islands, that she displays her most enchanting beauties; those who love her, but can not go so far to seek her, are reduced to offer her some violence, and to force her in some measure to come and dwell among them. This cannot be done without some little illusion." Let us conduct her then to our habitations, and engage her there to lavish all her beauties, where we can oftenest enjoy them.

Magnificence may sometimes be striking at first sight: the effect of nature, on the contrary, is never to surprise, but the more we dwell upon it, the more it is endeared to us; and the soft sensation which the simple view of it excites in us (by an analogy that no man can fail to observe in himself) insensibly pervades our souls with the most tender impressions of pleasure. And indeed, what human magnificence can be compared to the vast spectacle which nature opens to us? As soon as you cease, by long strait lines, dismal enclosures, and walks of yew, to shut out both earth and sky, you will see the azure vault of heaven displayed in all its majesty; the vivid phænomena of light will continually embellish the view; every cloud will vary the tints of colouring; and if the rays of the sun, by a more sensible opposition of light and shadow, throw a new lustre upon the varying verdure, you are immediately led to wander through walks where nothing has the appearance of confinement, where all the objects please, and those which are open to you, give you an interest in those which are concealed.

Unity is the fundamental principle of nature, and ought to be the principle of all the arts. In every work where the attention is divided, there is an end of all interest; it is like putting several pictures on the same canvas, or having discordant decorations on the same theatre, such as the sinking down of elysium, and rising up of the infernal regions on the opera stage.

All the objects which are seen from the same point, should belong to the same picture; they should only be component parts of the same *whole,* and by their connections and concord, contribute to the general effect and harmony of the landscape.

It is then necessary, in the first place, deliberately to consider the general outline: any errors in regard to this, would occasion insurmountable faults in the whole plan. . . .

Before you begin the work, make yourself well acquainted with the surrounding country, and secure the possession of such lands as are necessary to compleat your design.*

Take care not to begin with detached parts, and do not want to retain any particular things that are done, if they are incompatible with the general plan; and above all, do not fail to make a copy of the design yourself, or to get it done by another: when I say a copy of your plan, you understand that a landscape can neither be imagined, sketched, drawn, coloured, or retouched, by any but a landscape painter; and with regard to him, beware of the narrowness of the schools, or the sallies of imagination. To take what the situation offers, to know how to give up what it denies, and above all, to attend to the simplicity and ease of execution; these are the rules for the picture. Artists you know must be governed by *truth* and *nature,* for they govern us. . . .

ON THE CONNEXION WITH THE COUNTRY

I have already observed, that the fundamental principle of nature, and of picturesque effect, consisted in "*the unity of the whole, and the connexion of the parts.*" But it is not sufficient to have described the groundwork and basis of the general plan, and the manner of transposing the design from the original drawing, to the copy of it in nature; I must likewise enforce the necessity of uniting all the objects to each other: for since they make a part of the same view, they ought consequently to contribute to the general harmony.

If the size and consequence of the dwelling house require a large landscape, you can not give sufficient extent to your perspective, without going beyond the limits of your own territory for the back-ground, and multiplying the side scenes in the foreground which belongs to you, in proportion to the distance you wish to give. A fine distance, without intervening scenery to shew it to advantage, would be like a well-painted canvas at the end of the stage without the side scenes to give it effect.

You can never make the distance your own** but by well incorporating the adjoining ground. The least apparent separation would be a blot or scratch in the picture. To avoid the line which an inclosure must necessarily make, there is the resource of ditches filled with water, or common ditches with a palisade at bottom, which rises no higher than the level of the ground: or of an ha-ha.

*   If you meet with obstacles on one side of your house, you may change to another; for in this stile, which leaves all the points of the compass open to you, there is much more facility in chusing your views, and in the communication of your walks, than where a stiff line obliges you to keep the exact centre, without deviating to right or left.

**   To take possession of a country in this manner, by letting in a fine view of it, is a very satisfactory kind of property; for whilst it contributes to the general beauty, it belongs to every body, every body enjoys it, and nobody is offended. It would be very cold and narrow to imagine that an inclosure, or apparent separation of the particular property, however extensive, belonging to a castle, or even to a palace, could have more magnificence than the display of nature and the view of a fine country, which has no bounds but the horizon.

HUMPHRY REPTON
CONGRUITY OF STYLE AND CONCERNING CONTRASTS
(1806, 1816)

A man of great literary and artistic ability, Repton (1752–1818) became the leading English landscape gardener of his time. Greatly influenced by Lancelot "Capability" Brown, Repton designed notable gardens at Cassiobury Park, Ashton Court, Woburn Abbey, West Wycombe Park, Sheringham Bower, and many other estates. His essay "Congruity of Style" comes from his work *An Enquiry into the Changes of Taste in Landscape Gardening* (1806), and "Concerning Contrasts" comes from *Fragments on the Theory and Practice of Landscape Gardening* (1816)

CONGRUITY OF STYLE

Congruity of style, uniformity of character, and harmony of parts with the whole, are different modes of expressing *unity,* without which no composition can be perfect; yet there are few principles in gardening which seem to be so little understood. This essential unity has often been mistaken for symmetry, or the correspondence of similar parts; as where

> Grove nods at grove, each alley has a brother,
> And half the platform just reflects the other.
> —Pope

Indeed this symmetry in the works of art was perfectly justifiable under that style of gardening which confined within lofty walls the narrow inclosure appropriated to ancient grandeur.

When the whole design is meant to be surveyed at a single glance, the eye is assisted in its office, by making its divisions counterparts of each other; and as it was confessedly the object of the artist to display his labour, and the greatness of the effort by which he had subdued nature, it could not possibly be more conspicuous than in such shapes of land and water as were most unnatural and violent. Hence arose the sloped terrace, the square and octagon pool, and all those geometric figures which were intended to contrast, and not to assimilate with, any scenes in nature: yet within this small inclosure an *unity* of design was strictly preserved, and few attempts made to extend it farther than the garden wall.

From the difference of taste in Gardening betwixt the seventeenth and the eighteenth centuries, it seems at first sight almost impossible to lay down any fixed principles. It appears that in this instance, as in many others, mankind are apt to fly from one extreme to the other: thus, because straight lines and highly finished and correspondent parts prevailed in the ancient style, some modern improvers have mistaken crookedness for the line of beauty, and slovenly carelessness for natural ease: they call every species of regularity formal; and with the hacknied assertion, that nature *abhors a straight line,* they fatigue the eye with continual curvatures.

There appears to be in the human mind a natural love of order and symmetry. Children, who at first draw a house upon a slate, generally represent it with correspondent parts; it is so with the infancy of taste. Those who during the early part of life have given little attention to objects of taste, are captivated with the regularity and symmetry of correspondent parts, without any knowledge of congruity, or an harmony of parts with the whole: this accounts for those numerous specimens of bad taste, which are so commonly observable in the neighbourhood of great towns, where we see Grecian villas spreading their little Gothic wings, and red brick castles, supported by Grecian pavilions: but though congruity may be banished, symmetry is never forgotten. If such be the love of symmetry in the human mind, it surely becomes a fair object of inquiry, how far it ought to be admitted or rejected in modern gardening. The following observation from Montesquieu on Taste seems to place the subject in a proper light.

WOBURN ABBEY (12th century)
 and GARDENS (designed in 1802 by
Humphry Repton)
Woburn, Bedfordshire, England
Sandy Stockwell /CORBIS

Wherever symmetry is useful to the soul, and may assist her functions, it is agreeable to her; but wherever it is useless, it becomes distasteful, because it takes away variety; therefore things that we see in succession ought to have variety, for our soul has no difficulty in seeing them: those, on the contrary, that we see at one glance, ought to have symmetry; thus at one glance we see the front of a building, a parterre, a temple; in such things there is always a symmetry which pleases the soul, by the facility it gives her of taking the whole object at once.

It is upon this principle that I have frequently advised the most perfect symmetry in those small flower-gardens which are generally placed in the front of a green-house or orangery, in some inner part of the grounds, where, being secluded from the general scenery, they become a kind of episode to the great and more conspicuous parts of the place. In such small inclosures irregularity would appear like affectation. Symmetry is also allowable, and indeed necessary, at or near the front of a regular building; because, where that displays correspondent parts, if the lines in contact do not also correspond, the house itself will appear twisted and awry. Yet this degree of symmetry ought to go no farther than a small distance from the house, and should be confined to such objects as are confessedly the works of art, for the use of man; such as a road, a walk, or an ornamental fence, whether of wood or iron; but it is not necessary it should extend to plantations, canals, or over the natural shape of the ground.

In forming plans for embellishing a field, an artist without taste employs straight lines, circles, and squares, because these look best upon paper. He perceives not, that to humour and adorn nature is the perfection of his art, and that nature, neglecting regularity, distributes her objects in great variety with a bold hand. (Some old gardens were disposed like the human frame, alleys like legs, and arms

answering each other, the great walk in the middle representing the trunk of the body.) Nature indeed, in organized bodies comprehended under one view, studies regularity, which, for the same reason, ought to be studied in architecture. But in large objects, which cannot be surveyed but in parts and by succession, regularity and uniformity would be useless properties, because they cannot be discovered by the eye. Nature therefore, in her large works, neglects these properties, and in copying nature the artist ought to neglect them.

—Lord Kaims' Elements of Criticism

CONCERNING CONTRASTS

The first contrast here shewn is that in the shape of the trees, betwixt the straight, stiff, and upright forms to the right, and those drooping forms to the left; and though we may admire the stately and aspiring character of the hollyhock and larkspur among flowers, with the cedar and cypress among trees, yet if we turn to the opposite side, we shall confess the justice of Mr. Burke's remark, that a certain degree of weakness is not incompatible with beauty; and that in vegetables, as in the human form, the apparent need of support increases the interest we feel in what is graceful or beautiful....

The next contrast I shall mention is that of Light and Dark, not in shadow and shade, but of a variety in colouring observable in Nature, and well worth cultivating in the art of Gardening, although difficult to represent in painting. Of this I shall enumerate several kinds.

First, The difference of a leaf with the light *shining full upon it,* which renders it an opake object, and the same leaf seen transparent by the light *shining through it....*

Secondly, The Contrast produced amidst the more gaudy Colouring by the sort of repose that the eye derives, sometimes from white flowers, as of the jasmine, the passion-flower, and other plants, whose leaves are dark and not glossy: sometimes the same repose is produced by a mass of light foliage, at a little distance appearing without shape or colour, as in a bed of mignionette.

Thirdly, The Contrast in Texture; some plants and flowers appearing as if composed of silk, others of cloth or velvet; some smooth as satin, others harsh, rough, and prickly.

Fourthly, The contrast of Size; some like the aloe, the horse-chestnut, or the tulip-tree, bearing their blossoms above the reach of man; and others, like the diminutive rock plants, and miniatures of Nature, requiring to be raised, or placed on tables, and in flower-pots or baskets. Sometimes plants of the same species assume new dimensions, forming a contrast with their more common measurements....

The last contrast I shall mention is that of Cloud and Sunshine. There is perhaps nothing more reviving and delightful, than the sudden effect of a summer's shower, after a long continuance of dry weather: then all nature seems revived; the ground and the plants send forth new and grateful odours; the flowers, the birds, the insects, all join to express their pleasure; and even the gold fish in a globe, by their frolic motion shew that they partake in the general joy; splashing the water, and sometimes leaping out of it to meet the welcome drops. An assemblage of Contrasts, under such circumstances, I vainly fancied I could fix by my pencil's art; but a single drop convinced me how feeble is Art in her imitation of Nature.

ANDREW JACKSON DOWNING
UNITY, VARIETY, AND HARMONY (1841)

An American arbiter of taste on gardens and architecture, Downing (1815–1852) designed houses and gardens on both a grand and a small scale. He advocated the creation of public parks and cemeteries as recreation sites, and in collaboration with Calvert Vaux, Downing laid out the grounds for the White House, the Capitol Building, and the Smithsonian Institution. This selection is taken from *A Treatise on the Theory and Practice of Landscape Gardening*.

But there are many persons with small cottage places, of little decided character, who have neither room, time, nor income, to attempt the improvement of their grounds fully, after either of those two schools (Beautiful and Picturesque). How shall they render their places tasteful and agreeable, in the easiest manner? We answer, *by attempting only the simple and the natural;* and the unfailing way to secure this, is by employing as leading features only trees and grass. A soft verdant lawn, a few forest or ornamental trees, well grouped, walks, and a few flowers, give universal pleasure; they contain in themselves, in fact, the basis of all our agreeable sensations in a landscape garden (natural beauty, and the recognition of art); and they are the most enduring sources of enjoyment in any place. There are no country seats in the United States so unsatisfactory and tasteless, as those in which, without any definite aim, everything is attempted; and a mixed jumble of discordant forms, materials, ornaments, and decorations, is assembled—a part in one style and a bit in another, without the least feeling of unity or congruity. These rural bedlams, full of all kinds of absurdities, without a leading character or expression of any sort, cost their owners a vast deal of trouble and money, without giving a tasteful mind a shadow of the beauty which it feels at the first glimpse of a neat cottage residence, with its simple, sylvan character of well kept lawn and trees. If the latter does not rank

high in the scale of Landscape Gardening as an art, it embodies much of its essence as a source of enjoyment—the production of the Beautiful in country residences.

Besides the beauties of form and expression in the different modes of laying out grounds, there are certain universal and inherent beauties, common to all styles, and, indeed, to every composition in the fine arts. Of these, we shall especially point out those growing out of the principles of UNITY, HARMONY, and VARIETY.

UNITY, or the *production of a whole,* is a leading principle of the highest importance, in every art of taste or design, without which no satisfactory result can be realized. This arises from the fact that the mind can only attend, with pleasure and satisfaction, to one object, or one composite sensation, at the same time. If two distinct objects, or classes of objects, present themselves at once to us, we can only attend satisfactorily to one, by withdrawing our attention for the time from the other. Hence the necessity of a reference to this leading principle of unity. . . .

In Landscape Gardening, violations of the principle of unity are often to be met with, and they are always indicative of the absence of correct taste in art. Looking upon a landscape from the windows of a villa residence, we sometimes see a considerable portion of the view embraced by the eye, laid out in natural groups of trees and shrubs, and upon one side, or perhaps in the middle of the same scene, a formal avenue leading directly up to the house. Such a view can never appear a satisfactory whole, because we experience a confusion of sensations in contemplating it. There is an evident incongruity in bringing two modes of arranging plantations, so totally different, under the eye at one moment, which distracts, rather than pleases the mind. In this example, the avenue, taken by itself, may be a beautiful object, and the groups and connected masses may, in themselves, be elegant; yet if the two portions are seen together, they will not form a whole, because they cannot make a composite idea. For the same reason, there is something unpleasing in the introduction of fruit trees among elegant

ornamental trees on a lawn, or even in assembling together, in the same beds, flowering plants and culinary vegetables—one class of vegetation suggesting the useful and homely alone to the mind, and the other, avowedly, only the ornamental.

In the arrangement of a large extent of surface, where a great many objects are necessarily presented to the eye at once, the principle of unity will suggest that there should be some grand or leading features to which the others should be merely subordinate. Thus, in grouping trees, there should be some large and striking masses to which the others appear to belong, however distant, instead of scattered groups, all of the same size. Even in arranging walks, a whole will more readily be recognized, if there are one or two of large size, with which the others appear connected as branches, than if all are equal in breadth, and present the same appearance to the eye in passing.

In all works of art which command universal admiration, we discover an unity of conception and composition, an unity of taste and execution. To assemble in a single composition forms which are discordant, and portions dissimilar in plan, can only afford pleasure for a short time to tasteless minds, or those fond of trifling and puerile conceits. The production of an accordant whole is, on the contrary, capable of affording the most permanent enjoyment to educated minds, everywhere, and at all periods of time.

After unity, the principle of VARIETY is worthy of consideration, as a fertile source of beauty in Landscape Gardening. Variety must be considered as belonging more to the details than to the production of a whole, and it may be attained by disposing trees and shrubs in numerous different ways; and by the introduction of a great number of different species of vegetation, or kinds of walks, ornamental objects, buildings, and seats. By producing intricacy, it creates in scenery a thousand points of interest, and elicits new beauties, through different arrangements and combinations of forms and colors, light, and shades. In pleasure-grounds, while the whole should exhibit a general plan, the different scenes presented to the eye, one after the other, should possess sufficient variety in the detail to keep alive the interest of the spectator, and awaken further curiosity.

HARMONY may be considered the principle presiding over variety, and preventing it from becoming discordant. It, indeed, always supposes *contrasts,* but neither so strong nor so frequent as to produce discord; and *variety,* but not so great as to destroy a leading expression. In plantations, we seek it in a combination of qualities, opposite in some respects, as in the color of the foliage, and similar in others more important, as the form. In embellishments, by a great variety of objects of interest, as sculptured vases, sun-dials, or rustic seats, baskets, and arbors, of different forms, but all in accordance or keeping with the spirit of the scene.

To illustrate the three principles, with reference to Landscape Gardening, we may remark, that, if unity only were consulted, a scene might be planted with but one kind of tree, the effect of which would be sameness; on the other hand, variety might be carried so far as to have every tree of a different kind, which would produce a confused effect. Harmony, however, introduces contrast and variety, but keeps them subordinate to unity, and to the leading expression; and is, thus, the highest principle of the three.

REGINALD J. FARRER
PLANT COLLECTIONS VS. GARDENS (1909)

Botanist, plant-hunter, and influential gardener, Farrer (1880–1920) put his garden theories into practice at his ancestral home of Ingleborough House in Clapham, West Yorkshire, England. Yet Farrer spent much of his life in East Asia collecting plants. He wrote numerous books, including *The English Rock Garden* (1928), *Alpines and Bog Plants* (1908), and *On the Eaves of the World* (1916). The excerpt comes from *In a Yorkshire Garden*.

What did I see in Cornwall? Well, I saw, as I said, the perils into which too soft circumstances, and specialism, can lead a gardener. But I also saw, as I have not yet said, many a spectacle of bewildering gorgeousness and splendour. Holy souls, too, did I find, holy and humble ones, that loved their flowers and tended them as friends, and caused them to rejoice. But, will my Cornish friends allow me to say it, I saw no gardens. I saw a number of places, indeed, where a number of rare and exquisite plants were made to grow in luxury. I saw collections beyond price, and culture high beyond imagining. But of a garden I saw never a trace. Everything was aimless, formless, haphazard. Precious Rhododendrons dumped in a straight line through a wood, tree-ferns in a sort of square paddock-like clearing, Bamboos in a jostle down a glade, with no attempt to show up their individual graces or masses— nowhere, in fact, the least or most elementary notion of design, neither for garden-proper nor for garden-wild.

Of luxuriance and culture, indeed, as they are seen in Cornwall, I can give no adequate idea. Also, every species is the best of its kind, and priceless. Even the Polystichums are selected seedlings, beyond the dreaming of a millionaire. But there is no general effect, and no beauty except the individual beauty attained by each individual plant. And gardening, of course, is the art of bringing all these individual beauties into correlation so as to make the greatest beauty of all. But in Cornwall they think mainly of having a finer Gunnera than their neighbours, it seemed to me, or a bloodier scarlet seedling of Rhododendron. As for placing the Gunnera or the Rhododendron so as to enhance their glories by combination, there is rarely any notion. In fact, the gardeners there suffer the tyranny of the species and the specimen. If they could not grow everything so easily and so awfully well, they would be saved from this individualism, this cult of the separate rarity, which is the destruction of true gardening, that most purely democratic or actually communistic art ever elaborated by man.

I had not time to see all, or even very many gardens. But I found specialism rampant and haughty. It depressed me. All my

own cherished small people of the hills were swept out of consideration with a snort of contempt. And this offended my sense of decency. Perhaps it ruffled my vanity a little too. No, I won't admit that; I do maintain that the true gardener despises nothing. I cannot grow these refulgent Rhododendrons; but I don't despise them, I adore them. Why, then, should a Rhododendron-grower arrogate to himself the right of despising Gentian and Primula and Saxifrage? No, you may ignore, you may leave out, but you must never despise. And, of course, if I am to delve deep into my sensations, the sorrow that seized me amid the pomps of Cornwall has a stray fibre of its roots in envy. Think of me, worshipping *Cyclamen neapolitanum,* and overjoyed to grow it at all, with effort, sparsely, in chosen places of my garden; then think of me contemplating lawns of it at Caerhays, beneath secular cedars—and nothing regarded "(or so they would highly make you believe). From spectacle to spectacle of envy one swoons, and it does seem cruel that these people who cultivate rarity, ignoring effect and design, should so casually and without effort produce, and almost without knowing it either, such miracles of vegetation—as against an earnest, cramped striver like me, who wrestle so perennially for a result so puny.

Yes, these Cornish Paradises are collections. But they are not gardens. When I think of the missed, slighted opportunities, the ugly, stiff groupings, the total indifference that there reigns towards the glorious pictures that might be made, I am at last a little consoled. Otherwise, after a week, of it, I felt like the Queen of Sheba. There was no more spirit left in me. So many people, I seem to remember, had shown me "the finest *Embothrium* in the country," so many people had insisted to me on the size and uniqueness of their specimens, so many people had shrugged scorn at the myriad exquisite Daffodils that made their grass-slopes a flood of pale gold, that in the end I longed for any cottage-garden, where quite quite common little old plants are grown luxuriantly for their own sakes, and loved for their own sakes, and not because they are new—in from Yunnan or Hupeh, and bigger,

for their age, than Lady Tompkin's round the corner at Tre—something or other. . . .

So came I away at last from Cornwall; seduced into utter folly, of course. For now I am trying to grow *Embothrium* and *Tricuspidaria* and *Calceolaria violacea.* What an idiot one perpetually is—and how many awful failures it takes to kill Hope in one's heart—or even to wound her—as for killing her, it can't be done. This new folly, I dare not think of. However, since I planted *Embothrium,* there have been the most appalling frosts. And I notice that whereas the young shoots of the *Buddleia variabilis*—most indestructibly hardy of gorgeous plants—are very much shriveled and annoyed, the new shoots of *Embothrium* are perfectly untouched. After all, a moisture-loving Chilian might, conceivably, prove adaptable to my climate. Ah, so persuades me obstinate silly Hope—a garrulous persistent creature, whose flow of prattle is practically unquenchable. She lives in a garden, indeed, and though she has at least a hundred graves each year, she never stays quiet in any of them.

SYLVIA CROWE
A SINGLENESS OF THOUGHT (1958)

Dame Sylvia Crowe (1901–1997) established her private practice in England after World War II. Her work ranged from public parks to coastal reclamation and from corporate commissions to estate gardens. She gained recognition from her fellow landscape architects for her designs and for her service as president of the Landscape Institute and the International Federation of Landscape Architects. Crowe wrote numerous articles and books, including *Garden Design,* from which this excerpt is taken.

PRINCIPLES OF DESIGN
Perhaps the greatest of these, and the one most lacking in the aver-

age garden to-day, is a sense of unity. It is a quality found in all great landscapes, based on the rhythm of natural land-form, the domination of one type of vegetation and the fact that human use and buildings have kept in sympathy with their surroundings. When we say that a landscape has been spoilt we mean that it has lost this unity.

In the same way, all the great gardens of the world have a unity both of execution and conception which shows that they were created in singleness of thought. Their makers knew what they wanted and were able to express it as a complete whole. This quality can be seen in the progressive water-theme of the Villa D'Este, in the clear-cut compositions of Le Nôtre, and in the sweeping landscapes of Kent and Brown. It is equally apparent in the early gardens of every country; from the oasis garden of the East to the medieval cloister.

In the case of primitive gardens unity is achieved in the simplest possible way, first by limitation of materials and secondly by the strength of a single purpose, whether that purpose was to grow food for a monastic community, to find a place of seclusion in a warring world; or refreshment from the desert heat. But as desires and the means to satisfy them become more complex, this automatic unity has to be replaced by deliberate design, and the really great gardens all bear the impress of a mind or tradition which was strong enough to select only the forms and materials which would express one over-ruling idea. The result is that indefinable attribute called style....

Land-form gives basic unity to a garden, just as it does to a landscape. The sweeping lines merging gently into each other unite the ground-plane of the English landscape garden. They must not be broken by a harsh bank, nor a rock wall, nor by the sudden level rectangle of a tennis court. In contrast, the perfectly proportioned terraces at Vaux-le-Vicomte, with their clearly defined transition from one level to another, make a composition of even planes....

Unity may also be imposed by climate. The garden of Arnold Forster at Zennor, Cornwall, is an example of the unifying effect of exposure to the full force of the wind. The wind-clipped shape of the sheltering shrubs makes a pattern which gives a consistent character to the whole garden....

Even more important is congruity of form: the quality which brings the parts of a design together into one whole so that no part can be altered without reference to the rest. For example, a serpentine path at Vaux would be as unthinkable as a geometric bed cut in the grass at Stourhead or Stowe. In the English landscape garden a groundwork of grass flows like a sea through the composition. The continuity of this background is essential to the unity of the design. The Californian garden is less a pattern built up on a background than a mosaic of congruous shapes; the grass, the pool, the terrace, all closely related in form and interlocking to make one composition....

At the Tivoli gardens in Copenhagen, unity is given by the repetitive pattern of bubbling fountains in wooden bowls, and this repetition is strong enough to carry the varied and informal planting in the individual beds. In the Villa D'Este, water is the unifying theme. The Villa Lante is united by the proportion and logic of its progression from the woodland to the open parterre, and by the congruity of workmanship which gives a preciousness to all the elements and which would make a plain or coarse object out of place. In some of the modern Brazilian gardens, on the other hand, the surfaces are either plain or of coarse texture, and here a finely carved fountain figure would be equally incongruous...

Tone and color unify landscapes just as they do paintings. On a small scale it is often effectively used in grey gardens or, less happily, in blue borders or, with outstanding success, in Sorenson's all-yellow garden at Hellerup. On the larger scale it is one of the great factors in the English landscape garden, and at Stourhead the quiet greens are an essential part of the garden's beauty. Here the azaleas set within the framework of the woods are acceptable, partly because they are contained and muted by the wood and partly because they are on so great a scale that they light up the entire view in their season of flower, almost in the same way that

the whole tone changes with autumn colour. It is a general intensi-fication which does not spotlight one particular feature. On a quieter scale the same effect is given by the mantle of pale yellow cast over the hillside by the wild daffodils in early spring. On the other hand, isolated groups of colour, particularly if they are in the open and not within the woodland, destroy the unity of the composition.

In addition to the unity given by a pervading quality, it may also be imposed by a dominant feature to which all else is sub-ordinate. The house to which the garden is attached may set the tune to which all parts of the garden must conform. This is so at Montacute, where the garden is clearly an extension of the house both in the setting of its forthrights and in the strong echo of the architecture which is carried throughout the balustrades and gaze-bos. In other cases it may be the view which dominates. . . .

All gardens which show the greatest richness of design com-bined with simplicity have a common characteristic in the way in which the elements of their pattern interlock and overlap with each other. This not only gives them a close-knit unity, but imparts the quality of movement, one of the most emotionally stimulating attributes of a design. This interlocking can take place both in the ground pattern and on the different planes of elevation. . . .

The lack of unity, which has disrupted the majority of gardens of the last century and a half, is due to the same causes which have made chaos of our landscape; too many new things, ill-digested; new plants which we have not yet learnt to use; materials, such as Westmoreland rock and crazy paving, which are transported to all parts of the country and used in positions to which they are unsuited; foreign influences, copied without being assimilated or understood. But, above all, there is a lack of decision as to what each man really wants in his garden.

Decisiveness of intention was another factor which permeated the classic garden. The quiet refreshment of the oasis garden, the magnificence of the French, the spacious, ideal landscape of the leisured English landowner, were designed for one purpose and

one way of life. This was so well understood that if, in certain moods, a contradictory use was required, it was carefully concealed within the framework of the main theme, tucked away like the *giardino segreto* or, like the English kitchen garden, walled-off or embowered within the woods.

To-day, because there is not the same solidarity of taste, and also because gardens are spread through a far larger section of soci-ety, there is a greater diversity of needs. For this reason, a modern garden style, showing the same uniform characteristics as previous tradition, is unlikely to emerge and should not be encouraged, for it would contradict one of the bases of a true garden, in that it could not genuinely represent the character of its owner. Instead, the need of each owner should be developed into a garden individual to himself, and in the sincerity which such a garden expresses, it is likely also to give pleasure to others. . . .

There are, however, two types of pattern which may be con-sidered typical of this century. One is the composition of free forms, floating over each other and interlocking in different planes to form the rhythmic pattern of the abstract garden. . . . The other is the cellular, honeycomb design which has been developed to a high degree in Scandinavia. It is a true expression of the age because it allows diverse and small-scale uses to be welded into a unified composition, thus solving the modern problem of maintaining individual values within a world of crowd-organization.

This cellular construction also allows for that variety within the design which has always gone hand in hand with unity, for if lack of unity brings discord, lack of variety brings boredom. All the greatest gardens have shown that these two are not incompat-ible. Vaux shows endless invention in the design of the lateral gardens leading off the main axis while at Stowe the proportion and character of each view is different, the architecture of each arch and temple individual and distinct.

Surprise and hidden depths are part of the attribute of variety, whether it is the magnificently conceived hidden canal at Vaux or merely a curving path disappearing into the shadow of trees in a small private garden. A garden without mystery is not one to live with, although it may serve as a setting to some great building, to be seen purely as part of a view and not felt as an environment.

PETER WALKER
MINIMALISM IN THE GARDEN (2004)

In 1957 Walker (born 1932) co-founded with Hideo Sasaki the firm Sasaki, Walker and Associates and embarked on a variety of landscape architecture commissions. In 1983 he formed Peter Walker and Partners and has served as consultant and advisor to numerous public agencies and institutions: the Sydney 2000 Olympic Coordination Authority, the Redevelopment Agency of San Francisco, the Port Authority of San Diego, Stanford University, the University of California, and the University of Washington. He chaired the landscape architecture departments at both Harvard University and the University of California, Berkeley. He wrote the following essay especially for this book.

As with classicism and modernism, the minimalism of the 1960s and 1970s entered our fast-paced society to be further defined and redefined by varying artistic and cultural disciplines. Having always considered myself a modernist, by the early 1970s I was gradually becoming concerned at the increasingly picturesque tendencies in my work, which were in sharp contrast to the art I had been collecting: for example, the work of such minimalists as Frank Stella, Carl Andre, Sol LeWitt, Donald Judd, Dan Flavin, and Robert Morris. By analytically reaffirming and reviving the simplicity, formal strength, and clarity of modernism, these artists seemed to me to extend the work of my heroes, Mies van der Rohe, Louis Kahn, and the Los Angeles Case Study architects of the 1950s.

Despite my concern, my transition from appreciator of minimalist art to a designer of minimalist landscapes was a gradual one. I first noticed what I thought of as landscape ideas in the early striped paintings of Frank Stella: The internal design of the patterns was able to define the shape of a two-dimensional painting, obviating the frame and eliminating the possibility that it could be read as an abstracted image. This was like a garden without walls, able to exist in a spatial context while also existing as an object apart. Next I began to see Carl Andre's metal floor pieces as powerful metaphors for gardens: all flat ground plane and almost no third dimension, yet completely controlling the character and nature of the "empty" space above. They reminded me of the Persian carpets of the desert Bedouin: movable, intimate, ideal gardens. In one Andre work, *144 Blocks and Stones* (1973), all the gallery walls (read *architecture*) were emptied and the floor (read *landscape*) became a complex and mysterious totem. The materials were humble, even mundane, but the result was intensely compelling. Yet another Andre work, *Secant* (1977), was placed in an ordinary meadow. The meadow was naturally beautiful but hardly different from thousands in the region. Andre's profoundly simple placement of a series of cut timbers transformed it into a place that demanded—and generated—consciousness. Similarly Christo's *Running Fence* (1972–76) enlivened a generic California landscape into a condition of high celebration. I had grown up and lived most of my life in these same coastal hills, and yet I had never seen them in quite this way or felt so strongly a part of them before. That a string of silken sheets could accomplish such revision was astounding.

In 1911, when traveling through the Middle East, the youthful Le Corbusier was drawn to Turkish mosques, Byzantine monasteries, and Bulgarian houses by certain qualities of silence, light, and simple, austere form. On the acropolis of Athens, he was overwhelmed by the Parthenon, which he later interpreted as a distillation of form. A moment had been reached, he concluded, when nothing more could be taken away. It was a moment of perfection, a defining of the classic. In the 1970s I felt a similar response to

TANNER FOUNTAIN (designed in 1984
by Peter Walker)
Harvard University, Cambridge,
Massachusetts
Alan Ward

NASHER FOUNDATION SCULPTURE
CENTER (designed in 2003 by
Peter Walker)
Dallas, Texas
Tim Wight

André Le Nôtre's Chantilly, a great garden of stone, water, space, and light, another example of form reduced to its essential perfection. And it was following a summer tour of French gardens in the late 1970s that I began to try to make gardens in a new way. My first efforts were quite tentative. It quickly became apparent that the simple transfer of an idea inspired by artwork in a gallery or on specific site would not in itself be a successful strategy for landscape—because landscape must deal with the multiple dimensions of nature.

Despite the difficulty, an effort to extend minimalism into landscape design seemed timely. Developments during what has been termed our postmodern era questioned the legitimacy of modernist design, with some favoring a return to the vocabulary, if not the spirit, of classicism. Much thought focused on formal and decorative issues on the one hand and sociological and functional issues on the other.

As one of the manifestations of the last moment of high modernism in the visual arts, minimalism has many compelling affinities with classicism. But rather than focusing on design and functional issues as mutually exclusive, minimalism leads to examination of the abstract and the essential, qualities of both classicist and modernist design. In landscape architecture minimalism opens a line of inquiry that can guide us through some of the difficult transitions of our time: the simplification or loss of craft, transitions from traditional natural materials to synthetics, and extensions of the human scale to a larger scale in both space and time—all characteristics of our mechanically aided modern life. And minimalism in this context suggests as well an artistic approach to dealing with two of the most critical environmental problems we currently face: mounting waste and dwindling resources.

Minimalism in the landscape is concerned with the formal reinvention and the quest for primary purity and human meaning that constituted the spiritual strength of minimalism in art—an interest in mystery and nonreferential content that link it to the quest of classical thought. In this larger context, minimalism continues to imply an approach that rejects any attempt to overcome the forces of nature—intellectually, technically, or industrially. And yet it suggests a conceptual order and thereby tries to modify natural systems with geometry, narrative, rhythm, gesture, and other devices that can imbue space with a unique sense of place that lives in memory.

Perhaps the most important issue for the minimalist landscape is that of visibility: To be visible, an object must be seen in and for itself. If it is largely subordinated to context or if it is confused with the existing environment, the work is drained of its ability to be expressive, to carry meaning, to imprint itself on the memory. Even high decoration cannot gain conscious attention if it cannot achieve objecthood alongside other existing artistic presences. Reference to the quintessential minimalist artist points to the basic assumption of minimalist landscape. Donald Judd insisted that minimalism is first and foremost an expression of the objective, a focus on the object in itself, rather than on the surrounding context or on any interpretation. Minimalism, then, is not referential or representative, although some viewers will inevitably make their own historical and symbolic connections.

Similarly, the focus in minimalist landscape is on the designed landscape itself, its own energy and space, even though it exists in the context of the environment. The designer may employ strategies of interruptions or interaction or allow one to see beyond the designed "object" to the larger landscape. Nor, as is the case in minimalist art, is minimalist landscape necessarily reductivist, although these works often have few components and a directness that implies simplicity.

The problem of how to assure visibility cannot be isolated from the characteristics of the natural world. Objects in the landscape are seen within the larger environment, which includes not only the particulars of a site but, more comprehensively, the organic rhythms of the daily movement of the sun and moon, the changes of seasonal light and climate shifts, and, especially, the more random characteristics of birth, growth, and decline. This complex interaction between nature and even the simplest introduced or placed object magnifies and compounds the problem of placing objects on the land, making time as important a factor as place.

In the field of contemporary landscape design the element of time and the reality of unpredictability have not often been addressed in their primacy for three largely Cartesian reasons: first, a scientific/technological tendency to want to dissect, overpower, and control, rather than to celebrate, the mystery of nature; second, an inability or unwillingness to deal with natural complexity and change in our desire to offer "expert" service, predictability occupying perhaps too high a place in our value system; and third, an overemphasis on detail and specific program stemming from a questionable acceptance of modernist architectural thought. If "form follows function," then analyzing function becomes the highest priority. Form then merely expresses or reveals function rather than any other, higher ideal, and function becomes the measure of satisfaction of design goals. The more intuitive, artistic approach to designing in and with nature reveals—beyond function—a wonder-filled, even spiritual, interaction between a human physical act and the ever-changing world of open space.

In contemporary society, fragmentation, both physical and experiential, tends to break down our sense of natural order. Streams are interrupted and put in pipes; hills and mountains are cut, removed, or visually scarred. Pedestrian ways are rendered discontinuous. Buildings and chemical pollution block natural lines of sight to the major defining landforms, including the sea and even the sky. Natural distinguishing landscape units, for example the Los Angeles Basin, the island of Manhattan, the Charles River in Boston, as well as a myriad others, have been visually weakened by man-made roads, highways, building, and, in some cases, man-made landscapes. Such mutations diminish the human sense of order and, as a result, those feelings of stability—and of meaning—that premodern humans experienced in the natural—and agricul-

tural—landscape. In those landscape features humans discovered the spatial orderings that replicated their entire relationship to the universe as a whole.

In the fragmented circumstances of contemporary life, the reduction and focus offered by minimalism suggest a direction for the restitution of that spiritual sense of place. Ordering devices common to much minimal art and to traditional formal gardens include seriality and repetition, geometry (particularly liner and point grids), perceived extension of dimensions, liner gesture, and visual exploitation of edges and centers, including bilateral and asymmetrical symmetry. Other avenues to the reconstitution of the visible include the exploration of texture, color, pattern, and scale as well as such contrasts as synthetic versus natural, living versus inert. By these means, minimalism in the landscape can ultimately achieve the visibility that allows humankind to celebrate—without irony and cynicism—the mystery, the essential *quidditas,* of the physical world, the world we humans not only inhabit but of which we are only a part.

SHUNMYO MASUNO
ONE PATH, ONE FORM (1996)

Shunmyo Masuno, born in 1935, attended the Department of Agriculture at Tamagawa University in Japan with a major in forestry. Simultaneously he studied books on Japanese gardens and worked as an apprentice under noted garden designer Katsuo Saito. In 1979 he entered Daihonzansojiji Temple, where he underwent ascetic training to become a Zen priest. He established Japan Landscape Consultants in 1982 and is currently head priest of Kenko-ji Temple. A professor at Tama Art University in Japan, he also has lectured at Harvard, Cornell, and the University of Toronto. Professor Masuno has won numerous awards for his designs in Japan and abroad and has published many books, including two in English: *Ten Landscapes* and *Inside Japanese Gardens.* These excerpts are from *Process: Architecture,* Special Issue 7 (1995) and "Landscapes of the Spirit: The Gardens and Spaces of Shunmyo Masuno" by Kim Schuefftan in *Japanese Things* (1996).

Creating Zen gardens is not like a rich man's hobby, which attracts people's attention. You have to go straight to the heart of the matter and create something that will have a lasting impression on people. Zen gardens should be at one with the people who view them and an unforgettable garden is one that becomes an essential part of a person's life. This is also true of the lives of those looking at the garden and its creator for they are united by the garden, too....

When someone decides to create something, they are not aware of what and how they are going to make that thing up until the moment that they actually begin. However, once they have started, they become completely absorbed in what they are doing and the unconscious mind instantly takes over. In other words, when the mind, hands, body, time, and materials merge into one then an unconsciousness, which goes beyond the bounds of con-

sciousness, is responsible for creating things. This means that the spirit of the person, who has created the thing, becomes part of it. Having reached this state, they are able for the first time to perfect a work of art....

My designs are, as I have said before, expressions of my mind. Consequently, I devote much time to both developing a design concept as well as the design details in completing just one design. This is of course obvious to anyone who creates something but the big factor here is the way in which I pour my heart and soul into a design. When I consider a form then the problem is whether or not it has a philosophy. Obviously there is a great difference between a form, which only sets out to be beautiful, and one in which body and soul are united at the time of its creation. Even if the completed forms are very nearly the same, the impression of the viewer should differ greatly, too, because the mental energy, which exists within the work, is different. In either case, memories of the garden will linger with those who see it for a long time but when a garden has no soul, then even though it may catch the attention of many people for a time, they will completely forget about it as soon as something new comes along. Consequently we must question just how much of a creator's spirit is poured into a work. When I am creating a garden, I normally put most emphasis on this point. Naturally, it is necessary to be scrupulous about the minutest details but this is related to the fact that sufficient time is needed for design details too. In creating my work, I concentrate intensively on one form before going through each one of the above-mentioned processes....

The effort that is required to complete a single scheme is enormous.... Searching for and finding the right materials involves a basic process. It is something like intuition, but goes much deeper. I know what is needed from the detailed plan. Then I go to the mountains and search until I find a stone that speaks to me. Finding the right stone is something like meeting a person. Buddhism sees stones and trees as having souls [the Japanese word is *kokoro,* which is usually translated as heart/mind]. When I encounter a stone that

MUSHIN-TEI (designed and built in
1999–2001 by Shunmyo Masuno)
Ibaragi, Japan
Tabata Minao

seems right, whose voice and energy and heart are right for the garden, then I sketch it and take measurements and find its place in "the garden. No mistakes are made because I am not doing this by rules or abstractions, with my mind alone. I know what the energy and atmosphere of the garden is, and there is no rush. I search until stones are found that fit that energy and atmosphere. Here is one of the many instances in which my Buddhist training and practice are in complete congruence with the art of landscape design.

This process, this capturing the heart and life of a rock or a tree or a bush, is one of the most basic and important aspects of a landscape designer's work. Of course there is a plan. But a plan by itself is empty....

Construction work begins, when the design process is complete but supervision of this construction work is, needless to say, a very important part of the process as well as the work itself. This is because however good a design might be, if the finished product does not resemble the intended form then it will be meaningless. In order to create gardens in which the work and the creator are at one, using similar methods to mine, it is absolutely vital to be scrupulous about your ideas down to the very last detail. The creative process starts with a reappraisal of the composition of the site and continues with the allocation of land, the creation of land forms, positioning of stones and planting. Once you have been to see the site, the plan then becomes the criterion for making the garden. This is because the dialogue between the stones and plants, the appearance of the typography, the site and the view act as guidelines for the design. There are so many surprises in store at the site such as the unexpected expressions of stone and plants. It is impossible to anticipate such encounters as these and one cannot help smiling on discovering an unexpected quality, which was undetected on first inspection. Decisions about the positioning of elements are therefore made, while interpreting these expressions. At such times, it is mental concentration that is needed more than anything else, so I always prepare myself the day before I lay out stones and plants by meditating. Then once on site, I prepare my awareness by concentrating all my thoughts on my abdomen. In other words, I meditate in the Zen standing position, concentrating exclusively on abdominal breathing to rid my mind of all confusion.

Once I start arranging either the plants or stones, I become totally absorbed in the dialogue taking place between all the elements. I wonder just what kind of spirit a certain stone has and how it would prefer to be set out. This is also true of plants and I always consider how I think the plants would like to be displayed. I always feel at one with the plants, when I am planting them and with the stones, when I am arranging them. This is the moment when you know instinctively that everything is right, the moment of realization, which in Zen is called *jikishitanden.*

In this way, the whole composition of the garden gradually takes shape. When I am on site, I don't simply arrange stones and things like waterfalls or cascades to suit the forms of the retaining concrete. Instead, what I try to do is to make the landscaping and such things as retaining concrete walls fit in with the waterfalls, cascades, and other features that have been formed by the temporarily set out groups of stones, themselves arranged as a result of their dialogue with me....

I would also like to point out just what an important matter the supervision of the actual manual work involved in the layout of a garden actually is. Or to put it another way, it would be impossible to complete what might be called "a work of art" without this kind of supervision on site.

6

COLOR

My flowers grow up in several parts of the garden in the greatest luxuriancy and profusion. I am so far from being fond of any particular one by reason of its rarity, that if I meet with any one in the field which pleases me, I give it a place in my garden. Several spots of ground are covered with ten thousand different colours. The only method I observe in this particular is to range in the same quarter the products of the same season, that they make their appearance together, and compose a picture of the greatest variety.

Joseph Addison (1672–1719), English publisher, essayist, poet, and dramatist

No defect is more common than that of the proportion in which flowers of similar colours are distributed in a garden.... Add to this defect of proportion, the ill effect produced by placing together many species of flowers, which, although of the same colour, are not of the same tint.... Such arrangements as these cause the eye, accustomed to appreciate the effects of contrast of colours, to feel sensations quite as disagreeable as those experienced by the musician whose ear is struck with discords.

Michel Eugène Chevreul (1786–1889), French chemist and director of dyes, Royal Manufactory at the Gobelins

Knowledge of the laws of design need not imprison, it can liberate from indecision and vacillating perceptions. What we call laws of color, obviously, can be no more than fragmentary, given the complexity and irrationality of color effects.... If color is the chief vehicle of expression, composition must begin with color areas, and these will determine the lines. He who first draws lines and then adds color will never succeed in producing a clear, intense color effect. Colors have dimensions and directionality of their own, and delineate areas in their own way.

Johannes Itten (1888–1967), Swiss painter and Bauhaus teacher

previous spread:
TEXAS BLUEBONNETS IN MAHNKE PARK
San Antonio, Texas
Richard Cummins/CORBIS

opposite:
EDWARD S. HARKNESS ESTATE AND
GARDENS (design begun 1918 by Beatrix
Jones Farrand)
Waterford, Connecticut
Scott J. Tilden

ATTRIBUTED TO WILLIAM MASON
COLOR TRIADS (c. 1770)

Poet, essayist, and gardener, Mason (1724-1797) advocated a less formal, more picturesque style of garden design than his predecessors in England. He described his theories in his long poem *The English Garden* (1772-83). The following excerpt comes from "An Essay on the Arrangement of Flowers in Pleasure-Grounds," which is believed to have been sent by Mason to George Simon, 2nd Earl of Harcourt (1736-1809).

The ornament which a variety of flowers gives to edges of borders, & clumps of shrubs, in small pleasure-grounds, is great & universally acknowledged. Yet, variety is the only thing which is usually aimed at; & hence the general effect of them is by no means as beautiful and striking as it would be, were the Gardener to plant and sow under the direction of one natural and picturesque principle—what this principle is I will endeavour briefly to explain.

It is well known by Painters, & it ought to be known by the flower Gardener, that Red, yellow, & blue are the three primitive, or original colours in nature; from the blending of which all the rest are produced, except white, & black—the red & yellow produce Orange—red with blue, when the red is prevalent, produce Crimson—& when the blue prevails over the red the mixture is purple.

Yellow & blue, according to the increase of the one & decrease of the other, give every kind of Green, from Sea to Grass green; and all the three colours blended in different proportions, together, supply the Painter with every gradation of Brown.

But the Gardener has no occasion to regard these two latter colours, as the leaves of flowering plants, as of all others, are constantly Green; & I know of no flower the Petals of which are perfectly Brown, except, perhaps, some rare Auriculas. It is not, however, by rarities that the Gardener must hope, or attempt to produce the general effect here aimed at—those which are the most common & the most hardy are the best to be depended upon, and are therefore, exclusively, recommended to his use.

Having premised all this, I will now lay down the Principle itself, which is deduced from the above theory of Colours. It is simply this, that wherever a Flower of one of the three primitive hues is planted or sown, two others should be placed nearly contiguous to the first. The arrangement however, shalt be in the order above mentioned—Red the first—Yellow the second—Blue the third: for yellow being the most vivid of the three, will have the gayest effect in the center. The same principle applies itself to the three blended colours, Crimson, Orange, & Purple, in which the Orange (as the yellow before) claims the central position. Again, with respect to the streaked, or variegated Flowers, in which White usually intervenes. Those Flowers which have the greatest share of Red, & which predominates over White, the greatest of Yellow, or of Blue, or of Crimson, Orange, or Purple should have their places adjusted by the foregoing general rule.

White Flowers such as are perfectly so, I would wish the Planter to be sparing of: for in profusion they harmonize ill with Foliage. Therefore, whenever they are planted, they should as the painter terms it, be *kept down* by the real colours—for White and Black are in Optics deemed no colours. It may be thought, perhaps, that by closely, & uniformly persuing this principle, there would be an appearance of formality produced, which would ill accord, with our present natural mode of laying out Pleasure-Grounds; and it would be so, did all Flowers flow & fade, at one and the same time; but this is far from being the case. The judicious Planter may so arrange the Flowers, that when one trinal combination of hues fade, another may begin to flow....

It is highly necessary, that any person who chuses to follow this principle, should acquaint himself with the times of blooming, and withering, of those flowers which are best adapted to his purpose, and select those only, which are of a pretty equal size in point of height, that so their petals may intermingle of equal duration as to continuing in flower; & hues which are equally vivid; always preferring the brighter to the fainter, tho the latter may be more delicate—for as to delicate and rare flowers, they should always be placed separately. For however beautiful they may be in themselves, they can add nothing to that general effect, which is the sole thing aimed at by the principle.

There is another thing to be attended to, that Plants of a different Genus and Species, should be selected from these combinations, in order that their Genera may not bastardize one another; which might be the case, were they of the same family. Annual and Biennial Flowers should not be united with Perennial, for tho they may harmonize well, in point of colour, they will vary too much in size and in continuance of blossoming.

A Catalogue of Flowers formed upon this principle is a desideratum, which I am not sufficiently skilled in Botany to supply. I know enough of it, however, to foresee that a Catalogue, specifying such flowers as can properly be combined together with all the requisites of colour, size, and duration required by the principle, will not be very numerous; but there will be some difficulty as in ascertaining what combinations will in different months of the Summer season produce the best and most durable effect. Certain it is, that he who is directed by the Calendar, with which every Gardening-book from Miller's original one, will by no means succeed.

Every person, situated either in the Southern or Northern part of this Island must make one for himself, from such observations on the times, and duration of florescence, which his own garden, in the space of two or three years, will enable him to form for his own use—and perhaps the exploded system of Tournfort, which classes every flower by the number of its Petals (which are the colorific part of the plant) would assist him more for this purpose, than the more scientific system of Linnaeus, which arranges every plant by its organs of fructification....

CHRISTIAN CAY LORENZ HIRSCHFELD
TENETS OF COLORATION (1779–85)

C.C.L. Hirschfeld (1742–1792) was the most important writer on gardens and landscape in eighteenth-century Germany. His five-volume treatise, *Theorie der Gartenkunst* (Theory of Garden Art), was published simultaneously in German and French between 1779 and 1785 and was popular and influential among master designers and amateurs alike. This selection comes from a translation by Linda B. Parshall published in 2001.

COLOR

Nature did not wish mankind to view her works coldheartedly. She therefore employed light and color to endow the surfaces of things with such charm that they arouse pleasure and satisfaction and invite us to repeated contemplation. If everything in nature were the same hue, how quickly the eye would tire of looking and the spirit be surfeited and feel disgust, so it would be without the vivacity and gaiety of colors. In general, colors move us more than shapes; we need only open our eyes to color, whereas without comparison and judgment—that is, activity of the mind—a mere glance is insufficient to comprehend a form. Color is, so to speak, a kind of language, through which the inanimate objects of nature speak to the eye, a language understood everywhere and in every corner of the earth. Through color, objects acquire great power over our feelings; they excite such strong sensations of joy, love, peace and other emotions that it is easy to conclude that garden art can achieve color effects that are just as beneficial as those of nature herself.

It is true that nature has an astonishing variety of colors and displays them with intensity and restraint alike, with fiery brilliance and more muted degrees of brightness, through mixes and blends, through the variation and unexpected incidence of light, through play and reflection—presenting a spectacle as

following spread:
ROSENBORG PALACE (1606–34) and
GARDENS
Copenhagen, Denmark
Tibor Bognár/CORBIS

GOETHE'S GARDEN HOUSE AND
GARDEN (design begun 1776 by Johann
Wolfgang von Goethe)
Weimar, Germany
Richard Klune/CORBIS

splendid and beautiful as anything to be found in all of creation. And nature offers this delightful color display not just to the landscape painter, but to his rival, the garden artist, as well.

Cast your eye on an abundant field of flowers, especially when the regal tulip is blooming. What amazing splendor and diversity of color! It is hard to understand how the otherwise sensitive British eye seems to indulge so little in these beauties, whereas the Dutch regard them as the supreme charm of a garden. Although a park or garden can be beautiful without flowers, and a square filled with the most splendid blooms is still not a garden, nature offers enormous delight through the colors of flowers alone, not to mention their balsamic fragrances. To be fair, they cannot be entirely neglected in a garden.

However great the splendor of colors in the floral realm, it is surpassed by the most sublime and beautiful spectacle of color in nature: the rising and setting sun, with its endlessly changing complement of appearances. It is a sight that has moved poets to dazzling descriptions and inspired Lucas van Uden, Claude Gellée, and so many other geniuses among painters to the finest imitations of which art is capable; but it is also a spectacle of beauty that touches less refined eyes. I have often felt secret compassion for those country houses and gardens with encircling buildings, walls, or high trees that obscure a view of this supreme vision of nature. If only the architect and garden artist would always leave an opening through which the eye can enjoy this most splendid sight in creation!

Besides the passing grandeur of the colors to be seen in flowers and in the rising and setting sun, nature has provided for an admittedly less splendid but more enduring beauty of colors in the landscape's general attire. Green, agreeably strengthening and refreshing to the eye, is the predominant hue in a beautiful landscape. Yet even in a single area we can perceive an endless variation of color—heightened, subdued, and blended—not through the graduated effect of the hazy distance alone but as a result of the light in adjacent or nearby objects, in low-growing and taller

plants, in thickets, and in trees. Here nature does not simply retire, allowing the garden artist to captivate us through that same variety and alteration of greens in the natural landscape; she permits him to surpass her great if careless designs through a more measured blending of colors. She allows the garden artist to create a new whole by recombining her offerings, presenting, as it were, a painting of higher perfection.

The special beauty of colors includes: luminosity and vividness; modulation such as soft blue, rose pink, violet, light green; and variation, with imperceptible changes and gently unfolding combinations.

Whereas a garden artist may find he can achieve fiery color only by planting specific varieties of flowers, he can delight much more through pure, bright hues. Fiery colors produce joy; pure, bright colors bring happiness. Modulated colors offer refreshment and sweet feelings of repose (violet) or gentle merriment (light blue and rosy red). Variation entertains us with a sustained pleasure that fends off fatigue.

From these remarks, which must guide the thoughtful garden artist in his work, some general tenets of coloration arise.

1. Avoid using just one color, and know that you are acting contrary to nature's instructions if you choose just a single kind of green.

2. Never think that it is without consequence if you randomly intermix the colors of plants, shrubs, and trees; in fact, deliberation and choice are required if color is to be used with pleasing visual effect.

3. Concern yourself primarily with the luminosity and liveliness of color in order to arouse happiness. These qualities should not only enliven those objects close at hand but also dominate the color of your landscape painting.

4. Distinguish those parts of your site that require a different color either because of their natural location and condition, their purpose, or because of the character you want to give them through shaping the ground, placing the buildings, and so forth. A remote path into a thicket may be shaded with less cheerful green. A grotto and a hermitage require shrouding in dark and somber foliage.

5. Study the affinities of colors and seek to mix and combine related hues so that a perfect harmony arises. Pay attention not only to the effects of nearby and immediate color combinations, but ask also how they might appear at a certain distance, throughout the seasons, and even after several years.

6. As much as is possible, grant your objects, natural as well as artificial, a location and placement that enhances their beauty, one lit either through continuous, direct light or by intermittent sunlight, whatever site and intention allow and require. There is one important rule that is constantly broken, however: place the meadow of dew-covered flowers against the morning light, and let the bathing pond in the thicket be gilded by the soft rays of the retreating sun.

JOHANN WOLFGANG VON GOETHE
EXPERIENCING COLOR (1810)

Goethe (1749-1832), a brilliant German poet, novelist, playwright, courtier, and natural philosopher, believed that his principal contribution to culture was his scientific discoveries. His research spanned the fields of geology, meteorology, botany, and color perception; his studies of plants were informed by his visits to gardens in Italy between 1786 and 1788 and observations of his own gardens at his Weimar estate beside the Ilm River. Goethe authored many works on science, notably *The Metamorphosis of Plants* (1790) and *Theory of Color* (1810). This excerpt is from Charles Lock Eastlake's 1829 translation of the latter book, which greatly influenced scientists, painters, and garden designers. This passage describes the psychological impact of color on the viewer.

Since colour occupies so important a place in the series of elementary phenomena, filling as it does the limited circle assigned to it with fullest variety, we shall not be surprised to find that its effects are at all times decided and significant, and that they are immediately associated with the emotions of the mind. We shall not be surprised to find that these appearances presented singly are specific, that in combination they may produce an harmonious, characteristic, often even an inharmonious effect on the eye, by means of which they act on the mind; producing this impression in their most general elementary character, without relation to the nature or form of the object on whose surface they are apparent. Hence, colour considered as an element of art, may be made subservient to the highest aesthetical ends.

People experience a great delight in colour, generally. The eye requires it as much as it requires light. We have only to remember the refreshing sensation we experience, if on a cloudy day the sun illumines a single portion of the scene before us and displays its colours. That healing powers were ascribed to coloured gems, may have arisen from the experience of this indefinable pleasure. . . .

From some of our earlier observations we can conclude, that general impressions produced by single colours cannot be changed, that they act specifically, and must produce definite, specific states in the living organ.

They likewise produce a corresponding influence on the mind. Experience teaches us that particular colours excite particular states of feeling. . . .

The colors on the *plus* side are yellow, red-yellow (orange), yellow-red (minium, cinnabar). The feelings they excite are quick, lively, aspiring.

YELLOW

This is the colour nearest the light. It appears on the slightest mitigation of light, whether by semi-transparent mediums or faint reflection from white surfaces. In prismatic experiments it extends itself alone and widely in the light space and while the two poles remain separated from each other, before it mixes with blue to produce green it is to be seen in its utmost purity and beauty. . . .

In its highest purity it always carries with it the nature of brightness, and has a serene, gay, softly exciting character.

We find from experience, again, that yellow excites a warm and agreeable impression. Hence in painting it belongs to the illumined and emphatic side.

This impression of warmth may be experienced in a very lively manner if we look at a landscape through a yellow glass, particularly on a grey winter's day. The eye is gladdened, the heart expanded and cheered, a glow seems at once to breathe towards us. If, however, this colour in its pure and bright state is agreeable and gladdening, and in its utmost power is serene and noble, it is, on the other hand, extremely liable to contamination, and produces a very disagreeable effect if it is sullied, or in some degree tends to the *minus* side. Thus, the color of sulphur, which inclines to green, has a something unpleasant in it.

RED-YELLOW

All that we have said of yellow is applicable here in a higher degree. The red-yellow gives an impression of warmth and gladness, since it represents the hue of the intenser glow of fire, utmost purity and beauty. . .

YELLOW-RED

As pure yellow passes very easily to red-yellow, so the deepening of this last to yellow-red is not to be arrested. The agreeable, cheerful sensation which red-yellow excites, increases to an intolerably powerful impression in bright yellow-red.

The active side is here in its highest energy, and it is not to be wondered at that impetuous, robust, uneducated men, should be especially pleased with this colour. Among savage nations the inclination for it has been universally remarked, and when children left to themselves, begin to use tints, they never spare vermilion and minium.

In looking steadfastly at a perfectly yellow-red surface, the colour seems actually to penetrate the organ. It produces an extreme excitement, and still acts thus when somewhat darkened. A yellow-red cloth disturbs and enrages animals. I have known men of education to whom its effect was intolerable if they chanced to see a person dressed in a scarlet cloak on a grey, cloudy day.

The colours on the *minus* side are blue, red-blue, and blue-red. They produce a restless, susceptible, anxious impression.

BLUE

As yellow is always accompanied with light, so it may be said that blue still brings a principle of darkness with it.

This color has a peculiar and almost indescribable effect on the eye. As a hue it is powerful, but it is on the negative side, and in its highest purity is, as it were, a stimulating negation. Its appearance, then, is a kind of contradiction between excitement and repose.

As the upper sky and distant mountains appear blue, so a blue surface seems to retire from us.

NAUMKEAG ESTATE (designed in 1885 by Stanford White) and GARDENS (begun 1925 by Fletcher Steele)
Paul Rocheleau

But as we follow an agreeable object that flies from us, so we love to contemplate blue, not because it advances to us, but because it draws us after it.

Blue gives us an impression of cold, and thus, again, reminds us of shade. We have before spoken of its affinity with black.

Rooms which are hung with pure blue appear to some degree larger, but at the same time empty and cold.

RED-BLUE

Blue deepens very mildly into red, and thus acquires a somewhat active character, although it is on the passive side. Its exciting power is, however, of a very different kind from that of red-yellow. It may be said to disturb rather than enliven.

An augmentation itself is not to be arrested, so we feel an inclination to follow the progress of the colour, not, however, as in the case of the red-yellow, to see it still increase in the active sense, but to find a point to rest in.

In its very attenuated state, this colour is known to us under the name of lilac; but even in this degree it has a something lively without gladness.

BLUE-RED

This unquiet feeling increases as the hue progresses, and it may be safely assumed, that a carpet of a perfectly pure deep blue-red would be intolerable. On this account when it is used for dress, ribbons, or other ornaments, it is employed in a very attenuated and light state, and thus displays its character as above defined, in a peculiarly attractive manner....

RED

The effect of this colour is as peculiar as its nature. It conveys an impression of gravity and dignity, and at the same time of grace and attractiveness. The first in its dark deep state, the latter in its light attenuated tint; and thus the dignity of age and the amiableness of youth may adorn itself with degrees of the same hue.

History relates many instances of the jealousy of sovereigns with regard to the quality of red. Surrounding accompaniments of this colour have always a grave and magnificent effect.

GREEN

If yellow and blue, which we consider as the most fundamental and simple colours, are united as they first appear, in the first state of their action, the colour which we call green is the result.

The eye experiences a distinctly grateful impression from this colour. If the two elementary colours are mixed in perfect equality so that neither predominates, the eye and the mind repose on the result of this junction as upon a simple colour. The beholder has neither the wish nor the power to imagine a state beyond it. Hence for rooms to live in constantly, the green color is most generally selected.

FLETCHER STEELE
WHY PUT THE EYE ON A DIET? (1964)

The designer of more than seven hundred gardens, Steele (1885–1971) is widely regarded as a key figure in the transition from Beaux Arts formalism to modern American landscape design. In 1907, at the age of twenty-two, Steele studied briefly at the new Graduate School of Landscape Architecture at Harvard University and then went to work with Warren Manning, a former assistant to Frederick Law Olmsted. After completing a four-month tour of European gardens, he opened his own practice. His best-known design is the Blue Steps at Naumkeag. This passage from his book *Gardens and People* (1964) presents his ideas on color.

COLOR PROGRESS IN SUMMER

... Colors have their annual development, and all of their divergences influence our planting plans. The young landscape architect, putting away his color chart, decides that by and large he had better use vivid pink, red, yellow, and blue in spring and early summer, when they are clean and perky. In late summer he will forget the cherry side of red in favor of salmon and dull scarlet. Then, too, he will let blue turn to violet and purple, let bright yellow modulate to tawny gold and russet. In autumn he will not bother much about flowers, rather letting the garden play second fiddle in the grand color symphony that sweeps the countryside.

PREJUDICE STARVES EYE PLEASURE

Some people seem to think that refinement consists of a collection of prejudices—they will not have this, and they cannot bear that. Vulgar is their favorite epithet. They cringe at anything vivid. Their colors must be "soft" and they talk of "pastel shades"—which makes Rouault's pastels laugh.

The landscape architect was born at the time when his village shrieked with scarlet sage and golden glow. The aim of our gardeners then was to be fierce, that being before the "city people" came out to tell them how to make a garden. And to give them their due, it was they who discovered that intense colors are happiest when used with moderation. They banished our red and yellow combination, and few there be who dare to grow it now. It was never altogether forgotten, however, and the grown-up farmboy in the city, tired of palaces, dreams of an old red barn and cows and golden glow.

With the vigor of sprouting prejudice, all reds were soon kicked out along with scarlet sage. The Victorian censor's eye was blind to the value of scarlet and crimson sparkles among the flowers, even while it was being trained to tremble with joy under the glass at Chartres. "But glass is different," they said.

Once it got red out of sight, prejudice made a nuisance of other colors. Magenta was sent to the doghouse and bright yellow put on probation. In time even admittedly agreeable tones were stripped away by faddists till in the most expensive borders only blue flowers or white were allowed.

When this purge of color got well under way, all plants were outlawed whose foliage was not entirely green, on the pretext that they were "unnatural." (As though Nature could be ashamed by rules of etiquette!) The comprehensive variety of color, welcome to the healthy eye, was too violent for prejudiced vision and made the intelligentsia sick. Purple barberry, blue spruce, and golden arborvitae were put on the Plantsman's Expurgatory Index. White leaves or green streaked with yellow were regarded as some foul deformity, and scientists (who have their own blind spots) climbed on the bandwagon to encourage the distaste. Dislike became the lodestar of these gardeners, who had little time left for pleasure because of their constant annoyance with what the jaundiced eye was prejudiced against.

The unbiased artist knows that all colors and all foliage have a place somewhere in his work, like words in the dictionary waiting for a poet. To use color well is an arduous task, and not many will take the necessary trouble. Most of us are satisfied with knowing what we like, and we call that artistic good taste. After once making a mistake with magenta, for instance, we do not try again and again to contrive its proper use; instead, we blame the color itself, throw it out and forever after look at it down our noses. We say we cannot bear it in the garden. With less prejudice and more honesty we would admit that we lack the will to learn how to make the most of it.

All colors are beautiful or ugly according to their quantity and place in relation to other colors. Any arbitrary elimination removes a possible source of pleasure.

Why put the eye on a diet?

VITA SACKVILLE-WEST
THE WHITE GARDEN AT SISSINGHURST (1955)

A renowned English literary figure, Sackville-West (1892–1962) produced eight novels and five plays between 1906 and 1910. In 1913 she married the diplomat and critic Harold Nicolson, with whom she eventually purchased Sissinghurst Castle in Kent. She is remembered for her novels, but her most enduring work was perhaps the garden at Sissinghurst Castle. She wrote numerous articles and books about gardening, including *More for Your Garden* (1955), from which this selection is taken.

There comes a moment at twilight when white plants gleam with a peculiar pallor or ghostliness. I dare say of white, that neutral tint usually regarded as an *absence* of colour, that it is every bit as receptive of changing light as the blues and reds and purples. It may perhaps demand a patiently observing eye, attuned to a subtlety less crude than the strong range of reds and purples that we get in, say, the herbaceous phloxes which miraculously alter their hue as the evening light sinks across them. I love colour, and rejoice in it, but white is lovely to me forever. The ice-green shades that it can take on in certain lights, by twilight or moonlight, perhaps by moonlight especially, make a dream of the garden, an unreal vision, yet one knows that it isn't unreal at all because one has planted it all for effect. . . .

It is amusing to make one-colour gardens. They need not necessarily be large, and they need not necessarily be enclosed, though the enclosure of a dark hedge is, of course, ideal. Failing this, any secluded corner will do, or even a strip of border running under a wall, perhaps the wall of the house. The site chosen must depend upon the general lay-out, the size of the garden, and the opportunities offered. And if you think that one colour would be monotonous, you can have a two- or even a three-colour, provided the colours are happily married, which is sometimes easier

of achievement in the vegetable than in the human world. You can have, for instance, the blues and purples, or the yellows and the bronzes, with their attendant mauves and orange, respectively. Personal taste alone will dictate what you choose.

For my own part, I am trying to make a grey, green, and white garden. This is an experiment which I ardently hope may be successful, though I doubt it. One's best ideas seldom play up in practice to one's expectations, especially in gardening, where everything looks so well on paper and in the catalogues, but fails so lamentably in fulfillment after you have tucked your plants into the soil. Still, one hopes.

My grey, green, and white garden will have the advantage of a high yew hedge behind it, a wall along one side, a strip of box edging along another side, and a path of old brick along the fourth side. It is, in fact, nothing more than a fairly large bed, which has been divided into halves by a short path of grey flagstones terminating in a rough wooden seat. When you sit on this seat, you will be turning your backs to the yew hedge, and from there I hope you will survey a low sea of grey clumps of foliage, pierced here and there with tall white flowers. I visualize the white trumpets of dozens of Regale lilies, grown three years ago from seed, coming up through the grey of southernwood and artemisia and cotton-lavender, with grey-and-white edging plants such as *Dianthus* 'Mrs. Siskins' and the silvery mats of *Stachys lanata,* more familiar and so much nicer under its English names of Rabbits' Ears or Saviour's Flannel. There will be white pansies, and white peonies, and white irises with their grey leaves . . . at least, I hope there will be all these things. I don't want to boast in advance about my grey, green, and white garden. It may be a terrible failure. I wanted only to suggest that such experiments are worth trying, and that you can adapt them to your own taste and your own opportunities.

All the same, I cannot help hoping that the great ghostly barn-owl will sweep silently across a pale garden, next summer, in the twilight—the pale garden that I am now planting, under the first flakes of snow.

WHITE GARDEN AT SISSINGHURST
(design begun 1930 by Vita Sackville-West
and Harold Nicolson)
Kent, England
Eric Crichton/CORBIS

ROBERT DASH
COLOR, A POINT OF HUE (2000)

Born in 1934, Dash gained recognition for his painting, but he has devoted equal passion and creativity to the gardens of his estate, Madoo, on Long Island. For the past several years, he has written biweekly columns about gardening for the *East Hampton Star,* many of which were collected in his book *Notes from Madoo: Making a Garden in the Hamptons* (2000). This excerpt reveals Dash's ideas of color in the garden, clearly influenced by his work as a painter.

What is here now is mainly green garden. Foliant umbrage is silvery and cottony below and lanced, blunted, toothed, or indented; strap, ovate, and round; margined with white and yellow or speckled silver. Matte or shiny satisfactions take sun, wind, and wet, beginning ruby or tourmaline in spring and echoing them in autumn. The livery is so grave and complete and calming that I wish I were an herbivore. What is it if not superb glissando, rows of unornamented pewter plate on a dark wooden table or emerald crystals carving the very air? Bloom is an afterthought. Almost an impertinence.

But while this green flood was collecting, it soon became clear to me that this perfect color field would need some framing, and so the garden's inanimates—fences, railings, bowls, posts, arbors, doors, gates, benches, and tools—began to wear high hues of the sort that would make indoor eyeballs wince but were quite suitable outside. Didn't da Vinci say that the air does the painting?

What I have now are great brown Korean export bowls (oil and mustard), Aladdin size, bouqueted with green, and natural bamboo tying stakes and even scarlet surveyor's sticks, echoes of growth (or bloom, if you wish) so necessary to a small garden, where, unless one is a tireless plunger and lifter of annuals, it is impossible to expect unceasing display. Like italics, the geometry of framing is further satisfied by railings painted in matte char-

MADOO CONSERVANCY (design begun
1967 by Robert Dash)
Sagaponack, New York
Robert Dash

treuse, the color of infantile and autumnal foliage. All through the downs of August it sounds a fine note, and it is insouciant under hoar frost and snow.

A certain purple I mixed, one much barded with rose and cinder, became soft and hazy, very much like those grays beloved of landscape painters. A double tonality of it went up the gazebo, paled to two evening fogs on the roofs, remaining brusque and unmodified on the Chinese Chippendale railings below. It was Manet who thought the very color of the air was violet. A stained black octagonal table sits in the center, holding a disk of limestone on which is a blue pitcher and washbasin. There are eight black octagonal stools on the pale floor. The same dark purple went on a section of Carpenter Gothic fencing and on two eleven-foot arches made of plumbers' piping in the center of the potager. That a blue clematis twines on it seems irrelevant, for blooming or not, the arches never fade. The wheelbarrows became not fire engine red but more like drying tangerine skin. Three mirrors on each side of some outlying sheds counterpoint the effect. A curved bedroom door opening to a long path gets painted according to the viridity of the season—yellow in spring, dark blue when leaves adolesce. It takes a coat as orange as the barrows when the ginkoes go gold. And cream Panama hats sprout jauntily on the odd post and gate, and I have begun collecting lengths of hose in terra cotta. But I miss black. The winter and summer houses and the two studios attached have mintons and mullions of blue with green inserts. I begin to think that black eaves would look fine against the aging cedar shakes. A pale green fence abuts an even paler stile set above woodruff and epidemium. Goldfish circle under the new Chinese bridge, which is to be stained red and yellow on certain of its uprights, and the rest will be allowed to weather unadorned. But I think a shine of oil or wax might do. I path in faded earthen setts and bricks and on one rectangular terrace have placed purple and green boxes on dark wooden feet. In winter they are filled with prunings of red- and yellow-twigged dogwood, and the birds—cardinals, jays,

grackles, and mourning doves—assemble on the nearby stone bench washed in chick-cracked corn.

What I do may not be for others. We all practice seduction in unique fashion. Yet my heart leans on green for it is a world-class color, at once oasis and Eden. We agree, don't we, that the green gardens of the Italian Renaissance are unrivaled, unless by that most nearly perfect garden since . . . Rousham? "Green, green," said Lorca, " I would have you green/green hair/green branches." I take green to be not only the predominant color of a flourishing garden but the emblem of its aspiration, the barometer of its health, the very mirror of its finish. Green is its basic architecture clothed, which then becomes its ever-changing form. Great gardens have been green all through, with grass walks and mossed and vined walls enclosing generous, remarkably clipped yews like a great green house of grand green rooms roofed by the light of the sky. Green is the color that springs to mind when we think of Eden and the color one most anticipates as a garden is approached.

Of the other colors, I confess indifference to all of their seductive frailties. Never do I think consciously in terms of them, for they get in the way of form and are at their epitomes but the charming rewards of fine gardening (rather like those tan cities of northern Italy through which bright lines of washing sail out and then are drawn back in.) White, however, I do think of. White gates and benches and houses which are almost like canvas not yet covered, or the blaze of paper in Cézanne watercolors. A white clematis on an old piece of chipping white fence, pouring over and falling through a white rose. An enormous *soulieana* rose against hedge privet in bloom is a second bit of deliberate engineering I have tried and liked, and that annually works to great satisfaction. And wild daisies are making marvelous stops and explosions throughout the garden, and in the fields, glinting like felled clouds or crumbs of our mostly white, monitoring summer skies.

And now that I think of it, I do have another white, having thrown on a native holly I stemmed to a single fat trunk a large-flowered midsummer clematis. (The one over the rose is a double

early one and more like old piano keys or linen then white.) This one annually threads through the holly leaves and looks whiter for such dark backing, a carefully considered fountain effect that appears charmingly relaxed and casual to the point of seeming accidental. But the clematis, with its own contribution of lighter green leaves, looks quite splendid bare of bloom, the fountain form being just broad enough and high enough to fit the general elevations of the surrounding plantings. And yes, there is still another white clematis, the autumn *C. paniculata* (now *terniflora*) robing the yew hedge by the summer studio.

White seems to have a way of leading the eye to other whites, which reds and yellows and blues do not, and I have taken a walk around and around the garden and noted how many times and in how many subtly varied hues white appears. Dew will appear white in certain light. We have begun to have night fog. The countryside is mostly white houses in a green landscape with daisies and dog roses in hedgerows and field turns and of course potatoes blossoming, all as complete a large gardened landscape as one would ever wish to design, with pickets, too, and steeples all made whiter by graying shingled sheds and overarching elms and maples. Psychologists, when faced with the visually obsessed, call this alertness to seeing one color and only that color, as if it were everywhere and anything, the phenomenon of "setting."....

PENELOPE HOBHOUSE
DESIGN FOR COLOR (1985)

Born in Northern Ireland in 1929, Hobhouse is a garden writer, designer, historian, lecturer, and gardener. For fourteen years, until 1993, she and her husband, Professor John Malins, were in charge of the National Trust Gardens at Tintinhull House in Somerset, England. Today she lives in Dorset and travels in Europe, Australia, and the United States lecturing and designing gardens. This passage comes from *Color in Your Garden* (1985), one of her many books on gardening.

The plants available to gardeners are nowadays so numerous, and the quality of their color is so fundamental to the effect they produce, that they deserve careful choosing and arranging to give of their best. This is not just an aesthetic exercise which, in spite of theories of color harmony, must be mainly subjective. It calls for some consideration of the needs and behavior of plants, and their suitability as companions, so that they grow together to produce a healthy and flourishing picture throughout the gardening seasons.

The success of any particular plant color association or border color scheme will also depend essentially on the basic structure and design of the garden, which is the soberer background to brighter and more fleeting seasonal color effects. What we see depends not only on the hue or brightness of the color, but on the texture and form of the plants themselves and the nature of the daylight at the time: above all, colors are never perceived in isolation, but are always influenced by others that are present in the picture. Whatever the style of the garden, the framework planting, often in tones of green and gray, and the colors of building materials used for the house, paving, walls, paths, and steps must first be considered. It becomes the textured tapestry frame on which incidents or whole themes of flower and foliage color are then embroidered.

Before considering color in detail, take the garden as a whole. Whether the picture is formal or informal, manicured or casual, instinctive or self-conscious, even monochrome or multicolored, all its elements must come together to make a coherent composition. Buildings, walls, perimeter fence or hedge, and flat surfaces of lawn and paving should give architectural balance and unity of design. Color is everywhere, but look first at the relative darkness and lightness of the picture, the factors that a black and white photograph might reveal: these give architectural weight and define strong shapes, whether in hard manmade materials or in the softer textures of plant forms. Solid dark green yew gives strength, paler foliage of light green or feathery gray is more fragile, and mown lawns are pools of light. A balanced composition of these elements satisfies without the distraction of color. A garden in winter often reveals the strength and unity of the design; in summer, this coherence is obscured by billowing foliage and bright seasonal color. . . .

Color remains subjective; we can base our choice on a personal taste for pale "peaceful" tints, a desire to see something bright and cheerful from the windows of the house, a preference for the stimulation of color changes in different areas of the garden; changes which need a positive act of refocusing the eye and induce shifts of mood. One garden may have no bright colors at all, interest and stimulation given by subtle textural differences and dark or pale colors stressing shape and form; in another garden "color" effects dictate the style and the more minute differences of foliage surface become like the woven background to embroidered colors. Plant color becomes a tool to extend and reduce dimensions, to give sensations of warmth or coolness, to provoke stimulation or induce moods of restfulness. . . .

Where space is limited, perhaps to one border visible from the house all through the seasons, the choice of colors and how they are used becomes correspondingly more important. The border may be colorful during as much of the year as possible, or during only one or two seasons. Some color schemes are more appropriate to a confined area than others. Different ends of a relatively small border may effectively be devoted to separate color themes, each one perhaps at its best in a different season. The part nearest the house might be planned predominantly as a winter garden, the next area along for spring flowers, and so on, ending with late summer color where a warm sitting area is most used at that season.

How does the choice of color affect the seasonal aspect of the area being considered? In many ways a disciplined approach to color effects simplifies and dictates the choice of the actual plants. Choose a season, then make a list of the plants that flower in one or more colors at that time; do the same for another season, remembering that color themes can easily change throughout the year. A blue and yellow spring border can become predominantly yellow in summer, pink and gray or full of hot colors in late summer. Or just the reverse. Plant vivid red and scarlet tulip bulbs and orange or crimson wallflowers for spring, setting the plants or bulbs in autumn between the clumps of blue and pink Michaelmas daisies.

As you decide on plants for your wished-for color effects, consider also their contribution during the other seasons, their habits and cultural needs. Shrubs which give necessary structure do not like to be moved, and each year they grow in height and spread, casting shadows on neighboring areas, affecting the growing potential of near-by plants as well as altering the aesthetic balance of heights and shapes. Just as color masses are distributed through a scheme in contrasting association or in carefully contrived gradations of related tints and shades, so the size of the color area and relative heights of plants affect the composition. In a narrow border too many tall plants will make it seem even narrower; in a broad expanse too many plants at similar level give a flat two-dimensional effect, like a painting without the subtlety of cast shadows, as plants in different planes screen or expose each other. Yet each shadow alters color relationships as well as affecting how a plant may thrive. A background hedge in a narrow border may give the desired architectural stability, its visual continuity and strong color framing the grouped plants in front of it, yet it may equally well compete for light and air, and take much of the nutrition out of the soil. At the front of a border low planting with good evergreens will stabilize a scheme, linking a bed with lawn or pavement. Higher architectural plants link the area with trees or hedges of the garden framework yet compete for allotted space with plants chosen purely for limited seasonal effects. Remember as well as these three-dimensional effects, relative areas of plant color and their tonal and lightness/darkness contrasts can be as important as the actual color associations used—and that each individual composite scheme must equally fit in to the whole back-ground structure of the garden and any buildings.

7

PLANT SELECTION

Plants seem to be scattered profusely over the face of the earth like stars in the heavens, so that the lure of pleasure and curiosity should lead men to study nature. But the stars are far above us; we need preliminary instruction, instruments, and machines, which are like so many immense ladders enabling us to approach them and bring them within our grasp. Plants have been placed within our reach by nature herself; they spring up beneath our feet, in our hands so to speak, and even if their essential parts are sometimes so small as to be invisible to the naked eye, the instruments which bring them nearer to us are far simpler to use than those of the astronomer.

Jean-Jacques Rousseau (1712–1778), French novelist and philosopher

A flower-garden is an ugly thing, even when best managed: it is an assemblage of unfortunate beings, pampered and bloated above their natural size, stewed and heated into diseased growth; corrupted by evil communications into speckled and inharmonious colours; torn from the soil which they loved, and of which they were the spirit and the glory, to glare away their term of tormented life among the mixed and incongruous essences of each other, in earth that they know not, and in air that is poison to them.

John Ruskin (1819–1900), English writer and art critic

A garden is a complex of aesthetic and plastic intentions; and the plant is, to a landscape artist, not only a plant—rare, unusual, ordinary, or doomed to disappearance—but it is also a color, a shape, a volume, or an arabesque in itself.

Roberto Burle Marx (1909–1994), Brazilian painter and landscape architect

previous spread:
PRESIDIO PARK (designed in 1929 by
Roland S. Hoyt)
San Diego, California
Lowell Georgia/CORBIS

opposite:
COURTYARD GARDEN OF GETTY
MUSEUM (based on Villa dei Papiri near
Herculaneum, first century)
Malibu, California
Robert Holmes/CORBIS

PLINY THE YOUNGER
MY GARDEN IN TUSCANY (1ST CENTURY A.D.)

Gaius Plinius Caecilius Secundus, known as Pliny the Younger (c. 62–c. 113), a Roman senator and a nephew of the orator Pliny the Elder was famed for his charming letters. They give an account of upper-class Roman life in the first century and include many references to his own gardens in Tuscany and Laurentum, near Rome. The letters are among the clearest and most intelligible accounts of garden plans from antiquity and were much studied during the Renaissance as an authentic source of information on Roman gardens. The excerpt below is from one of Pliny's garden letters, translated by Betty Radice.

TO DOMITIUS APOLLINARIS

I am touched by your kind concern when you try to dissuade me from my intention of staying in Tuscany in summer. You think the place is unhealthy, but while it is perfectly true that the Tuscan strip of seacoast is relaxing and dangerous to the health, my property is some distance away from the sea, and is in fact at the very foot of the Apennines, which are considered the healthiest of mountains. So to rid you of all your fears on my account, let me tell you about the climate, the countryside, and the lovely situation of my house, which will be a pleasure alike for me to tell and you to hear. . . .

The countryside is very beautiful. Picture to yourself a vast amphitheatre such as could only be a work of nature; the great spreading plain is ringed round by mountains, their summits crowned by ancient woods of tall trees, where there is a good deal of mixed hunting to be had. Down the mountain slopes are timber woods interspersed with small hills of soil so rich that there is scarcely a rocky outcrop to be found; these hills are fully as fertile as the level plain and yield quite as rich a harvest, though it ripens rather later in the season. Below them the vineyards spreading

down every slope weave their uniform pattern far and wide, their lower limit bordered by a belt of shrubs. Then come the meadows and cornfields, where the land can be broken up only by heavy oxen and the strongest ploughs, for the soil is so stiff that it is thrown up in great clods at the first ploughing and is not thoroughly broken until it has been gone over nine times. The meadows are bright with flowers, covered with trefoil and other delicate plants which always seem soft and fresh, for everything is fed by streams which never run dry; though the ground is not marshy where the water collects, because of its downward slope, so that any surplus water it cannot absorb is drained off into the river Tiber flowing through the fields. The river is navigable, so that all produce is conveyed to Rome by boat, but only in winter and spring—in summer its level falls and its dry bed has to give up its claim to the title of a great river until the following autumn. It is a great pleasure to look down on the countryside from the mountain, for the view seems to be a painted scene of unusual beauty rather than a real landscape, and the harmony to be found in this variety refreshes the eye wherever it turns.

My house is on the lower slopes of a hill but commands as good a view as if it were higher up, for the ground rises so gradually that the slope is imperceptible, and you will find yourself at the top without noticing the climb. Behind it is the Apennine range, though some way off, so that even on a still and cloudless day there is a breeze from the mountains, but one which has had its force broken by the distance so that it is never cutting nor boisterous. It faces mainly south, and so from midday onwards in summer (a little earlier in winter) it seems to invite the sun into the colonnade. This is broad, and long in proportion, with several rooms opening out of it as well as the old-fashioned type of entrance hall.

In front of the colonnade is a terrace laid out with box hedges clipped into different shapes, from which a bank slopes down, also with figures of animals cut out of box facing each other on either side. On the level below there waves—or might I have said ripples—a bed of acanthus. All round is a path hedged by bushes which are trained and cut into different shapes, and then a drive, oval like a racecourse, inside which are various box figures and clipped dwarf shrubs. The whole garden is enclosed by a dry-stone wall which is hidden from sight by a box hedge planted in tiers; outside is a meadow, as well worth seeing for its natural beauty as the formal garden I have described; then fields and many more meadows and woods....

The design and beauty of the buildings are greatly surpassed by the riding-ground. The centre is quite open so that the whole extent of the course can be seen as one enters. It is planted round with ivy-clad plane trees, green with their own leaves above, and below with the ivy which climbs over trunk and branch and links tree to tree as it spreads across them. Box shrubs grow between the plane trees, and outside there is a ring of laurel bushes which add their shade to that of the planes. Here the straight part of the course ends, curves around in a semicircle, and changes its appearance, becoming darker and more densely shaded by the cypress trees planted round to shelter it, whereas the inner circuits—for there are several—are in open sunshine; roses grow there and the cool shadow alternates with the pleasant warmth of the sun. At the end of the winding alleys of the rounded end of the course you return to the straight path, or rather paths, for there are several separated by intervening box hedges. Between the grass lawns here there are box shrubs clipped into innumerable shapes, some being letters which spell the gardener's name or his master's; small obelisks of box alternate with fruit trees, and then suddenly in the midst of this ornamental scene is what looks like a piece of rural country planted there. The open space in the middle is set off by low plane trees planted on each side; farther off are acanthuses with their flexible glossy leaves, then more box figures and names.

...These are my reasons for preferring my home in Tuscany to one in Tusculum, Tiber, or Praeneste. And I can add another reason: I can enjoy a profounder peace there, more comfort, and fewer cares; I need never wear a formal toga and there are no neighbours to disturb me; everywhere there is peace and quiet, which adds as much to the healthiness of the place as the clear sky and pure air. There I enjoy the best of health, both mental and physical, for I keep my mind in training with work and my body with hunting. My servants too are healthier here than anywhere else; up to the present I have not lost a single one of those I brought here with me—may I be forgiven for saying so, and may the gods continue to make this the pride of the place and a joy to me.

PO CHU-I
PINE TREES (9TH CENTURY)

The most prolific Chinese poet of the Tang Dynasty, Po Chu-i (772–846) was a member of the Han-lin Academy. He wrote more than three thousand poems—brief topical verses expressed in very simple, clear language. Po-Chu-i also occupied several important government posts, rising to the presidency of the imperial board of war. Banished on several occasions for arguing against government policies, he retired in 832 to the Hsiang-shan monastery a few miles from Lo-yang, the eastern capital. Throughout his life, he gained inspiration and refreshment from looking at gardens. The poem was translated by Arthur Waley.

Below the hall
The pine-trees grow in front of the steps,
Irregularly scattered—not in ordered lines.
Some are tall and some are low:
The tallest of them is six roods high;
The lowest but ten feet.
They are like wild things
And no one knows who planted them.
They touch the walls of my blue-tiled house;
Their roots are sunk in the terrace of white sand.

following spread:
PINE TREE AT MORTON ARBORETUM
(design begun 1921 by O.C. Simonds, Joy
Morton, and Charles Sprague Sargent)
Lisle, Illinois
Scott J. Tilden

RED FORT (1565–73) and FLOWER
GARDENS
Agra, Uttar Pradesh, India
Brian A. Vikander/CORBIS

Morning and evening they are visited by the wind and moon;
Rain or fine—they are free from dust and mud.
In the gales of autumn they whisper a vague tune;
From the suns of summer they yield a cool shade.
At the height of spring the fine evening rain
Fills their leaves with a load of hanging pearls.
At the year's end the time of great snow
Stamps their branches with a fret of glittering jade.
Of the Four Seasons each has its own mood;
Among all the trees none is like another.
Last year, when they heard I had bought this house,
Neighbours mocked and the World called me mad—
That a whole family of twice ten souls
Should move house for the sake of a few pines!
Now that I have come to them, what have they given me?
They have only loosened the buckles of my care.
Yet even so, they are "profitable friends,"
And fill my need of "converse with wise men."
Yet when I consider how, still a man of the world,
In belt and cap I scurry through dirt and dust,
From time to time my heart twinges with shame
That I am not fit to be master of my pines!

NUSRATI
ROSE GARDEN OF LOVE (1657)

**Nusrati served as poet of the Adil Shahi court at Bijapur, India. He
composed the long poem *Gulshan-I 'Ishaq* (Rose Garden of Love),
one of the major works of the Muslim Sufi sect written in Deccani
Urdu. An illuminated version of the poem is in the collection of the
State Hermitage Museum in St. Petersburg. Nusrati died in 1684.
The translation is by Ali Akbar Husain.**

Farah Bakhsh was a garden exceedingly green
Every flower was a scar on the breast of the sky

Its plots, illuminated, shone like polished mirrors
The sky full of stars, the garden appeared

The sight of new buds in the garden trees
Caressed the heart of the beloved gently

(Interplanted) with violets, the tulips seemed ruby idols
Their red cheeks aglow like Judas tree blossoms

Touched with Spring's exhilaration, the Artabotrys flower was like
wine
The eyes of the narcissus were also heavy with wine

The Mesua flower outshone the henna-dyed hand
And henna-worked patterns paled beside the (Mesua-dyed)
scarves

The white of the moonflower scarred the breast of the moon
Beside the yellow sunflower, the sun's garden seemed withered

The fragrance of *kewra* the air permeated
It seemed both the rising and invisible stars

More comely than the beloved's were the basil's ringlets
Their knots as though braided by the hands of the beloved

Entangled in Love's knot was Beauty wholly
The knots of all tresses forgotten wholly?

The hyacinth field rejoiced the heart fully
The flaming Celosias lit it up brightly

The bed of Gomphrena was a bed of light
Or, say, like an ornament of ruby and glass

The marigold bushes seemed all aglow
Or, say, they were candles of a brilliant light

The stately cypresses that rose all around
Seemed a row of *houris* in Paradise....

The safflower that filled up all the tulip cups
Brightened its own red bodice in turn

With the white of sandalwood from the tuberose
The pigeons and ring doves brightened their clothes

From the violet's cup, distilled afresh,
The black bees and *bhangraj* brought ambergris

The aloeswood incense sticks from the musky willow
Made the fragrance of basil seem like ambergris glow

The flower buds like bottles of rose water scent
Scattered rose water wherever they bent

...Sweet lote-fruit, and grape clusters,
Were brighter and clearer than Pleiades clusters

Fragrant apple, and fig, mango, and jackfruit
Durian, and banana, *jamun,* mulberry, and pineapple

The clusters of *tindu,* sweet-smelling, soft guava
As though bathed clear in a shower of dew

Citron, sweet and sour, lime and oranges
Quince, and star-fruit, and more citrons delicious

Sweet, soft and supple, sweet-smelling sugarcane
With knots tied up, more stately then the beloved

As for the pine nut, walnut and the almond

WILLIAM MORRIS
FLORIST FLOWERS (1882)

British craftsman, designer, writer, typographer, and socialist, Morris (1834–1896) attended Exeter College at Oxford, where he formed the Brotherhood, which included Edward Burne-Jones and Dante Gabriel Rossetti. Morris and his Pre-Raphaelite friends formed their own company of designers and decorators that specialized in producing stained glass, carving, furniture, wallpaper, carpets, and tapestries. The company's designs and Morris's writings brought about a complete revolution in public taste and gave life to the Arts and Crafts Movement in England. His designs drew inspiration from nature as did his unaffected and informal designs for the gardens at his three homes. This selection is from a lecture entitled "Making the Best of It," first published in *Hopes & Fears for Art: Five Lectures* (1882)

Before we go inside our house, nay, before we look at its outside, we may consider its gardens, chiefly with reference to town gardening; which, indeed, I, in common, I suppose, with most others who have tried it, have found uphill work enough—all the more as in our part of the world few indeed have any mercy upon the one thing necessary for decent life in a town, its trees; till we have come to this, that one trembles at the very sound of an axe as one sits at one's work at home. However, uphill work or not, the town garden must not be neglected if we are to be in earnest in making the best of it.

Now I am bound to say town gardeners generally do rather the reverse of that: our suburban gardeners in London, for instance, oftenest wind about their little bit of gravel walk and grass plot in ridiculous imitation of an ugly big garden of the landscape-gardening style, and then with a strange perversity fill up the spaces with the most formal plants they can get; whereas the merest common sense should have taught them to lay out their morsel of ground in the simplest way, to fence it as orderly as might be, one part from the other (if it be big enough for that) and the whole from the road, and then to fill up the flower-growing space with things that are free and interesting in their growth, leaving nature to do the desired complexity, which she will certainly not fail to do if we do not desert her for the florist, who, I must say, has made it harder work than it should be to get the best of flowers.

It is scarcely a digression to note his way of dealing with flowers, which, moreover, gives us an apt illustration of that change without thought of beauty, change for the sake of change, which has played such a great part in the degradation of art in all times. So I ask you to note the way he has treated the rose, for instance: the rose has been grown double from I don't know when; the double rose was a gain to the world, a new beauty was given us by it, and nothing taken away, since the wild rose grows in every hedge. Yet even then one might be excused for thinking that the wild rose was scarce improved on, for nothing can be more beautiful in general growth or in detail than a wayside bush of it, nor can any scent be as sweet and pure as its scent. Nevertheless the garden rose had a new beauty of abundant form, while its leaves had not lost the wonderfully delicate texture of the wild one. The full colour it had gained, from the blush rose to the damask, was pure and true amidst all its added force, and though its scent had certainly lost some of the sweetness of the eglantine, it was fresh still, as well as so abundantly rich. Well, all that lasted till quite our own day, when the florists fell upon the rose—men who could never have enough—they strove for size and got it, a fine specimen of a florist's rose being about as big as a moderate Savoy cabbage.

They tried for strong scent and got it—till a florist's rose has not unseldom a suspicion of the scent of the aforesaid cabbage—not at its best. They tried for strong colour and got it, strong and bad—like a conqueror. But all this while they missed the very essence of the rose's being; they thought there was nothing in it but redundance and luxury; they exaggerated these into coarseness, while they threw away the exquisite subtlety of form, delicacy of texture, and sweetness of colour, which, blent with the richness which the true garden rose shares with many other flowers, yet makes it the queen of them all—the flower of flowers. Indeed, the worst of this is that these sham roses are driving the real ones out of existence. If we do not look to it our descendants will know nothing of the cabbage rose, the loveliest in form of all, or the blush rose with its dark green stems and unequalled colour, or the yellow centred rose of the East, which carries the richness of scent to the very furthest point it can go without losing freshness: they will know nothing of all these, and I fear they will reproach the poets of past time for having done according to their wont, and exaggerated grossly the beauties of the rose. . . .

So much for the over-artificiality in flowers. A word or two about the misplacing of them. Don't have ferns in your garden. The hart's tongue in the clefts of the rock, the queer things that grow within reach of the spray of the waterfall; these are right in their places. Still more the brake on the woodside, whether in late autumn, when its withered haulm helps out the well-remembered woodland scent, or in spring, when it is thrusting its volutes through last year's waste. But all this is nothing to a garden, and is not to be got out of it; and if you try it you will take away from it all possible romance, the romance of a garden.

The same thing may be said about many plants, which are curiosities only, which Nature meant to be grotesque, not beautiful, and which are generally the growth of hot countries, where things sprout over quick and rank. Take note that the strangest of these come from the jungle and the tropical waste, from places where man is not at home, but is an intruder, an enemy. Go to a

botanical garden and look at them, and think of those strange places to your heart's content. But don't set them to starve in your smoke-drenched scrap of ground amongst the bricks, for they will be no ornament to it.

As to colour in gardens. Flowers in masses are mighty strong colour, and if not used with a great deal of caution are very destructive to pleasure in gardening. On the whole, I think the best and safest plan is to mix up your flowers, and rather eschew great masses of colour—in combination—I mean. But there are some flowers (inventions of men, i.e. florists) which are bad colour altogether, and not to be used at all. Scarlet geraniums, for instance, or the yellow calceolaria, which indeed are not uncommonly grown together profusely, in order, I suppose, to show that even flowers can be thoroughly ugly....

And now to sum up as to a garden. Large or small, it should look both orderly and rich. It should be well fenced from the outside world. It should by no means imitate either the willfulness or the wildness of Nature, but should look like a thing never to be seen except near a house. It should, in fact, look like part of the house. It follows from this that no private pleasure-garden should be very big, and a public garden should be divided and made to look like so many flower-closes in a meadow, or a wood, or amidst the pavement....

WILLIAM ROBINSON
THE WILD GARDEN (1883)

An Irish gardener and author, Robinson (1835–1935) secured positions early in his career at the National Botanic Garden at Glasnevin in Ireland and the Royal Botanic Garden in Regent's Park in London. His first two books resulted from a garden tour of France in 1867. In 1870 Robinson published his influential book *The Wild Garden,* in which he attacked the formal artificiality of high Victorian gardens and passionately advocated the planting of hardy native and exotic flowers. The excerpt originally appeared in his book *The English Flower Garden and Home Grounds.*

O universal Mother, who dost keep
From everlasting thy foundations deep,
Eldest of things, Great Earth, I sing of thee.

In a rational system of flower gardening one of the first things to do is to get a clear idea of the aim of the "Wild Garden." When I began to plead the cause of the innumerable hardy flowers against the few tender ones put out in a formal way, the answer sometimes was, "We cannot go back to the mixed border"—that is to say, to the old way of arranging flowers in borders. Thinking, then, much of the vast world of plant beauty shut out of our gardens by the "system" then in vogue, I was led to consider the ways in which it might be brought into them, and of the "Wild Garden" as a home for numbers of beautiful hardy plants from other countries which might be naturalised, with very little trouble, in our gardens, fields, and woods—a world of delightful plant beauty that we might make happy around us, in places bare or useless.

The term "Wild Garden" is applied to the placing of perfectly hardy exotic plants in places where they will take care of themselves. It has nothing to do with the "wilderness," though it may be carried out in it. It does not necessarily mean the picturesque garden for a garden may be picturesque and yet in every part the result of ceaseless care. What it does mean is best explained by the winter Aconite flowering under a grove of naked trees in February; by the Snowflake abundant in meadows by the Thames; and by the Apennine Anemone staining an English grove blue. Some have thought of it as a garden allowed to run wild, or with annuals sown promiscuously, whereas it does not meddle with the flower garden proper at all.

I wish the idea to be kept distinct from the various important phases of hardy plant growth in groups, beds, and borders, in which good culture may produce many happy effects; from the rock garden or borders reserved for choice hardy flowers; from growing hardy plants of fine form; from the ordinary type of spring garden. In the smaller class of gardens there may be little room for the wild garden, but in the larger gardens, where there is often ample room on the outer fringes of the lawn, in grove, park, copse, or by woodland walks or drives, new and beautiful effects may be got by its means.

Among reasons for advocating this system are the following:

1. Because many hardy flowers will thrive better in rough places than ever they did in the old border. Even small ones like the Ivy-leaved Cyclamen, are naturalised and spread all over the mossy surface of woods. 2. Because, in consequence of plant, fern and flower and climber, grass, and trailing shrub, relieving each other, they will look infinitely better than in stiff gardens. 3. Because no ugly effects will result from decay and the swift passage of the seasons. In a semi-wild state the beauty of a species will show in flowering time; and when out of bloom they will be succeeded by other kinds, or lost among the numerous objects around. 4. Because it will enable us to grow many plants that have never yet obtained a place in our "trim gardens"—multitudes that are not showy enough to be considered worthy of a place in a garden. Among the plants often thought unfit for garden cultivation are a number like the coarser American Asters and Golden Rods, which overrun the choicer border-flowers when planted among

them. Such plants would be quite at home in neglected places, where their blossoms might be seen in due season. To these might be added plants like the winter Heliotrope, and many others, which, while interesting in the garden, are apt to spread so rapidly as to become a nuisance. 5. Because in this way we may settle the question of spring flowers, and the spring garden, as well as that of hardy flowers generally; and many parts of the grounds may be made alive with spring flowers, without in the least interfering with the flower garden itself. The blue stars of the Apennine Anemone will be seen to greater advantage when in half-shady places, under trees, or in the meadow grass, than in any flower garden, and this is but one of many of sweet spring flowers that will succeed in like ways.

Perhaps an example or two of what has already been done with Daffodils and Snowdrops may serve to show the way, and explain the gains of the wild garden, and there is no more charming flower to begin with than the Narcissus, which, while fair in form as any Orchid or Lily of the tropics, is as much at home in our climate as the Kingcups in the marsh and the Primroses in the wood. And when the wild Narcissus comes with these, in the woods and orchards of Northern France and Southern England it has also for companions the Violet and the Cowslip, hardiest children of the north, blooming in and near the still leafless woods. And this fact should lead us to see that it is not only a garden flower we have here, but one which may give glorious beauty to our woods and fields and meadows as well as to the pleasure grounds. . .

All planting in the grass should be in natural groups or prettily fringed colonies, growing to and fro as they like after planting. Lessons in this grouping are to be had in the woods, copses, heaths, and meadows, by those who look about them as they go. At first many will find it difficult to get out of formal masses, but they may be got over by studying natural groupings of wild flowers. Once established, the plants soon begin to group themselves in pretty ways.

In the cultivation of hardy plants and especially in wild gardening the important thing is to find out what things really do in the soil, without which much good way cannot be made. Many people make errors in planting things that are tender in our country and very often fail in consequence; but apart from such risky planting perfectly hardy plants may disappear owing to some dislike of the soil. They flower feebly at first and afterwards gradually wane in spite of all our efforts. The Narcissus, which is so free and enduring in cool damp soil, does little good on warm, light or chalky soil. Some things are so omnivorous in their appetites that they will grow anywhere, but some, the more beautiful races of bulbous and other early flowers, will only thrive and stay with us where they like the soil. It should be clearly seen therefore that what may be done with any good result in the wild garden cannot be determined beforehand, but must depend on the nature of the soil and other circumstances which can be known only to those who study the ground.

Where the branches of trees, both evergreen and summer-leafing, sweep the turf in the pleasure grounds many pretty spring-flowering bulbs may be naturalised beneath the branches, and will thrive without attention. It is chiefly in the case of deciduous trees that this can be done; but even in the case of Conifers and Evergreens some graceful objects may be dotted beneath the outermost points of their lowest branches. We know that a great number of our spring flowers and hardy bulbs mature their foliage and go to rest early in the year. In spring they require light and sun, which they can obtain abundantly under the summer-leafing tree; they have time to flower and grow under it before the foliage of the tree appears; then, as the summer heats approach, they are overshadowed, and go to rest; but the leaves of the tree once fallen, they soon begin to reappear and cover the ground with beauty.

GERTRUDE JEKYLL
MIXED FLOWER BORDER (1899)

The influence of Gertrude Jekyll (1843–1932) on garden design remains pervasive to this day. In addition to her work with Edwin Lutyens, she also collaborated for more than fifty years with William Robinson, who founded *The Garden* magazine in 1871. Jekyll became editor in 1899 and contributed many articles to this and other publications. Jekyll also wrote many books. This excerpt appeared originally in her first book, *Wood and Garden*.

I have a rather large "mixed border of hardy flowers." It is not quite so hopelessly mixed as one generally sees, and the flowers are not all hardy; but as it is a thing everybody rightly expects, and as I have been for a good many years trying to puzzle out its wants and ways, I will try and describe my own and its surroundings.

There is a sandstone wall of pleasant colour at the back, nearly eleven feet high. This wall is an important feature in the garden, as it is the dividing line between the pleasure garden and the working garden; also, it shelters the pleasure garden from the sweeping blasts of wind from the north-west, to which my ground is much exposed, as it is all on a gentle slope, going downward towards the north. At the foot of the wall is a narrow border three feet six inches wide, and then a narrow alley; not a made path, but just a way to go along for tending the wall shrubs, and for getting at the back of the border. This little alley does not show from the front. Then the main border, fourteen feet wide and two hundred feet long. About three-quarters of the way along, a path cuts through the border, and passes by an arched gateway in the wall to the Pæony garden and the working garden beyond. Just here I thought it would be well to mound up the border a little, and plant with groups of Yuccas, so that at all times of the year there should be something to make a handsome full-stop to the sections of the

following spread:
GREAT DIXTER HOUSE AND GARDENS
(design begun 1910 by Edwin Lutyens and
Gertrude Jekyll)
East Sussex, England
Eric Crichton/CORBIS

border, and to glorify the doorway. The two extreme ends of the border are treated in the same way with Yuccas on rather lesser mounds, only leaving space beyond them for the entrance to the little alley at the back. . . .

The western end of the flower-border begins with the low bank of Yuccas, then there are some rather large masses of important grey and glaucous foliage and pale and full pink flower. The foliage is mostly of Globe Artichoke, and nearer the front of *Artemisia* and *Cineraria maritima.* Among this pink Canterbury Bell, Hollyhock, Phlox, Gladiolus, and Japan Anemone, all in pink colourings, will follow one another in due succession. Then come some groups of plants bearing whitish and very pale flowers, *Polygonum compactum, Aconitum lycoctonum,* Double Meadowsweet , and other Spiræas, and then the colour passes to pale yellow of Mulleins, and with them the palest blue Delphiniums. Towards the front is a wide planting of *Iris pallida dalmatica,* its handsome bluish foliage showing as outstanding and yet related masses with regard to the first large group of pale foliage. Then comes the pale-yellow *Iris flavescens,* and meanwhile the group of Delphinium deepens into those of a fuller blue colour, though none of the darkest are here. Then more pale yellow of Mullein, Thalictrum, and Paris Daisy, and so the colour passes to stronger yellows. These change into orange , and from that to brightest scarlet and crimson, coming to the fullest strength in the Oriental Poppies of the earlier year, and later in Lychnis, Gladiolus, Scarlet Dahlia, and Tritoma. The colour-scheme then passes again through orange and yellow to the paler yellows, and so again to blue and warm white, where it meets one of the clumps of Yuccas flanking the path that divides this longer part of the border from the much shorter piece beyond. This simple procession of colour arrangement has occupied a space of a hundred and sixty feet, and the border is all the better for it.

The short length of border beyond the gateway has again Yuccas and important pale foliage, and a preponderance of pink bloom, Hydrangea for the most part; but there are a few tall Mulleins, whose pale-yellow flowers group well with the ivory of the Yucca spikes and the clear pink of the tall Hollyhocks. These all show up well over the masses of grey and glaucous foliage, and against the rich darkness of dusky Yew.

Dahlias and Cannas have their places in the mixed border. When it is being dismantled in the late autumn, all bare places are well dug and enriched, so that when it comes to filling-up time, at the end of May, I know that every spare bit of space is ready, and at the time of preparation I mark places for special Dahlias, according to colour, and for groups of the tall Cannas where I want grand foliage. . . .

I have no dogmatic views about having in the so-called hardy flower-border none but hardy flowers. All flowers are welcome that are right in colour, and that make a brave show where a brave show is wanted. It is of more importance that the border should be handsome than that all its occupants should be hardy. Therefore I prepare a certain useful lot of half-hardy annuals, and a few of what have come to be called bedding-plants. I like to vary them a little from year to year, because in no one season can I get in all the good flowers that I should like to grow; and I think it better to leave out some one year and have them the next, than to crowd any up, or to find I have plants to put out and no space to put them in. But I nearly always grow these half-hardy annuals; orange African Marigold, French Marigold, sulphur Sunflower, orange and scarlet tall Zinnia, Nasturtiums, both dwarf and trailing, *Nicotiana affinis,* Maize, and Salpiglossis. Then Stocks and China Asters. The Stocks are always the large white and flesh-coloured summer kinds, and the Asters, the White Comet, and one of the blood-red or so-called scarlet sorts.

Then I have yellow Paris Daisies, *Salvia Patens,* Heliotrope, *Calceolaria amplexicaulis,* Geraniums, scarlet and salmon-coloured and ivy-leaved kinds, the best of these being the pink Madame Crousse.

The front edges of the border are also treated in rather a large way. At the shadier end there is a long straggling bordering patch of *Anemone sylvestris.* When it is once above ground the foliage

remains good till autumn, while its soft white flower comes right with the colour of the flowers behind. Then comes a long and large patch of the larger kind of *Megasea cordifolia,* several yards in length, and running back here and there among the taller plants.... If the edging threatens to look too dark and hard, I plant among or just behind the plants that compose it, pink or scarlet Ivy Geranium or trailing Nasturtium, according to the colour demanded by the neighbouring group. *Heuchera Richardsonii* is another good front-edge plant; and when we come to the blue and pale-yellow group there is a planting of *Funkia grandiflora,* whose fresh-looking pale-green leaves are delightful with the brilliant light yellow of *Calceolaria amplexicaulis,* and the farther-back planting of pale-blue Delphinium, Mullein, and sulphur Sunflower; while the same colour of foliage is repeated in the fresh green of the Indian Corn. Small spaces occur here and there along the extreme front edge, and here are planted little jewels of colour, of blue Lobelia, or dwarf Nasturtium, or anything of the colour that the place demands.

The whole thing sounds much more elaborate than it really is; the trained eye sees what is wanted, and the trained hand does it, both by an acquired instinct. It is painting a picture with living plants.

JENS JENSEN
NATIVE PLANTS (1939)

Danish-born landscape architect, Jensen (1860–1951) became one of America's greatest landscape designers and conservationists. Using native plants and designs suitable for the Midwestern landscape he loved, he introduced the influential Prairie Style of landscape architecture. He served for many years as superintendent of public parks in Chicago and later created a private practice designing parks and estates throughout the Midwest. The *New York Times* obituary referred to Jensen as the "dean of American landscape architecture." This passage comes from his book, *Siftings*.

It is often remarked, "native plants are coarse." How humiliating to hear an American speak so of plants with which the Great Master has decorated his land! To me no plant is more refined than that which belongs. There is no comparison between native plants and those imported from foreign shores which are, and shall always remain so, novelties. If, however, as is said, our native landscape is coarse, then as time goes by we, the American people, shall also become coarse because we shall be molded into our environments....

My first acquaintance with the redbud dates back a quarter of a century. It was on an excursion to the historic spot of Starved Rock on the Illinois River. Everywhere the bluffs were covered with the blossoms of the redbud. To me, who had never seen this plant before, it was a delightful experience.

Memory brings back a little incident in connection with this trip. Luncheon had been prepared for us in a little town nearby. The proprietor of the hotel had been kind enough to decorate our tables with carnations, but it was rather a weak greeting after seeing the blossoms of the redbud. How gay the dining room would have been if a little spray of this native plant that now was making the valleys of the Illinois River gay and festive had been placed

on each table. Instead, we had a manufactured greenhouse flower. Man still seems far from understanding and appreciating the beauty of his native land....

Every plant has its fitness and must be placed in its proper surroundings so as to bring out its full beauty. Therein lies the art of landscaping. When we first understand the character of the individual plant; when we enjoy its development from the time it breaks through the crust of mother earth, sending its first leaves heavenward, until it reaches maturity; when we are willing to give each plant a chance fully to develop its beauty, so as to give us all it possesses without any interference, then, and only then, shall we enjoy ideal landscapes made by man. And is not this the true spirit of democracy? Can a democrat cripple and misuse a plant for the sake of show and pretense? I am asking these questions because there are people on this earth who have used such methods in developing gardens that are admired by many. But these gardens exemplify none of the freedom which every democracy should possess.

Plants, like human beings, have their own individuality. Some plants to be at their best need association in a small colony or group; others love the company of multitudes, forming a carpet on the forest floor or in the open. Some speak much more forcefully alone, as, for instance, the cottonwood with its gray branches stretching up into the heavens as a landmark on the plains. Some plants express their beauty in a lowland landscape and some on the rocky cliffs. Some fulfill their mission in the rolling hilly country, and some belong to the vast prairies of Mid-America. Others sing the song of sand dunes, still others of rocky lands. A grove of crab-apple trees on the edge of the open prairie landscape gives a distinct note to the plains. The timid violet sings its song and fits into a different composition from that of the robust aster....

The Chinese say that a gardener must be a wise man because he must know the trees he uses and their growth for hundreds of years hence. How short a lifetime is to complete the study of the character and the beauty of the plants used in the composition of landscapes. Only last spring the real loveliness of our red maple was shown to me. A group of these trees were in bloom against the purple and gray background of the oak-covered sand hills across a marshy stretch. I had seen them singly scattered amongst oaks and sugar maples, but never had I seen them in groves forming a rosy mist over a dune landscape....

On a hill in southern Wisconsin stands a little group of birch trees which we visited for many consecutive years at the time the shad was in bloom. To see the fleeting white blossoms of the shad entwined with the white bark of the birch trees was a sermon we were willing to go more than one hundred miles to listen to, and we always felt we were more than repaid for the trouble....

Swamps in the north are really the gayest of gay in early spring and late autumn. Here grow the small willows in various colors, together with sumac, dogwood, and huckleberry. Grasses and sedges in different shades of brown on the edges of the swamps become a tapestry of beautiful hues, warm and pleasing in the crisp air of spring and autumn. Man often tries to imitate this wealth of color by using exotic plants with differently colored branches, but he utterly fails in his purpose because he does not take into consideration that the coloring of these native plants is just for a short period. After that, they change into a somber green, quiet and restful for the warm summer days....

I might go on indefinitely speaking about these many plants I have met throughout the years, each having a sermon for me. There are but few plants that do not love company. On the other hand, most of them are particular about their associates. The spiritual message or character of the individual plant is often enhanced by its association with other plants which are attune with it. Together they form a tonal quality expressed by an orchestra when certain instruments in chorus bring out a much higher and a much finer feeling than a combination of others. The different plants are then given a chance to speak their best.

SHIGEMORI MIREI
PLANTS IN THE JAPANESE GARDEN (1949)

A historian trained in painting and flower arranging, Shigemori Mirei (1896–1975) is increasingly admired for his contemporary Japanese garden designs. Believing that the Japanese dry landscape garden had fallen into cliché, he applied modernist shapes, colors, and materials to create stunning avant-garde works that also celebrated the ancient gods and rituals at the heart of Japanese culture. He created designs for more than ninety religious and residential gardens. This essay comes from his book, *Gardens of Japan*.

Plants are so superbly important to the Japanese garden that many experts say that, if the rock-composition is the bone of the garden, the plants are the flesh. Since the purpose of the Japanese garden art is to reproduce beauty of nature, it is only natural that the trees and flowers should be given the place of honour.

Nevertheless, the flower-beds such as seen in the gardens of America and the European countries are not very popular in Japan. Flower-beds existed even in the early days; but they are limited in number and are used for the cultivation of a small group of special flowers like tree peony, grass peony, or chrysanthemum.

This may seem strange in view of the fact that Japan is practically buried in trees and flowers. Still, in this fact is revealed interesting psychology of the Japanese people. The people of Japan prefer foliage to flowers. They favor the trees with attractive foliage like pine, cedar, fir, oak, camphor tree, maple, cycamore willow, but are not very appreciative of the flowering trees, except cherry, plum, peach, camilia, magnolia, and azalea. Comparatively speaking, they are partial to white flowers, and, if they take a red one, they take the kind that is not deeper than pale pink. Not that they dislike red—they have intense love for crimson maple trees— but that they do not want garish flowers to be superabundant in their gardens.

The Japanese love to build their gardens near the forest of pine trees or other large trees, for such forest gives depth to the gardens. When such forest is not available, however, they plant huge trees for the background.

Large trees are used not only as a background, but also as the central spectacles in various sections of the garden. In the early ages, these central trees were honored because of the belief that they would be used by the descending gods as their abode, although nowadays they are cherished because of the scenic beauty they compose.

Large trees are used in many parts of the garden principally because they give antiquity to the whole composition. This is important inasmuch as an ancient garden is a living testimonial of the long history honoring the temple or the home to which it belongs. There is a kind of beauty age alone can bring. The old trees bearing the vestiges of countless years have the kind of quality no young trees can rival. Moreover, the things that have survived the ravage of time are bound to be superior to the others, because, barring a few exceptions, only the best are likely to be preserved for so long.

These old trees are planted mainly in vicinity of the gate, the artificial hill, or the waterfall as well as beside the pond and on the island. These trees each forms the center of the pattern composed by smaller trees. When this central tree is a cherry or another of a similar kind, it is planted at the eastern or the southern part of the garden, while the one that sheds leaves, like a maple, is planted at the western or southwestern part. The reason for this is that the trees so placed shield the garden against summer heat as well as admit winter sunshine.

Not many trees are planted in the center of the Japanese garden. Although, in some cases, this central area is given to the central tree, ordinarily it is covered with a few trimmed shrubs or small trees. Herein we see an evidence of the love for empty space as described already.

Although few of the central trees are of the flowering kind, the small trees known as *Shita-kusa* (undergrowth) consist of many that bear blossoms. Especially popular are the varieties of azalea and camilia. However, as these plants are beautiful only during the blossom time, they are used mainly as the complementary parts of the pattern.

The trees in the Japanese garden are treated in such manner that they each brings out a natural characteristic of its own. Here "naturism" reigns supreme, giving each tree an opportunity to be true to its own nature and to attain its own type of beauty. This naturistic technique, however, is not applied in the case of trimming, for there the branches and leaves are sheared to form a certain pattern. In this, the garden experts are impelled by a higher purpose, such as that of enhancing scenic beauty of the garden or sustaining symphony of the features.

GRAHAM STUART THOMAS
OLD ROSES IN THE GARDEN (1955)

A horticultural artist, author, and garden designer, Thomas (1909–2003) studied at the University Botanic Garden at Cambridge and later worked for several nurseries. He was the instigator of garden conservation in Britain and became gardens adviser for the National Trust. Thomas's greatest creation was the rose garden at Mottisfont, which he created in the 1970s. He had gathered together an unrivaled collection of pre-1900 roses that was to form the National Collection of Old Roses. A popular garden writer, Thomas wrote *The Old Shrub Roses*, from which this excerpt is taken.

From early spring onwards we watch our favourites appear; how keen we are to see the snowdrops, and to grow six or more varieties to prolong their flowering season; then the daffodils—what flower

more expressly trumpets the coming of spring?—the tulips, giving off redoubled energy when the sun's rays rebound from their richly hued cups; and later the glistening crystalline irises; each new flower of the year more abundantly endowed than the last in colour and form. We pass, too, from the sudden awakening of forsythia to the sweet fragrance of *Viburnum Carlesii,* and before we are fully aware of it the great family of rhododendrons is upon us, imparting grandeur to the scene. The flowering cherries and crab-apples give way to May and laburnum, and the whole horticultural world is ablaze with colour and fragrance. I await these arrivals every year with intense delight, but the coming of the rose is to me the very crown of the year. From the first delicate-flowered pale yellow species and Scots Roses that open, in company with the Cherokee and Banksian Roses on warm walls, to the last poignant autumn blooms, the rose gives unequalled beauty. There is a rose for every taste. Whether we are newly awakened to flowers and delight in the dazzling display of Floribundas, or the more exquisite blooms of the classy Hybrid Teas; or whether our senses have developed still further and embrace the perfect roses of a more refined and elegant age; or whether we go back to the exquisite grace and charm of the original species, there is, I repeat, a rose for every taste.

Roses have so much "fullness" about them; they are full of vigour if the most suitable kinds are planted and reasonably treated; they are full of contrast, their rounded flowers, sprinkled over the network of leaves, create a delightful effect; they are often full of petals, of a good texture of rich velvet or of shining silk; and they are full of scent. They are rich throughout in qualities which have been favourites with gardeners of all ages. Listen to M. Cochet-Cochet: "Le Rosier est de beaucoup le plus important de tous les arbustes cultivés pour l'ornement des jardins."

This paean of praise from a worthy French nurseryman may perhaps require a little qualification. Roses are certainly the favourite flowering shrubby plants of today, but with few exceptions they cannot form the framework of a garden. Evergreens are needed for such positions. Roses are more suitable for foreground colour-work, the filling-in of bays between heavier material, the covering of stumps, hedgerows, and banks with their long trails, and for growing near to the eye and nose, that their beauties may easily reach the senses. Apart from their loss of leaves in winter the Rugosa Roses and the new hybrid 'Nevada' are flowering shrubs of the heaviest calibre, and can be used in important positions governing the design of beds and borders. Most species are more airy, with a dainty refinement that I feel prompts one to place them well away from buildings. The modern and the old florist's roses are more suitable for use in conjunction with formality, whether it be of wall, path, or hedge. When the wall can be of grey Cotswold stone, or the hedge of a blend of holly and box and copper beech, the contrast is superb. A visit to Hidcote will convince intending hedge-planters of the tapestry background that can be obtained from mixed hedges. For informal hedges the roses themselves present several varieties and species of great value.

It cannot be denied that a garden full of one thing can be boring to all but the ardent collector himself. While we are all entitled to do as we like with our gardens I would suggest a careful disposal of old roses, so that the eye may not tire of their qualities in perspective. The old roses create a delightful pattern of flower and foliage at six yards' distance, but at a greater distance give a rather spotty effect. This is due to their small leaves and the regular dotting of flowers along their branches. I feel they very much need the foil of other foliage and the contrast of other flower shapes and styles. Particularly successful with these old roses are foxgloves—just the common wild type and the white, with a few of 'Sutton's Primrose' placed near the dark purple forms. Their spikes give the right contrast in form, and their colours blend happily. Also I like to use *Lilium candidum* and some of the daintier delphiniums in light colours, and the tall irises of the Ochroleuca section. The striking contrast of leaf and flower in these gives just the relief and "uplift" that is needed. Foliage of *Iris pallida* and *Sisyrinchium striatum; Eryngium giganteum,* the silvery-grey biennial 'Sea Holly,' sages, the ordinary culinary and the purple-leaved form;

Hosta or plaintain lily of which the best is *Hosta sieboldiana;*
Stachys olympica, and *Santolina neopolitana* and *chamaecyparis-*
sus—all are splendid subjects for underplanting and mixing
with the old roses. The blatant yellow blooms of the Santolina or
'Cotton Lavender' need never interfere with the colour scheme
if the plants are clipped over in February. For bold corner-work,
especially against paved paths, the Megasea saxifrages (*Bergenia*)
provide the very best of materials, their big broad leathery leaves
of dark green matching the stones' solidity.

These foliage plants can blend an otherwise jumbled mass
of flowers and leaves into an harmonious and satisfying whole.
The use of white flowers with the roses cannot be too strongly
emphasized. For this purpose I have already mentioned foxgloves
and *Iris ochroleuca,* and to them will add Philadelphus or Mock
Orange. A great range of these is available from small shrubs of
two-three feet to giants up to fifteen feet, and the blend of their
fragrance with that of the roses can be almost overwhelming on
a still summer evening. A quantity of pinks—a seed-raised garden
strain is the best, embracing all the tones that are found in the
'Highland Hybrids'- 'White Ladies' and others will provide the
most ideal display at just the right time, and their fragrance again
enters into the scheme. White flowers will intensify the purples
and enrich the pink roses; pale lilac, as may be obtained from
Campanula lactiflora, will purify pink roses. Various contrasts,
such as the clouds of greenish yellow stars and velvet leaves of
Alchemilla mollis with 'Tuscany', will be found, and over them all
a solid garden quality should reign. Flimsy annuals and ordinary
daisy-flowers, so often the body of the average herbaceous border,
may well be avoided.

It will be apparent from the above that I like my old roses
mixed with other plants, rather than arrayed in beds by themselves.
They can be very pleasingly grown in this way, but the general
blend of flower and foliage which is apparent in a mixed border is
to my mind more satisfying and appealing. In addition to creating
a glorious picture at midsummer, many of the foliage plants will

produce flowers earlier or later; a suitable grouping of spring bulbs,
followed in late summer by Galtonias (summer hyacinths), the
hardy *Agapanthus campanulatus* and hybrids, and the free-flower-
ing dwarf *Yuccas flaccida* and *filamentosa* will provide interest
through the year. Over my more stalwart roses I have just planted
some of the small hardy *Clematis Viticella* varieties. These can
be cut to the ground every February and will provide a canopy of
glorious maroons, mauves, and whites to blend with fuchsias and
agapanthus in late July and August. With the old roses, therefore,
may I suggest a generous blend of flowers and foliage, to create
a "cottage garden" mixture and to give colour and interest from
April to October.

RUSSELL PAGE
ON PLANTING SHRUBS (1962)

**English landscape architect Page (1906–1985) studied at the Slade
School of Art in London and in Paris, but his passion for plants soon
led him into a career as a professional garden designer. From 1945
until 1962, Page lived and worked in France and enjoyed an international practice, undertaking commissions in Europe, the Middle
East, and North and South America. The following essay comes from
Page's eloquent book *The Education of a Gardener*.**

When he comes to consider shrub plantings, the garden-maker
might forget his catalogues and alphabetical lists and, to clear
his mind and eye, devise his own and different classification. So
much has been written on shrubs, their descriptions, cultural
needs, and so on that one may soon become fuddled by an excess
of information.

I would try to classify shrubs according to the places and parts
of the garden for which they are most suited by their nature and

their appearance. For example, whatever the climate and the site, there will be a range of shrubs which belong to the fringes of the garden, species whose form and habit are such that they will "mix" well with the natural growths of the place and cause no sense of shock at points where garden merges into woodland or meadow. They may, of course, have other uses too and many will find a place in the more civilised and elaborate parts of the garden. For example, *Rhus cotinus,* the smoke or wig bush, is one of these: native to the rocky slopes of the Alps and South East Europe, and like many of the berberis species suitable for the fringes of a wild garden on certain sites, it is also interesting enough in its habit, its foliage and its flowering to star in an important position in a more sophisticated part of the garden. There are many different species of shrubs, that you can use as native plants, if you are sure that they will look in no way exotic in their setting. There are, indeed, certain plants for which I can find no other use. The yellow and red-twigged willows, pollarded each spring and planted in quantity, will enliven a flat wet site with their winter glow of greeny yellow and smoky red as will *Cornus alba sibirica* and other varieties, but these are plants only for distant use. Individually and seen in detail they lack interest and are altogether too dull to look more than weeds inside the limits of a garden. One can make a short list of such plants useful for blending with the indigenous vegetation on the outer fringes of the garden proper.

On the other hand there is another group of shrubs which I think are often misused, since their proper place is in an enclosed garden. These include philadelphus, weigela, deutzia, and the hybrid lilacs. These plants make most unsuitable neighbours for ericaceous plants like rhododendrons and azaleas, for instance, though I have constantly seen them so used and even mixed with brooms, heathers, and Japanese maples. To my mind they belong somewhere between flower garden, orchard, and kitchen garden where they can be associated with such old-fashioned flowers as paeonies and lilies and pansies. They are perhaps a little dull when not in flower and so need the support of flowering herbaceous plants. But when they are in blossom they have an air of sophistication which belongs well inside the garden enclosure. Lilacs look their best and are easier to prune and keep shapely when you grow them as half-standards. For the first two or three years they will be disappointing, but after they will make great rounded heads covered with flowers. Weigelas need grouping in mixed colours of white and pink and crimson, but they become unsightly unless you ruthlessly cut out old wood as soon as they have flowered. The philadelphus hybrids, too, are apt to grow into unmanageable thickets unless you take out as much old wood as possible each July. Weigela, philadelphus, and deutzias merit a fair space of ground in sun or even in half-shade where their effectiveness can be prolonged and strengthened by groups of the old *Paeonia officinalis* white, hot pink and deep crimson with perhaps an edge planting of *Campanula portenschlagiana* or *C. carpatica.* I would not make the same reservations about the lilac species which are quite suitable for the wilder parts of the garden, as are the Preston hybrids, while the charming dwarf *Philadelphus microphyllus* fits in almost anywhere.

Rose species in the main belong to the wild garden, though amongst them again are some which have such character and colour that I use them in many different ways. I have seen *Rosa rugosa* growing as pheasant-cover in the Yorkshire dales, its single mauve-rose flowers and red hips blending perfectly with thickets of brambles. Its many hybrids though, are more strictly garden plants. Rose 'Blanc Double de Coubert,' 'Roseraie de l'Hay' and 'Conrad Meyer' are three superb doubles to use with herbaceous plantings or in a garden of shrub roses....

Other shrub families are more adaptable and you can use their different species and varieties in all sorts of ways and in all sorts of positions. In acid soil and a mild climate few plants are as useful as the hydrangea. The aquamarine and sapphire blue of *Hydrangea macrophylla* combined with the indigo of wet slate roofs and the dark green of *Cupressus macrocarpa* and *Pinus radiata* is a lovely combination, common enough in Cornwall and Brittany. I like to see these same hydrangeas massed in moist and shady woods where they look no more exotic than *Rhododendron ponticum.* The vinous purple red, the crimson and pink and white varieties are perhaps better inside the garden but in large masses, associated with evergreens only and in a setting of grass and nearby trees. I find their weight of flower colour altogether too overpowering for me to attempt to use other flowering shrubs or plants anywhere near them. . . .

We might consider how to use evergreens shrubs in the garden to make a composition which will stand by itself before any flowering plants are brought in to add colour and diversity. First in Western Europe, I would place the ordinary yew, *Taxus baccata,* as an evergreen of many garden uses. You may use it as a feathery bush and then tree, to grow on through the centuries and be handsome at every stage. You may clip it into hedges from three to fifteen feet in height or give it any shape you like. Lightly clipped over each year, you can use it as a close-textured green background for other plantings or for a formal or informal barrier between two different parts of the garden. Never believe those who complain that it takes too long to grow. After the first three years it will give you increasing satisfaction which is as much as can be said for most trees and shrubs.

Box in its many varieties is the slowest-growing of our evergreens; left wild it makes a warm and satisfying greenery under wintry trees and there is perhaps no need to enlarge on its uses for hedging. I remember working in a Northhamptonshire garden which had a double box hedge about fifteen feet high which you could walk under. Next to box and yew I like best *Laurus nobilis,* the bay laurel, although only in Southern Europe is it hardy enough to use freely to thicken a wood or to clip into high and fragrant walls of foliage. Farther north it needs a sheltered corner in which to make a green buttress. I think of it always as a symbol of Mediterranean civilisation and I do not like a garden to be without it. . . .

I turn more and more towards shrubs as an alternative to herbaceous plants because they seldom need staking or splitting up,

two operations that take a great deal of time as well as skill. Used for this purpose shrubs give you the means of achieving agreeable variations of texture and form, although you cannot usually manage the sudden and recurrent contrasts and harmonies and the close and rapid changes of colour which herbaceous plantings will provide. I prefer to think of shrub plantings as exercises in the assembling of texture and shape, with leaf colour as a secondary consideration and flower colour as an additional and more ephemeral satisfaction. When there is no place for a separate garden you may design a border of shrubs, perhaps against a hedge (but not so close to it as to obscure its crisp wall of sunny or shadowed foliage) or else under a wall or simply rising from a breadth of lawn. It will be a tapestry woven of leaves from the five continents in associations that are visually pleasing but in quite a different way from the far more cautious and restrained use that one would make of them when planting for a natural or wild effect.

ROSEMARY VEREY
GROUND COVER AND LOW-MAINTENANCE PLANTS (1990)

British author of many garden books, Rosemary Verey (1919–2001) based many of her design principles on the experience she gained while creating her personal gardens and her commissions. Verey advised HRH Prince Charles on his garden at Highgrove and also designed gardens at Woodside, the estate of Sir Elton John. The following passage is excerpted from *Good Planting*.

Walk around your garden and notice those areas which have had little time spent on them; they may be occupied by ground cover or low-maintenance plants. There will be flat ribbons or pools of low evergreens—obvious plants like ajuga and lamium—used at the edge of the border, under shrubs and trees, under the overhang

HERB AND VEGETABLE GARDEN AT
NATIONAL CENTRE FOR ORGANIC
GARDENING
Ryton, near Coventry, England
Michael Boys/CORBIS

of a hedge or at the base of a wall; or plants like heathers or prostrate junipers which need little attention. Both ground cover and low-maintenance plants are very wide subjects. To a certain extent they overlap, but there are subtle difference between the two: ground-cover plants are low-maintenance in that the area of soil that they cover requires scant attention and very little weeding, whereas with a low maintenance plant, it is the plant itself which is trouble free and demands little attention....

GROUND COVER

The great virtue of ground-cover plants is that they will take care of themselves, without digging or dividing, not only season by season but also over several years. If initially they are planted in clean ground, this should solve the weeding problem, for annual re-seeding will be inhibited by the vigorous spread of the ground cover. A yearly tidy will improve the look, but even this may not be essential.

Grass, of course, is the quintessential ground cover—but one which requires plenty of attention. A burning question is whether to have or not to have a lawn, and if not, what could be a reasonable substitute. Grass has great ecological benefits. According to the 1948 United States Department of Agriculture Year Book, it is unparalleled in its ability to convert carbon dioxide into oxygen, thereby improving the air we breathe....

Some ground-cover plants lack horticultural interest and, used unimaginatively, may give away the fact that the owner has called in a contractor to do his planting for him. But used with skill and imagination, they can be as versatile and eye-catching as any shrub or perennial and there are always associates to add interest at different seasons. The ajugas and lamiums, for instance, keep their main rosettes of leaves in winter, sending out longer arms and flowering shoots in spring and summer. The early bulbs are good companions for them: chionodoxas, scillas, *Iris reticulata, Anemone nemorosa,* and puschkinias which come through from February to April. Used with discretion, lamiums can be some of

the most useful and adaptable garden plants. Their leaves are small and attractive, their flowers vary in colour from white to darkish pink, and, provided that you keep them clipped back after they have flowered, they will remain discrete....

LOW MAINTENANCE PLANTS

Whereas ground-cover plants tend to occupy extensive and difficult places and are usually evergreen, minimum upkeep plants can feature in any part of the garden, including mixed and herbaceous borders. When you are planning these borders, it is wise to keep "an eye to the future so that you will not find yourself having to do major upheavals, sometimes every autumn. This is when low-maintenance plants are useful. Whereas some are relatively short-lived, others improve with age, rather than deteriorate, when they are left undivided. But I am not advocating that you should not use plants such as delphiniums and asters, which need a lot of attention, for they include some of the most beautiful perennials which are essential ingredients of summer borders.

Herbaceous peonies—have we not all seen and coveted them?—dislike disturbance. In fact, they will take two years to settle back into a flowering routine after replanting, so choose their position and their neighbours carefully. Once planted, all they require is an annual mulch of farmyard manure or leaf mould in autumn and a bone meal feed in spring. Their wonderful double flowers may need staking if they get wet and heavy with rain, and for tidiness you can control their leaves, which often turn a rich bronze and crimson in autumn....

ROSE BED UNDERPLANTINGS

Shrub roses, so called because they do not need the drastic pruning of Hybrid Tea roses, are becoming increasingly popular. A single Hybrid Tea or even a small group of them looks out of place in the shrub border—each individual bloom is too big and blowsy to associate well with the flowers of graceful shrubs. As the Victorians did, and when space allows and taste demands, Hybrid Teas should have beds of their own. But both old and modern shrub roses fit in admirably with other border plants. They do not need pruning to their stumps or bare bones each winter, their stems are graceful and often arching and many have attractive hips to add to the autumn effect. . . .

It is well to consider a few golden rules. First, I think it is essential in a rose bed for the underplanting to be of a single species. This is not the occasion for a tapestry effect—the roses must always take a leading role. Second, you are adding another layer in order to hide the knobbly lower stems of the roses and to clothe the bare soil, so the ground cover must be quite low. Third, I recommend that, although possibly evergreen, it should either be cut back sufficiently or its edges lifted back to allow an autumn mulch or manuring to be put round the roses. I have always found well-rotted horse manure much the best for this—best for the rose and for the gardener, as it does not blow around. Fourth, choose a plant that is sufficiently interesting in flower or leaf while the roses look like dead stumps; if the two are in flower at the same time, the colours must be complementary. . . .

SHRUBBERIES

If you are a weekend gardener and must keep your work to a realistic minimum, or if you have a large garden with parts quite far from the house where you do not want to spend too long working, straightforward shrub border, with no underplanting, is an ideal solution. It requires a different approach. Once planted, it should involve minimum upkeep, but first you must make sure the ground is clear of perennial weeds. In the autumn the bed should have a mulching when the soil is damp. . . .

When you are choosing the plants for your shrub border, consider their different characteristics. Some shrubs are a natural ground cover and are also low-maintenance, as I have already explained. Plants such as the horizontal junipers, *Lonicera pileata,* and *Cotoneaster microphyllus* cover the ground with their spreading evergreen branches and these require no pruning to keep them

shapely. Choose some of these, but remember that they are basically green, and that you will want to include colour in the whole picture, for instance with spring blossom such as *Spiraea 'arguta'* and forsythia, or with summer flowers like *Kolkwitzia amabilis* and tree peonies. For autumn colour *Acer japonicum, Viburnum opulus* and *Euonymous alatus* all change dramatically in October. If you like berries for flower arranging, *Viburnum opulus* will again be useful, and you could choose the variety *V.o.* 'Fructu-luteo' for yellow berries, and the varying colours of the berrying forms of pernettya. Do not forget the charm of coloured stems in winter months.

HEIDI GILDEMEISTER
MEDITERRANEAN GARDENING (1995)

Gildemeister (born 1937) is a resident of Majorca, Spain, where over the past twenty years she has converted a maquis-covered landscape into a thriving ten-acre garden. She is a founding member and past president of the Mediterranean Garden Society and lectures and writes extensively all over the world on subjects related to mediterranean-climate gardening. She is a gardener of long and varied experience in Europe and South America. These edited passages come from her first book, *Mediterranean Gardening: A Waterwise Approach*.

There is no need to sacrifice beauty for the sake of water conservation. Contrary to the popular image of a water-saving landscape consisting solely of cacti in a dusty area of rocks and pebbles, drought-tolerant Mediterranean natives are very attractive. They fit every landscape and offer the same variety of shape, texture and colour as the water-demanding plants. Such gardens will gain in radiance as drought-tolerant plants stand up to dry summers and, when well-chosen, look as good in midsummer as in spring. Many colourful plants in existing gardens (glorious wisteria, heady jasmine) are drought-tolerant.

Waterwise gardens are attractive yet do not demand constant attention. Reduced maintenance is matched by significant savings in expenditure (water, fertilizer, labour). And such gardens promote health as plants respond vigorously to practices which copy their native habitats.

A change to a low-water-requiring garden is often quite easy and it is not always necessary to design from the beginning again. You are already on your way if you use plants of low water requirements, reduce the lawn, change watering from a time schedule to a need schedule and if you apply water carefully to avoid runoff. Success is assured by careful planning. Consider the Eight Steps.

STEP 1 PLANNING YOUR GARDEN
STRUCTURING THE LAND
Whatever your garden is intended for, give it structure and backbone. In a Mediterranean climate the garden is a significant living space where one may spend most of one's time. Do you want to work in it or rest, collect plants or acquaint children with nature? Service areas planned as carefully as the garden, allotting each function its place, turn into attractive sites. Locate the compost pile, a place for mulch preparation, a sand pit for children to play. Anchor your house to its grounds, balance the garden with its mass. . . .

PREVENTING EROSION, SHELTER FROM THE WIND
A well-planned garden, large or small, has pronounced horizontal lines. They give structure to the garden, define its areas, improve the precious rainwater's infiltration and above all: prevent erosion. The horizontal backbone (patio, terrace, wall, path) often requires stonework. Retention walls hold up soil, providing soil depth. While formerly extensive terracing was done to this effect, on a small scale a leveled trail might do. Hard-surfaced "horizontals"

can substitute the controversial lawn and render gardens more user-friendly, permitting garden pleasures and tasks to continue once rain stops.

STEP 2 CREATING PLANT COVER AND SHADE
While British gardeners ponder about shape, texture, or variegated leaves, "covering the ground" is at the forefront on Mediterranean gardeners' minds. Evergreen vegetation retains soil, protecting it year-round from dehydration. The resulting soil humidity encourages a flourishing soil life which in turn stimulates vigorous growth. A lush plant cover suppresses competing weeds. It cools the atmosphere and plants, also the gardener! Where under a blazing noon sun the air stands still, a single tree on a lawn or paving creates a refreshing breeze. Midsummer days (or nights) are never unbearably hot if trees and climbers surround the house. By establishing a lush plant cover, you create a better environment and simple beauty.

STEP 3 USING DROUGHT-TOLERANT PLANTS
Plants from others areas of the world with a Mediterranean climate may be satisfactorily grown together with the Mediterranean natives. They include drought-tolerant trees, shrubs, and bulbs from the California chaparral, the South African fynbos, or the Australian heathlands and grow in the same climate we garden in. These plants, often referred to as exotics, are natives too—in their homeland. Carpenteria, one of the most beautiful flowers and given a choice site in English gardens, in California is considered a weed from the wild. The same is true of South Africa where such lovely bulbs as *Ixia, Sparaxis,* and *Watsonia* are on the verge of being lost to construction sites, while Westringia, one of the most useful plants for Mediterranean gardens, would turn nobody's head in its native Australia.

STEP 4 REDUCING THE LAWN, ALTERNATIVES
Should you opt for drought-tolerant alternatives to grass, ever-

HOME AND GARDEN OF GARDEN
DESIGNER HEIDI GILDEMEISTER
(begun 1995)
Mallorca, Spain
Heidi Gildemeister

green low-lying foliage plants (single species in large patches) achieve the tranquil effect lawns provide. Yet open spaces do not necessarily require treatment as lawns. Broken up by ground-covering vines, shrubs of varying heights, low walls, paths, or such constructions as pergolas, they offer diversion. Take time out to search for inspiration or seek professional advice.

Paving, even extensive, is an excellent lawn alternative and may double as patio, courtyard, or terrace. Open, sunny stretches heat up, but a tree together with arbour or pergola gives cooling shade. Wooden decks, bordered by bench-railings, are Californian alternatives. Adjoining chaparral or maquis vegetation is improved by selective pruning or trimming. Gravel, another non-vegetative lawn alternative, requires maintenance and is not really satisfactory. Weeds grow in it while the gravel in its turn invades plantings.

STEP 5 GROUPING PLANTS FOR WATER NEEDS

You will achieve important savings in water (and labour!) if you divide your garden into areas with high, medium, and low water requirements, according to the specific needs of the plants.

Winter rain takes care of Mediterranean climate plants and generally carries them through summer without further attention. These plants qualify for low-water regions and make up the non-irrigated area.

Yet many plants do not come from a Mediterranean climate and show improved performance with weekly watering in summer. They make up the second group.

Species from tropical or summer rain regions require ample supplies. Planted near the house, they constitute the water-intensive area.

STEP 6 PLANNING WATER MANAGEMENT

Rain, absent over long periods, is nevertheless an important element in planning for water-saving gardening. While blue summer skies are overhead, try to foresee where winter downpours may make a stream. You may not see real rain for years, but when it comes, it can be destructive, washing away your garden's fertile soil. . . .

Rainwater, if retained and stored on your land, brings relief in dry periods, providing the best water, free of charge. So-called ground water recharge is achieved by natural drainage. It is improved by the soil's water retention, by soil-protecting vegetation and mulch. Reduce the water, flowing along a drive or steep path, by diverting it over the widest possible area. Cisterns store rainwater from roofs and terraces.

In Mediterranean climates, natural rain replaces irrigation efficiently. But even drought-tolerant or waterwise gardens need a tap while plants become established. It is easy to lay a pipe to a distant corner. When considering irrigation, use efficient equipment. This may mean single sprinklers for small lawns as much as sophisticated apparatus which is improving all the time. Have all equipment in place before planting. Also change irrigation from a time to a need schedule and consider "grey water."

STEP 7 USING WATER-SAVING PRACTICES
The closer one can cater for plants' requirements, the better they are equipped to withstand drought and the less water they will need. Such requirements include:

Water loss through leaves is reduced by choosing suitable sites. Keep shade plants in the shade, water-loving ones at the bottom of slopes or adjacent to lawns. Exacting sites (midday and afternoon sun) are reserved for sturdy plants. Separate thirsty plants from those with low water needs.

Many colourful native plants grow in infertile, rocky soils with poor water-holding capacity . . . yet excellent drainage is essential for all waterlogged roots lack soil oxygen and rot.

Grouping plants close together creates micro-environments for moisture retention, shades the ground, protects small plants from wind, discourages water-stealing weeds.

Deep root runs for those demanding it, keep roots cool.

Give careful attention to mulch, one of the pillars of low-water gardening.

When planted in early autumn, root systems adjust over humid mild winters and plants often enter the summer drought period already well-established. Plants from 2- to 4-liter containers establish best. If smaller, they need too much coddling over harsh summers.

STEP 8 A WATERWISE GARDEN FOR ALL SEASONS
Although water may be scarce, enjoy vigorous greenery and flowers all year round by planning your garden for the four seasons.

Cooler nights and the first autumn rains awaken the plants from summer dormancy and trigger off new growth. Take advantage of autumn-flowering bulbs (*Amarine, Colchicum, Sternbergia, Urginea*) and climbers (*Bignonia, Passiflora, Plumbago, Solanum jasminoides*). . . .

Winter bloom is the great benefit of Mediterranean gardening. Exploit it, for so much is in bloom at this period. White flower clusters after Christmas cover laurustinus (*Viburnum tinus*), a Mediterranean basic plant. Carob's (*Ceratonia siliqua*) young, lemon-green foliage looks from afar like *Acacia,* ready to bloom. *Chasmanthe*'s sword-like leaves look as unruffled by wind as if grown in a conservatory and the tall flowers last for weeks, while *Aeonium* lights dull areas with yellow radiant flowerheads. . .

Spring gardens thrive on winter rain, when native vegetation is usually seen at its best. Exuberant flowering is breathtaking and many trees (*Cercis siliquastrum, Crataegus, Styrax officinale*) and shrubs (lilac, spiraea) are covered with bloom. Choose early-flowering ones (the wide range of *Prunus*), growing spring bulbs beneath (crocus, cyclamen, fritillary, muscari, tulips).

After flowering, let your evergreen garden rest under hot summer skies while you retire to cool shade. Pines' resinous scent or rock roses' ethereal oils will greet you. Drought-tolerant evergreen foliage prevents a dried up midsummer look (box, lentisc, myrtle, oak, *Grevillea, Taxus, Thuja, Westringia*). Also enjoy the summer flowers. With little or no water bloom *Agapanthus, Amaryllis belladonna, Crinum,* accompanied by Coreopsis, Gaillardia, and climbing Bignonia.

STEVE MARTINO
DESERT GARDENS (1992)

American landscape architect Steve Martino (born 1946) has conducted pioneering work with native plant material and the development of a desert-derived aesthetic. He studied art and architecture at Arizona State University, and his work ranges from urban development and remote large-scale communities to private gardens. His projects have received more than eighty local, regional, and national design awards, including seven National Design Awards from the American Society of Landscape Architects. This essay originally appeared in 1992 in *The Environmental Gardener,* a publication of the Brooklyn Botanic Garden.

I grew up in Phoenix, in the heart of the Sonoran Desert, and I've stayed on to design gardens here.... I began to strive for gardens which evoke the special qualities of the desert. Appropriate plant selection, placement and massing, along with appropriate mulches and paving materials, can quite poetically express the ecology of the desert and its sense of place. Using native plants was also the simplest way to make a home fit comfortably into the desert environment. As a bonus, desert natives are genetically suited to the soil and rainfall of the region, so water conservation follows. Creating functional and beautiful outdoor spaces that integrate human activity with the natural processes of a site—that's what my gardens are all about.

WILDNESS AND ORDER
Site research forms the foundation for all my designs. I take soil samples and have them tested at Al Lengyel's agricultural lab in Phoenix. Our central Arizona soils are alkaline, high in salts, low in organic matter and microorganisms, and usually riddled with layers of calcium carbonate or caliche that you either have to work around or jackhammer to make hospitable for plants. The water here is also alkaline and high in bicarbonates, compounding the problem. Organic matter must be added to soils with a high pH to give the plants the best possible start in their new environment. When I do a site analysis, I also look at the "big picture"—not just the site itself but also the streetscape, the neighborhood, and the region. I tailor my designs to all of these to make the gardens feel at home.

In my designs I use the "hardscape"—paving, walls, fences— to structure and define space. I like the juxtaposition of these refined and ordered man-made elements with the wildness of an ever-changing natural garden. The right kind of mulch, or what I call "desert pavement," is crucial for a natural-looking landscape. Because rainfall is so sparse and plants must compete for water, the ground is not thickly carpeted with plants like the prairie or the eastern forests. Consequently, matching the rock types, sizes, and colors of the surrounding landscape is important and requires an artistic eye.

Before I think about specific plants, I think in terms of plant forms or masses that will be needed to perform specific functions. What sculptural form or massing, for example, will provide privacy, a sense of enclosure, and refuge? Where do I need to locate trees to cast cooling shade?

PRIVATE RESIDENCE (designed in 1985
by Steve Martino)
Paradise Valley, Arizona
Steve Martino

ARID ZONE TREES (designed in 1988
by Steve Martino)
Queen Creek, Arizona
Steve Martino

EXPLORING THE DESERT

When I first started using native desert plants, the landscape industry knew little about them. There was even less interest among gardeners and nurserymen. I was fortunate to meet Ron Gass, early in my career. Ron is a naturalist, native plant specialist, and nurseryman. I must have driven him crazy when I started hanging around his nursery. I would ask what seemed like a hundred times what each plant was. Most plants didn't have common names, and I could never remember the Latin nomenclature.

Ron and I became good friends and I traveled with him on several seed collecting expeditions throughout the Sonoran Desert. Several times we even ventured into northern Mexico. Ron had an intimate knowledge of desert plants. He knew the exact location and elevation where each of his nursery plants grew in the wild. He'd say something like, "I found this growing in Pepper Sauce Canyon north of Tucson in the Catalina Mountains." You can bet when I found myself hiking in that canyon ten years later, I was on the lookout for Arizona yellow bells. This kind of first-hand knowledge has made me a much more skillful and intuitive desert garden designer. However, until I developed some confidence in using these "unknown" plants, I'd show my designs to Ron and ask him what he thought about my plant combinations and whether he felt that they all fit together. Ron Gass's Mountain State wholesale nursery provided dozens of plants for my back-yard designs in the early years. Today, he grows thousands of native plants for my large-scale desert restoration projects. Several of these species have no commercial market yet.

DESERT SHAPES AND SHADOW PATTERNS

I try to capture the character of the arroyo or desert "wash" in my garden designs. The wash is my favorite part of the desert. It's where the action is. These natural drainage ways are where the plants are dense and lush and animals come to seek shelter.

Whenever I saw a group of plants in nature that appealed to me I'd try to analyze what it was about them that I liked. I'd even photograph the scene for future reference. It was always the combination of texture, leaf pattern, and color that made these combinations so remarkable. I especially like the effect of cactus growing out of plant masses.

Plants with bold shapes also play an integral role in my desert gardens. The relentless Arizona sun is a major element of desert gardening—in fact, I consider it an absolutely basic design tool. The blinding midday sun tends to flatten forms and colors. Only the strongest shapes remain distinct. The light doesn't soften and color doesn't return until late afternoon. The bold, distinctive shapes of spiked agaves (*Agave* spp.) ocotillo (*Fouquieria splendens*), and prickly pears (*Opuntia* spp.) hold their own against the brilliant midday light. They also cast wonderful shadows. Also basic to desert gardening is creating intricate shadow patterns on walls and paving—I'd go as far to say that a tree's shadow is as important as the tree itself.

PENSTEMONS AND PRICKLY PEAR

One of my favorite plants is the versatile mesquite tree. In fact, I use several different mesquites in either standard or multi-trunk forms—mostly the relatively small and slow-growing velvet mesquite (*Prosopis juliflora*) but also a new cultivar, *Prosopis alba* 'Colorado', developed by Mountain States nursery, which looks a lot like the popular Chilean mesquite but is more cold hardy, and the western honey mesquite (*Prosopis glandulosa var. torreyana*), which has the largest leaves and is the most open and airy tree. Mesquites grow from twenty to fifty feet tall, are handsome and extremely drought-tolerant, and provide the most leaf area, and therefore shade, per gallon of water, according to studies by the University of Arizona. Their seedpods are a favorite food for many rock and antelope squirrels, as well as javelina. Blue palo verde (*Cercidium floridum*) is another favorite tree. This spiny deciduous tree, which grows fifteen to thirty feet high and wide, has distinctive blue-green bark and leaves and very showy yellow flowers in spring. I also like the sculptural form of prickly pear cactus, especially when contrasted with soft spreading ground covers. These plants have wonderful flowers and require no supplemental water. I most often use the native *Opuntia engelmannii,* which has yellow, pink, and red flowers, the non-native *Opuntia ficus-indica,* an upright thornless tree-forming cactus with yellow flowers and big pads (leaves) and *Opuntia violacea,* which has red-violet pads and brilliant yellow flowers.

Arizona has the greatest representation of hummingbird species in the United States, and we also have the plants to attract them. My favorites, the penstemons, are even pollinated by hummingbirds. I typically use the hot pink *Penstemon parryi,* which produces an incredible show during March and April with its multiple three-foot-high flower spikes. I also use the orange-flowered *P. superbus,* the deep red *P. eatonii* and the lavender-blue *P. spectabilis.*

The chuparosa or hummingbird bush (*Justicia californica*) with its bright red flowers, the brittle-bush (*Encelia farinosa*) with its brilliant yellow blossoms, and the strongly scented, olive green creosote bush (*Larrea tridentata*) form the basis of the simple plant palettes typical of my gardens. Other favorites are the ocotillo, staghorn cactus (*Opuntia acanthocarpa*), jojoba (*Simmondsia chinensis*), wolfberry (*Lycium fremontii*), indigo bush (*Dalea bicolor* var. *argyraea*), *Viguiera deltoidea,* native verbenas *Verbena goodingii* and *V. pulchella,* and desert marigold (*Baileya multiradiata*), along with *Salvia coccinea* and *Salvia greggii* from the nearby Chihuahuan Desert.

Soil conditions dictate suitable species for a particular site. I always try to match the plants to the particular soil types in which they occur naturally in the wild. Except for the cacti, virtually all the plants need supplemental water until they become established...

RICK DARKE
DESIGNING THE WOODLAND GARDEN (2002)

American writer, photographer, and landscape-design consultant Darke (born 1952) has studied and photographed North American plants in their native habitats. He graduated from the University of Delaware with a degree in plant science and subsequently worked at Longwood Gardens for twenty years. His efforts with international plant exploration and introduction have taken him to Japan, South Africa, England, Germany, Brazil, Australia, New Zealand, Costa Rica, and the Canary Islands. Much of his research on North American plants is based on his own gardens near Newark, New Jersey, and in the rolling piedmont of Landenberg, Pennsylvania. He wrote *The American Woodland Garden: Capturing the Spirit of the Deciduous Forest,* from which this excerpt is taken.

A garden designed to capture the spirit of the deciduous forest need not be a faithful replication of the forest community. The emotional and persuasive power of art results from selection, distillation, and enhancement, and so the most artful, evocative woodland gardens may borrow from any number of patterns and signatures that define the native forest—its lines and framework, its layers, luminous qualities, color cycles, sounds, and scents—melding them into an insightful yet livable landscape....

ABSTRACTING THE FOREST

The visual complexity of the unedited native forest is sometimes so great that it overwhelms the eye, appearing beautiful but chaotic. In the woodland garden, reducing the complexity and drawing out one or a few distinct motifs can result in a landscape that is powerfully reminiscent of the forest, but is more easily read and more accessible....

FRAMING AND ENCLOSING

Whether creating vistas or enclosing and defining garden spaces, the natural architecture of the deciduous forest can be as effective as any made of masonry or steel. Sometimes there is an opportunity to frame views or spaces through the selective removal of existing trees. In other situations, tree plantings can be made to define and organize garden vistas and rooms. In most instances, utilizing trees and other natural elements of the forest is considerably less expensive than traditional architectural means. . . .

WORKING WITH LAYERS

The natural layering of the deciduous forest may be emulated and enhanced through the art of the garden. Working imaginatively with layers will make the most of any garden space, resulting in powerful compositions and rich plant combinations on both large and small scales. . . .

CELEBRATING AND ENCOURAGING NATURAL FORM

Though some amount of pruning and shaping is always necessary in even the most informal, naturalistic gardens, working as much as possible with natural plant forms is usually the most practical and often the most visually interesting approach. . . .

GARDENING AT THE EDGE

Though shaded interior conditions dominate native forests, sunnier settings typical of the woodland edge are common in many private gardens and park landscapes. Some edge areas are more or less permanent, due to clearings which must be maintained for driveways, walks, dwellings, and other utility structures, and these offer opportunities to plant species requiring greater sunlight than the interior environment affords. Many interior, shade-tolerant species flower more freely at the sunny edge, and their fall foliage colors are often richer and more varied.

In suburban gardens, particularly those on land once cleared for agriculture, edge conditions are often temporary, gradually giving way as sunny lawn areas are reduced in favor of woodland plantings. Plants which can make this transition an attractive process are important elements in the evolution of such gardens.

INTEGRATING EXOTICS

Even among gardeners ardently devoted to growing and conserving North American native plants, few would be so purist as to say that exotics have no place in the designed landscape. The exotic species that is an old family favorite or is a reminder of a visit to a far-away garden is often an innocuous addition even in the native garden. Most importantly, the places in which we make gardens have sometimes been so changed by human influence that certain growing conditions on the site are no longer suitable for the native plants they might once have supported, and in some cases carefully selected exotics may actually be better suited to the design purpose and less consuming of natural resources. . . .

WORKING WITH TEXTURES AND WITHIN THE COLOR GREEN

The rich diversity of woodland textures and green hues offers myriad opportunities for enduring, eye-catching combinations, and if elements such as rocks, garden structures, and local relics are added to the composition, the design possibilities are virtually limitless.

THE INFLUENCE OF EVERGREENS

A drive-by evaluation of the landscapes in a typical suburban housing development, even those built on land that was formerly forest, will reveal a heavy reliance on evergreen trees and shrubs. The reasons for using evergreens are varied. The color green, generally taken for granted by many gardeners in spring and summer, takes on greater cachet in the winter landscape. Also, evergreens are often perceived as more "alive" in the winter landscape than deciduous plants. Perhaps most commonly, evergreens are valued for the constant screening effect they can provide. The downside of these evergreen-filled landscapes is that they are relatively

HOME OF GARDEN DESIGNERS RICK
DARKE AND MELINDA ZOEHRER (begun
1988) Landenberg, Pennsylvania
Garden design and photography
© Rick Darke

static, possessing little of the seasonal drama of a predominantly deciduous landscape. If the purpose of the garden is to evoke the deciduous forest, evergreen trees and shrubs must be used carefully and sparingly, so the garden emulates the open, luminous characteristics of a native woodlands as much as practical. The ground layer is an appropriate place to indulge in native evergreens including ferns, mosses, club mosses, sedges, wood-rushes, and herbaceous perennials, which will add their verdant hues to the winter landscape without diminishing the vistas, as well as the light and shadow play of the woods.

CELEBRATING NATURAL LIGHT IN THE WOODLAWN GARDEN

To the uninitiated, the woodland garden might seem a place of darkness, but in truth, it can be among the most radiant landscapes on earth. One magical aspect of deciduous woodland plants is that their thin foliage is translucent, particularly in spring and fall, and capable of all manner of incandescent effects....

Observe your existing garden landscape and make note of specially lit moments you want to celebrate. Organize pathways, garden seating, or views from inside the dwelling to provide the needed focus at the appropriate time. When creating new parts of the garden, place an emphasis on plants with foliage or flowers that are particularly capable of accentuating the sun's rays, and position them where you are likely to view them glowing against dark-colored backgrounds, shadows, or reflective surfaces.

WOODLAND WALKS AND PATHWAYS

On more than one occasion I've listened to the suggestions of British gardeners that Americans are too willing to set a few native plants along a path and call it a garden, and there is some truth in these observations....

Certainly, the American woodland garden should be more than a simple "walk in the woods," but deciduous trees are among the greatest structural elements in any natural landscapes. If recognized as such in the garden and put to imaginative use, they can play a significant role in organizing artful experiences that are both evocative of the native forest and easier on the budget....

THE WOODLAND GARDEN DWELLING

I am often perplexed by talk of "connecting to nature" through the garden when no mention is made of the house. Since woodland nature is so tied to cycles of light, sounds, scents, and other seasonal nuance, it is especially important that that connection between a woodland dwelling and garden be made as strong as imagination and resources allow. Given the complexity and hurried pace of contemporary life in North America, with so many stimuli competing for our attention, the phrase "out of sight, out of mind" applies ever more certainly to the great outdoors, including the garden in its quiet but necessary moments. Fortunately, technological advances in modern building materials, particularly those associated with glass, in windows, walls, and skylights, have made it economically and ecologically sound to provide views from all parts of the house into beautiful living phenomena of the woodland landscape.

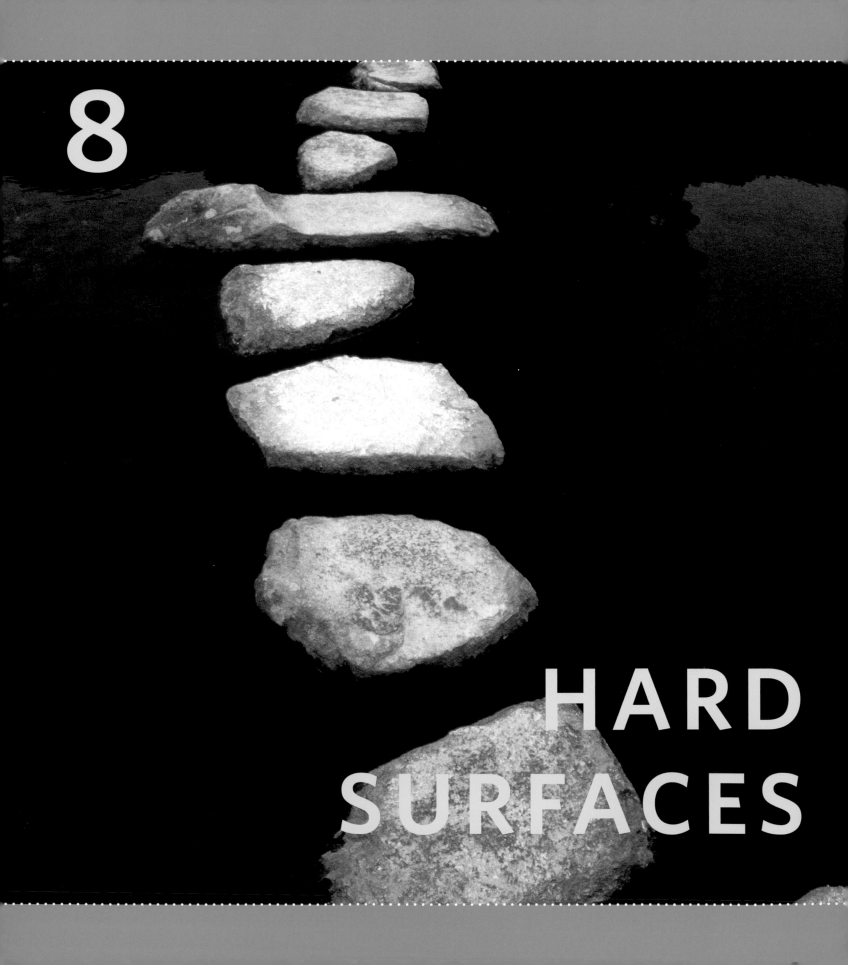

8

HARD
SURFACES

In America a fence . . . is very necessary for protection, *for* shelter, *and for* shade. *As to the first, gardeners may scold as long as they please, mankind never will look upon taking fruit in an orchard or a garden as* felony *nor even as* trespass. *Besides, there are, in all countries, such things as* boys; *and every man remembers, if he be not very forgetful, that he himself was once a boy. So that, if you have a mind to have for your own use what you grow in your garden, the only effectual security is an insurmountable fence. . . .*

William Cobbett (1762–1835), English publisher and journalist

A word should be said about the steppingstones in Japanese gardens. They have what seems the purely practical function of providing a firm, clean surface to walk on, but as a rule they are shaped so irregularly that if one does not watch every step one makes one is likely to slip and fall. Since it is necessary to look down each time one moves, the changes in one's line of vision are especially vivid. Gardeners do everything they can to see that their landscape will stand up under the close scrutiny of a person circumscribed in this fashion. After walking from stone to stone for a time, one usually comes to a place where one looks up in surprise at an unexpected vista. There is an attempt in the placing of the stones to emphasize these changes in the landscape; they serve not merely as pavement but as a guide for the viewer.

Kenzo Tange (1913–), Japanese architect

ATTRIBUTED TO TACHIBANA NO TOSHITSUNA
SETTING STONES (c. 1050)

Scholars have attributed the text of the classic Japanese garden treatise *Sakuteiki* to Tachibana no Toshitsuna (1028–1094). One of the Four Great Families during the Heian period, the Tachibana family enjoyed grand palaces and gardens. Toshitsuna gained knowledge of garden design through his exposure to these properties and headed a government office responsible for construction and repair of imperial estates. This excerpt is taken from a translation by Jiro Takei and Marc P. Keane.

SECRET TEACHINGS ON SETTING STONES

When setting stones, first bring a number of different stones, both large and small, to the garden site and temporarily set them out on the ground. Set those that will be standing stones with their "heads" upright, and those that will be reclining stones with their best side facing out. Compare the various qualities of the stones and, keeping the overall garden plan in mind, pull the stones into place one by one.

Choose a particularly splendid stone and set it as the Main Stone. Then, following the request of the first stone, set others accordingly. Choose one with a well-balanced head and then set other stones in front of this in succession, culminating in the Fore Stone. If a stone that does not have a well-balanced head is chosen, set it so that it shows its best side. Do not be concerned if it leans a little.

For a stone that will descend from the shoreline to the depths of the pond, or ascend from the depths out to meet the shore, a majestic stone of grand proportions is best. If this is to be constructed, then gather stones of the same color, the shapes of which seem like they will fit each other well, and set them together so that they make one huge, composite form.

Set a splendid stone that will balance well with the Bracketing Stones and Fore Stone when they are set, and then set the Rear Stone following the request of the first stone set.

ANONYMOUS SECRET TEACHINGS

The stones of steep mountain cliffs rise in the angular manner of folding screens, open shutters, or staircases.

The stones at the base of a mountain or those of a rolling meadow are like a pack of dogs at rest, wild pigs running chaotically, or calves frolicking with their mothers. As a rule of thumb, when setting stones, if one pair "flees" from the group, then seven or eight should "chase" after them, like children playing tag.

It is considered common sense that Buddhist Trinity arrangements shall be made with standing stones while arrangements in the "shape of piled boxes" shall use horizontal stones.

Retaining stones should be amply set in places where hillsides have been deeply cut away. In areas that will abut an expanse of lawn, such as the boundary where a hillside meets the flat courtyard, or the edges of the lawn itself, set some low stones, scattered this way and that, some upright and some laid flat.

There are many names of stone groupings, including Multilayered Shape, Crown Shape, Writing Desk Shape, Bucket Type, and so on.

If there are stones that "flee" then there should be stones that "chase" after; if there are stones that lean, there should be those that lend support; if some proceed then others should acquiesce; if some face up, then others should face down; and to balance with stones that stand upright there should also be those that recline.

Stones must be set powerfully, which means that the "roots" of the stone must be set deeply. However, even if a stone is deeply set, if it is not balanced with the Fore Stone, then it will appear weak. Even a stone set too shallowly will appear strong if it is well balanced with a Fore Stone. There is a Secret Teaching about this.

When setting a stone, soil must be packed in all around the bottom of the stone so that there is not room for so much as a speck of dust left. If the soil is compacted only around the perimeter of the stone then the soil will run away when it rains, leaving empty pockets beneath the stone. Use a slim pole and ram the soil bit by bit from the bottom up.

TABOOS

Regarding the placement of stones there are many taboos. If so much as one of these taboos is violated, the master of the household will fall ill and eventually die, and his land will fall into desolation and become the abode of devils.

The taboos are as follows:

Using a stone that once stood upright in a reclining manner or using a reclining stone as a standing stone. If this is done, that stone will definitely become a Phantom Stone and be cursed.

Taking a flat stone that once was reclining and standing it upright to face toward the residence. Whether it is set in a high or low place, far or near, it will make no difference. This will result in a curse.

A stone that is 1.2 to 1.5 meters tall should not be placed in the northeasterly direction. This will become a Phantom Stone, and, since it would become a landmark to aid the entry of evil spirits, people will not be able to live there for long. However, if a Buddhist Trinity is placed in the southwest, there will be no curse, neither will devils be able to enter.

JI CHENG
WALLS, PAVING, AND RAISING MOUNTAINS (1631–34)

Born in 1582 in China's Jiangsu Province, Cheng was a prominent Ming dynasty landscape and rock artist whose designs included gardens south of the Chiangjiang (formerly the Yangtze River). Between 1631 and 1634, he wrote *Yuan Ye* (The Craft of Gardens). It is believed to be one of the first general manuals on landscape gardening in the Chinese tradition. The excerpt is from the translation of the work by Alison Hardie.

WALLS

Most surrounding walls for gardens are made of earth tamped between shuttering, or of blocks of stone, or take the form of thorny hedges. Now thorn hedges are better than flowering shrubs in that they look wilder and give the garden quite a flavour of the mountain forests. Walls within a garden, for example in front of a flowerbed or beside the water, along a path or around a hill, may be built perhaps of stone, or of brick, decorated with openwork or plain and polished; in fact they can be satisfactorily designed in many different ways. As long as they are elegant and contemporary, and worthy of appreciation, they will add to the beauty of your garden. Traditionally it has been considered that if a wall is decorated at the mason's pleasure with carvings of flowers, birds, fairies or monsters, this is really artistic; in fact not only is it ugly in a garden, it is unacceptable even in front of a dwelling-house. Sparrows build their nests among the carvings, which is most annoying; weeds accumulate all over them like creepers. Though you may try to drive the sparrows away you can never get rid of them; if you try to knock the weeds down, you risk damaging the wall. There is absolutely nothing you can do about the situation. Such decoration is the sort of thing that vulgar townies and stupid rustics go in for; the man of enlightened tastes will be more cautious.

When ordinary people build walls, if the ground is sloping or cramped, this limits their construction. But why not make the wall wider at one end than the other, in order to fit in with the regular proportions of the buildings? This is something that neither masons nor landowners understand. . . .

PAVING

Generally speaking, in laying paving or making a path, there is a slight difference between what pleases in gardens and in dwelling-houses. It is only in the midst of main halls and large buildings that you should pave the ground completely with polished bricks; a winding path or walk can be cobbled with various unworked stones of an oblong shape; in a central courtyard it may be appropriate to lay an interlocking zig-zag pattern; near steps you can also use a pattern of concentric squares. If you intersperse octagons with squares, and select pebbles to set among them, you can obtain an effect like Sichuan brocade. The verandah outside a tall building, studded with flowers, will rival the glory of the Qin Terrace. With a patterned fabric of tiles, and a terrace covered in stone slabs, you can sit on the ground and recite poetry to the flowers, or spread out a rug and raise your glass to the moon. Even shattered pieces of tile may come into their own: they can be chipped into shape and arranged in a rippling wave pattern, like stones on the floor of a lake. Even broken bricks may have their uses: they can be carved and fitted together around a plum-flower shape, in a random pattern like cracked ice. Walks and paths may be laid in a very conventional way, but steps should always be something out of the ordinary; lotuses seem to bloom under one's feet, as footsteps are heard all around. As you pick up kingfisher feathers in the depths of the woods, a feeling of springtime arises from who knows where.

A narrow way set around with flowers is better paved with stone, while an open courtyard surrounded by buildings should be laid with bricks. Paving of all kinds, square or round, should be laid in an appropriate way. Shaping the paving-stones should be

the work of a specialist tiler, but unskilled labour may be used for the odd jobs.

UNWORKED STONE WALKS

When laying walks in a garden, you should use small stones of irregular shape, fitting them together like the seeds in a pomegranate; this is both hardwearing and elegant. A winding road running from high to low and leading from hill to valley can be given unity by this method. Some people set pebbles among the stones to make a pattern on the road; however, this is both not very durable and rather vulgar.

PEBBLED AREAS

Pebbles are suitable for laying on paths that are not frequently used. It is best if you can intersperse large stones with small, but I am afraid most workmen are incapable of this. It is also effective to use bricks or tiles, and inlay them to form various brocade-like patterns. But if you lay them in the form of cranes or deer or lions playing with a ball, and the lion ends up looking like a dog, it is just ridiculous. . . .

VARIOUS TYPES OF BRICK PAVING

Paving can be laid with various types of brick. Within a house, you should use shaped bricks, and lay them flat; in a courtyard, you should lay them on end. Square, repeated, or stepped interlocking zig-zag patterns were conventional in the old days. Modern patterns such as herringbone, woven matting, or woven hat pattern are all possible provided the bricks are found in a suitable length. . . .

PRINCE CHARLES-JOSEPH DE LIGNE
STATUES AND ORNAMENTATION (1781)

A Belgian nobleman, Ligne (1735–1814) influenced garden design through his writings and counseled Marie-Antoinette on the Petit Trianon, the Duc de Chartres on the Parc Monceau, and the Baron de Monville on the Desert de Retz. But Ligne's real passion was for his garden at Beloeil, which he called "the handsomest garden in Europe . . . if it weren't for Versailles." This excerpt is from the 1991 translation by Basil Guy of Ligne's 1781 book *Coup d'œil sur Beloeil et sur une grande partie de jardins d'Europe* (A Look at Beloeil and Many of the Great Gardens of Europe).

If you are not rich, you will still have all that is necessary if you own a neat house with but one story, a hidden roof, a colorful wash, a few plaster bas-reliefs, or a rustic frame; a wide and flowing brook, issuing from genuine rock; a swaying bridge like Aline's; a few benches; perhaps a stone table; a shepherd's hut; a mobile salon on four wheels; a few proud but not arrogant pines alongside tall and simple poplars, slim and supple; a weeping willow; a Judas tree; an acacia; a plane tree; three beds of flowers, sown at random, with daisies on a section of your lawn; a small field of poppies and cornflowers; a few hieroglyphics on a small monument with a couple of inscriptions, for I do not want to abuse this fashion. [There should be] no commonplaces, no vague or petty ideas, which are often wrong. Do not put a label on each tree. Do not force the visitor to reflect, but assist the lazy. Let thinking be increased, expanded, and inspired. Let the philosopher find consolation in it, the lover sensitivity, and the poet novelty and liveliness. You must always give prime consideration to those three types especially. With all that and an unexpected ha-ha as a boundary to allow you full enjoyment of the hillsides, the plains, the woods, the meadows, the villages, and the old castles of the surroundings, I would surpass Kent and Le Nôtre. With twenty thousand francs for the

work and two hundred for maintenance, I would attract every traveler from at least ten leagues around. Must we be Croesus to dwell in the woods or fields? From a certain distance a house that cost five hundred ducats yet looks odd seems merely to have an error of petty magnificence. A reed colonnade can have the appearance of marble. You must think almost exclusively of pleasing only the eyes. You may even fool them; but let it not be with some sort of theatrical decoration, painted planks, wooden pyramids, and so forth. Such tricks are unworthy, vulgar, and mean.

If the owner's wealth allows him to spend a million, he need only develop what I have just said on a larger scale. But let there be no half measures to conspicuous consumption.

He must not say, I have not done this or cut down that in order to save money. As soon as you decide in favor of magnificence, you must avoid all such questions as, Why is this here? Why not somewhere else? And so forth. A gardenist is well rewarded when, sitting unobserved beneath a great oak, he overhears visitors walking past say that his garden leaves nothing to be desired, that the soul is satisfied. Let me repeat: I am laboring only for this. After having been busied but uninspired in town, the soul must be able to take wing in the country.

If you are wealthy, I would want you to have an obelisk sixty feet high; three valuable statues each in the depths of its own grove; four handsome, beautifully carved vases; an antique bath; a few ancient bas-reliefs; a balustrade for a bridge thrown across one of your many streams—all in white marble. Leave no stone unturned in Paros or Carrara, and have one of your ships, on returning from the isles of Greece, bring back to you a few of the famous remains of learned antiquity, while another, sailing full speed for America, should there seek out the rarest birds and plants for you. Have a yacht transport whole fields of tulips from Delft and Haarlem. Vary the color of your lawn with gold and silver grass.

I would also want you to have magnificent galleys, flying bridges, sluices made from cut stone, bronze busts, a closed saloon

STATUE AND COLUMNS AT HADRIAN'S
VILLA (118–138)
Tibur, near Rome, Italy
Macduff Everton/CORBIS

STONE CARVING OF THE GIANT TIBER
IN VILLA LANTE GARDENS (designed in
1573 by Giacomo Barozzi da Vignola)
Viterbo, Tuscany, Italy
Craig Lovell/CORBIS

surrounded by a gallery of eight columns that support a dome of gilded copper or a lead terrace. And I would like all that to be spaced over great distances in your garden, where there should be an interplay between the water, the greensward, and the finest oaks…

I have statues in high regard, but those of marble are soon stained, those of stone split, those of plaster make a wretched appearance. We should be mediocre in nothing, but especially not in these matters. Unless you can afford to put one hundred thousand crowns' worth of statues in a garden of one hundred acres, it is better to say you do not like them. That is what I say myself, but I fib.

Statues ennoble and give life. It is well, too, to place a few busts in retired places, without pretension; still, they must seem to be a fancy or an act of friendship. If of love, so much the better. A statue dear to one's heart is better than the Horses of Victory or of the Sun; but it must be placed only in a temple of mystery, and mystery for mystery, it is better to keep the spirit of the beauty we adore. Invoke that spirit in your gardens; after satisfying your heart, it will inspire you even with taste; for we must love and be loved in order to create beauty. All the works of love are perfect. Poems and gardens that breathe of it cannot fail to charm.

But is it to frighten children that colossal white figures are set out symmetrically, ranged like a regiment? With money or an unprincipled Priapus (since we esteem morality more than ever now that it no longer exists) or else some Minerva with a burning lance, it might be possible to create a perfect garden, more suitable to another sort of regiment. Do not visitors recognize the harm done by the great volume of space that these statues occupy? Rather, let each white divinity stand relieved against dark masses of trees, displaying the talents of him who was so cruel as to cut into the block. And in place of those alignments of Roman emperors and Greek philosophers (with whose heads I long to play ball) let us place in leafy bowers a Venus amid myrtle, a Mars enclosed in laurel and pomegranates, and even a Vulcan protecting a forge

or some fire-breathing machine, if we are fortunate enough to be able to combine the agreeable with the useful.

How pained I am by these gods who are almost all poorly endowed, these emperors and philosophers always standing in the sun, always exposed to the stares of the curious! Let them be grouped together sometimes; let them lie down, and give them an air of victory, or beneficence, or gallantry!

JEAN-CLAUDE NICOLAS FORESTIER
TERRACES, PERRONS, *AND STEPS* (1920)

The French landscape architect J.-C. N. Forestier (1861–1930) trained with Jean-Charles-Adolphe Alphand, the director of public works in Paris. Forestier rose to the rank of commissioner of parks in Paris. His commissions included an arboretum at Vincennes, gardens of the Champ-de-Mars, projects in South America, and the Maria-Luisa Park in Seville. This selection is drawn from Forestier's 1920 book *Jardins,* which describes his ideas on walled gardens, trellises, hedges, and terraces. Helen Morgenthau Fox translated the work in 1928 as *Garden: A Notebook of Plans and Sketches.*

Laying out variations in the levels of the land artificially is sometimes necessary.

This requires the building of terraces and stairways, which add greatly to the beauty of the garden.

In England, in the last century, some landscape architects advised that terraces be avoided and replaced with gentle ramps and inclines, over which the walks were to descend as gradually as possible.

They wished to avoid steps for those who objected to them, in their leisurely walks, and for the gardeners, who have to wheel

LINDERHOF CASTLE AND GARDEN
(1870–79)
Bavaria, Germany
Archivo Iconografico, S.A./CORBIS

their carts and barrows over them. Besides, they thought the architectural structures would mar the rustic look of their country-side.

It does not seem possible to equal the beauty of terraces by any substitute. Wide, level, and restful, they command the distant views or the loveliness of the nearby garden. Repeated in successive levels, on the side of the hill, they beautify the slope and emphasize the lines of the garden with their light and shade. One terrace may be a distinct garden in itself.

Many interesting effects may be secured on stairways by various combinations of stone, brick, water, vines, vases, bushes, and flowers. It is easy to adapt the stairs to all the undulations of the garden. They provide places for statuary or a sun-dial, for pools and fountains.

Alongside of some stairways are gentle inclines of easy access for wheelbarrows, carriages, and carts. Those in the gardens of Versailles were made for the roll-chair of the king.

Stairs are a means for reaching different levels and take the place of walks that would be too steep. If there is too much of an incline in a walk, this may be corrected by inserting a few steps here and there. A continuous stairway without landings for rest not only is tiring but creates a very disagreeable impression in descending.

Formerly a landing place was considered necessary every twelve steps; to-day we think that, for the comfort of the walker, one is needed for every seven or at most nine steps.

Wide steps lessen the steepness of the gradient. The tread should not be uncomfortably wide, but should fit the natural gait. The riser should be neither too low nor too high, but in proportion to the width of the tread. This is accomplished by giving the steps such a height that the sum of twice that height added to the width will come to between 130 and 140 centimetres.

Stairways of turf are not recommended for general use, as they are not very solid or durable. Though the ones at Marly, which were considered masterpieces, have completely disappeared, others remain and some are now being constructed. For example,

those at the end of the parterres of the Château de Raba (near Bordeaux) leading to the pavilion of the Muses. These stairs are always green, and easy to make, if not to maintain.

Stairs are usually constructed of stone or brick. They may be against terrace walls or descend in imposing, vast parrons with straight steps as at the Tuileries and Versailles. At the Villa d'Este they form semicircles around the pools and fountains.

They may be designed in ovals or complete circles with concave or convex steps, and with a central landing uniting the oval or circular form.

Any of these forms may be used, the circular, with lines radiating toward or away from the centre, or the straight design, either simple or flanked with ornaments, such as vases, pyramids, and balls. Where stone is rare, stairs are often constructed of brick; its joints forming a pattern on its red surface, harmonize well with the greens of foliage and flowers. Sometimes they are topped with red, brightly painted or clay color flower pots.

After a short while, the white or grey joints are colored light green by the mosses, delicate grasses and wall plants, which seed themselves.

In England, they often try to produce this look of age on brick or stone stairs; instead of using a mortar, which would be too hard, they use a mixture of earth and seeds; they also plant perennials and all the thousands of wall plants here. Once a Campanula pyramidalis was found in the joint of a step; it seemed to have seeded itself between the bricks during the summer, and decidedly blocked the stairs with its very high stalks and blue flowers.

Is not this trying too hard and being too ingenious to attain the picturesque?

The dimensions of the steps have to be carefully studied. Formerly a good medium height for each of them was 15 centimetres; their depth 38 centimetres. These measurements are not used for inside stairs, and cannot be adhered to rigorously in all cases. They vary within certain limits, according to the difference in the level to be spanned, the number of steps, the form and number of landings and many other circumstances.

KARL FOERSTER
ROCKS AND ROCK GARDENS (1955)

Born in Berlin, Germany, Foerster (1874–1970) studied under the plant breeder and landscape architect Ludwig Winter. Foerster's goal at his nursery in Berlin and later at Potsdam was to simplify the vast assortment of available plant material, particularly perennials, and select a limited number for maximum beauty, resilience, and endurance. Together with the landscape architects Hermann Mattern and Herta Hammerbacher, he formed the working alliance Garten-gestaltung Bornim in 1927. Foerster wrote many important books about his garden theories. This excerpt comes from a translation by Kenneth A. Beckett of Foerster's writing on rock gardens published as *Rock Gardens Through the Years: An Illustrated Guide for Beginners and Experts* (1987).

What role do rocks play in the garden? What task is performed by the huge numbers of perennials, of mainly dwarf form, that we know as rock-garden plants?

Most natural rocks have the sculptural and artistic beauty, sometimes even the grandeur of the rocky mountain landscape and form a wonderful backdrop for the flowers of the rock garden.

The role of stone in the garden is and will remain an incredibly rich one. Stone offers a framework for the best in garden design, a practical means, while enhancing the plants themselves, of dealing with variations in height. It can serve both as a solid and attractive pathway beneath our feet and protection from the eroding and softening effects of time....

The natural rock garden should as far as possible form a natural outcrop amongst specially selected shrubs and plants. There are many ways of using stone in the form of paved paths or stepping stones—often a partly buried large rock will be sufficient—to lead into other parts of the garden and to link them with the actual rock garden. But such links are by no means essential. As I have already said, one must rid oneself of the mistaken idea that most alpine plants can only be used to full effect in some kind of rock garden. This misconception causes gardeners a lot of worry, robs them of their courage, and stifles their imagination. There is a whole host of small perennials which will be quite at home in a rock-free natural or formal garden. Of course there are a few species which really only look right amongst rocks. I hope these remarks may lead to greater freedom of thought on the subject of rock gardens.

Rock gardens for many years have been developing from their small, timid beginnings. They began with small stalactite gardens where alpine plants were grown in carefully prepared soils and slowly spread beyond the alpines with their short spring flowering time. Today one can speak of a universal art of rock gardening extending throughout the course of the whole year.

Today we use small perennials which grow wild in all parts of the world so that there is scarcely a month of the year when the garden need be empty of blossom. Added to these are the specially cultivated varieties or cultivars.

From woods and mountains, from the edges of fields, from steppes, beaches, heaths, dunes, and moors, from nurseries, plantations, and botanical gardens come hosts of plants which, over the years, will grow well in our gardens without any trouble and without any time-consuming preparation of the soil. Many of them are only suitable for wild gardens, a good number are more suited to the formal rock or water garden. There are of course others which, correctly planted, will suit both the formal and the natural garden and which for this very reason are extremely popular....

PREPARING THE SOIL FOR ROCK GARDENS

The preparation of soil for rock gardens is essentially the same as for flower-beds, differing only in that if the soil is very water retentive it should be placed over a layer of gravel, pebbles, or rubble to assist drainage. With a light, very dry soil the opposite approach is necessary, with a layer of loam preventing water from draining away too quickly. This need not be friable loam; ordinary loam will serve the same purpose equally well. Heavy soils can be made lighter before planting by adding sand, peat compost, or manure. Light soils will bind better if you add friable loam and old manure, old peat, and fairly heavy compost or old root-free pasture soil.

CHOICE AND POSITIONING OF ROCKS

Avoid dull-coloured rocks where at all possible, since these can look really miserable, especially in wet weather, whereas bright slabs of stone will give the opposite effect in sunny areas, such as seating areas or patios—rather like the choice of a white tablecloth for meals. The most common mistake of all is to choose rocks that are too small; it is far better to use fewer, larger, more impressive rocks, the same being true of dressed slabs of stone.

Any natural stone or rock has its own rules which determine the best position for it in the rock garden, each possessing inbuilt advantages and disadvantages for any individual site. Rocks do not always have to be placed flat, half-covered in soil. You can stand the occasional rock on end and plant around it accordingly, taking care to avoid the danger of an unattractive spiky effect. Rocks placed too low to the ground will soon be overgrown by the plants.

There are two essential guidelines to be kept in mind: rocks at higher elevations should project higher from the soil, while rocks in hollows and crannies should be placed flatter. They should also be grouped in such a way as to avoid any sloping areas of soil. This is done by making terraces of earth supported by rocks or stone walls and incorporating pockets where plants can be positioned to hang down over the wall. The area at the base of the wall is ideal for plants that need extra protection and moisture.

I have often found the evening to be the best time for planning and positioning rocks and earth to the fullest effect.

An extremely useful feature is the inclusion of stepping stones or natural stone steps which allow comfortable access to any part of the rock garden without having to stand on the soil. Alternatively you may prefer a continuous path climbing up through the garden and forking around any steep elevation. On occasions I have used a path of this kind to great effect, with the earth above and below supported with lumps of granite, and paved quite simply with smaller pieces of stone. It only needs a little imagination to create a highly pleasing impression. The pleasure to be obtained from imitating wild natural features on a small scale and from incorporating miniaturized works of man, such as sunken roads or a mountain pass, is so great in itself that in laying out the rocks and earth one tends to overlook the next and finest stage— that of planting. This is a task which reveals to the full our dormant knowledge of stone and moss, mountain and valley, wild plants and natural forms. Proportion is everything and once you have mastered this you have established a wonderful bridge between the small-scale and the large. Few other areas of garden design can bring us so closely in touch with the earth's varying surfaces, and over the years all the different areas of the rock garden develop in their attractiveness as they become more richly covered with vegetation. . . .

In the case of stones and rocks surrounding pools and ponds one often finds large, tall stones projecting far into the water while flatter stones are restricted to the banks. Here we should take a lesson from our fellow-gardeners in the East, where the experience of many centuries should not be overlooked.

FLETCHER STEELE
MOST GARDEN SEATS ARE BAD (1964)

The designer of more than seven hundred gardens, Steele (1885–1971) is widely regarded as a key figure in the transition from Beaux Arts formalism to modern American landscape design. In 1907, at the age of twenty-two, Steele studied briefly at the new Graduate School of Landscape Architecture at Harvard University and then went to work with Warren Manning, a former assistant to Frederick Law Olmsted. After completing a four-month tour of European gardens, he opened his own practice. His best-known design is the Blue Steps at Naumkeag. This passage from his book *Gardens and People* presents his ideas on garden seating.

MOST GARDEN SEATS ARE BAD

There are two ways of sitting in gardens. One is to perch, thus relieving the legs a moment; the other is to lounge. A hard, transitory perch is usually all that is proffered by the gardener.

Making a seat by placing a stone slab on two other rocks used for legs must have been one of the less imaginative inventions of the Neolithic Age. But only the elegant demands of the Mauve Decade could have introduced it to America, made of sawed white marble, bedaubed with insipid carving.

Such a thing is worse than no perch at all. In form, color, and decorative treatment it is out of harmony with our domestic environment, for it is the bastard of palaces and is happy only when associating with statues and urns. Repulsive to touch, it is either too hot or too cold. The human form will not fit its harsh, flat surface, squirm as one will. Its height never suits and its location seems cunningly chosen to exhibit one's wriggling to the world. Fancy stone benches in most gardens are placed at the ends of walks or opposite verandahs where the sitter's wretchedness is the cynosure of all observers.

Sometimes, to be sure, they are tucked away to exploit a vista or patronize a mountain. Then they demand that the visitor compliment the view. They arouse mental discomfort, for it is a nuisance to know that the hostess expects one to say: "How sweet the moonlight sleeps upon this bank," when all one really wants is to get up and go home.

From every angle, marble slabs are a mistake. Along with starched collars and derby hats, they belong to the order of vestigial nuisances. Unfortunately while those same uncomfortable habiliments were in fashion, marble slabs became the standard definition of a proper garden bench, so their feeble imitations in concrete are still widely seen and avoided.

After the fin de siècle thirst for elegance was exhausted, however, common sense emerged in the American garden and settled down on a wooden bench—the counterpart of the indoor sofa, with perishable upholstery omitted. It is bearable when shaped to fit the human frame and if its back is tipped to accommodate the recline sought by our backs when sitting down. When it is properly designed, the sitter forgets it, and no more can be asked of any apparatus.

Wood is a natural building material for Americans to use. It maintains a comfortable temperature under most conditions. And while the man from Mars might not believe it, no garden law requires us to paint wooden benches white.

SIT WHERE YOU LIKE

Aunt Dolly used to have a little French chair taken out to the middle of her big drawing room and there she would sit, far from neighbor, lamp, or table. To callers it looked like some strange mistake, but she liked it. She was used to it. Most people get the habit of using some particular chair indoors, which comes to be recognized as theirs. They feel at home in it. Not until they insist on having their own chair in its fixed place in the garden can we be sure that living out of doors in America is more than a pastime of our decade, like vitamin hunting.

BENCH IN MOTTISFONT ABBEY (13th
century) and ROSE GARDEN (designed in
1972 by Graham Stuart Thomas)
Hampshire, England
Clay Perry/CORBIS

It is hard to tell ahead where the favored place will be for sitting in the garden, just as it is futile to attempt to force people to go here or there. They are like horses led to water when it comes to settling down; they will or they won't. Beauty of view, careful furnishing, even food and drink will not hold them long. The favorite location is more often found by chance. A breeze is discovered in some odd corner. The dog stops there to drink at a pool, and a wall keeps the sun off one's book. A chair is brought out; it is pleasant. The gardener returns the next day and the next habit forms. After a week no other spot occurs to mind. More chairs and tables appear, and the family settles down.

The problem of the designer is to provide cozy places ready to be discovered, even though it may be years before they are much used. Whether people know it or not when they build, they will want sunny nooks in spring and autumn; a refuge in shade for summer days; places that get the breeze and places out of the wind. There must be retreats for the solitary and plenty of rooms for crowds, both in the open and under cover.

It is impossible to foretell the program of any family far in advance. They build a house for summer use and later occupy it the year round. They start with no thought but tennis, then get arthritis and do considerable sitting. Or they hate games, and along comes a flock of children who must play. Where will they sit to watch the youngsters?

Such developments are not exceptional. They are among the hundred legitimate reasons why people change their minds after they have lived a few years in a garden. What pulls one member of the family will drive another away; yet all must be satisfied. So the landscape architect asks:

"Do you like to hear the telephone bell? Where will the baby-carriage go? Do you want to keep an eye on the weeds or get out of their way? Where will you put things down? Do you like supper al fresco? And where will you sit to be with the stars?"

SITTING IN DISCOMFORT

Most of the time man envies his dog, though not always. When he explores an unfamiliar drawing room, his soul becomes at one with that of an uncertain canine. Mentally he turns around and round in search of a spot to curl up. If a place next to a strange hostess is indicated, then he knows how it feels to be told to lie down.

In most of our gardens, conditions are even worse. But few seats are provided and they are glued down. The only endurable fixed seating for an American is a reservation in a train or a theater from which all but the buyer can be kept at bay. In a garden nobody wants to be told where to sit. Yet an immovable bench does just that by saying: "Here or not at all."

LIU DUNZHEN
CHINESE GARDEN BUILDINGS (1936)

An architect and a scholar, Liu (1896–1968) studied architecture and engineering at Tokyo School of Higher Education and later taught in the Department of Architecture of the Technology Institute of Nanjing University. He made fundamental contributions to the study of historical Chinese architecture and garden design. In 1993 McGraw-Hill published the translation by Chen Lixian of Liu's book *Chinese Classical Gardens of Suzhou*, from which this passage is taken.

In the classical gardens in Suzhou, buildings are put up to serve the dual functions of habitation and appreciation. Together with hillocks, pools, flowers, and trees, they contribute to the composite garden scenery. In certain scenic areas, they sometimes constitute major scenic themes. Hillocks and pools are the main elements in classical gardens, but their scenic beauty is usually viewed from the inside of buildings. Buildings, therefore, are not only places for rest but also observation posts for scenic appreciation. The different

types of buildings and their relation to each other to a great extent depend on the life styles of the garden owners, and the number of buildings in proportion to other elements in the gardens. These factors have become an outstanding feature in garden construction in China.

In small and medium-size gardens, the total space occupied by buildings would take up 30 percent of the total garden space, as in the cases of Hu Yuan (Kettle Garden), Chang Yuan (Carefree Garden), and Yongcui Shanzhuang (Mountain Villa of Embracing Emerald). In most of the larger gardens, all the buildings together would occupy no more than 15 percent of the entire garden space, as in the cases of Canglang Ting (Surging-Wave-Pavilion Garden), Liu Yuan (Lingering Here Garden), and Shizilin (The Forest of Lions Garden). Because of this, the architectural design of buildings and their artistic arrangement in relation to each other are of special importance in planning each garden as a whole.

The buildings in the classical gardens in Suzhou not only are differently shaped and located, but also vary as to type, decoration, and adaptation to the surroundings. The basic types of buildings designed for gardens usually include:

Halls (*Ting* or *Tang*)

Lounges surrounded by windows (*Xuan*)

Guest houses (*Guan*)

Two- or three-story buildings (*Lou*)

Two-story pavilions (*Ge*)

Waterside pavilions (*Xie*)

Landboats (*Fang*)

Pavilions (*Ting*)

Corridors or covered ways (*Lang*)

…The shape and arrangement of buildings in the gardens are usually designed to make these edifices appear light and delicate, small and lovely, and full of variety. Yet there are no rigid conventions about their form. In Chinese architecture, ordinary living quarters usually require three to five rooms, but for the buildings in gardens, one room or even half a room should suffice, as long as it is deemed suitable and proper. Square wooden blocks to support beams and girders are rarely used, and buildings generally are not fitted with carvings of phoenixes or gold leaves. Efforts are made to attain simplicity and good taste.

In the treatment of space in garden buildings, openness and good air circulation are generally the aim. This applies to the free arrangement of courtyards and compounds and to such devices as open corridors, cave openings, open windows, tracery windows, transparent screens, and paper or wooden partitions for rooms. The more skillfully designed Suzhou gardens achieve and maintain both desirable separation of space, and continuity of space between buildings, and between buildings and other scenic objects. … This sense of free space gives the observer a feeling of infinite depth in the scenery.

Wide stretches of whitewashed walls matched with black-grey tile roofs and chestnut-brown pillars, railings, and overhanging ornaments, generally are the keynote colors for the garden buildings. The interior fittings usually are light brown with natural wood graining. With the white walls as their foil, the grey door and window frames made of water-polished bricks appear simple, elegant, and bright. The white walls not only serve as foils for flowers and trees but, more interestingly, are screens of innumerable and ever-changing scenes when the sun hits the ensemble from different directions and in varying intensity.

Buildings also play their roles in the creation of garden scenery. They may bring about a diversity of contrapositional and borrowed scenes as well as changes in and combinations of scenic objects.

Various devices are employed to use buildings as elements in contrapositional scenery. For instance, Yuanxiang Tang (Distant-Fragrance Hall) in Zhuozheng Yuan (The Humble Administrator's Garden) faces Xuexiangyunwei Ting (The Pavilion of Fragrant-Snow-and-Colorful Clouds), directly to the north, and faces Xiuyi Ting (The Embroidered-Silk Pavilion) to the east. From

Xuexiangyunwei Ting (The Pavilion of Fragrant-Snow-and-Colorful Clouds) one may look southward and enjoy a panoramic scene of Yuanxiang Tang (Distant-Fragrance Hall) and Yiyu Xuan (Leaning-on-Jade Hall) in the distance. This technique of interweaving and merging one entity with another is an excellent device in the art of classical gardens in Suzhou.

There are different ways for buildings to "borrow" scenery:

Borrowing from afar
Borrowing from adjacent objects
Borrowing from scenery underneath
Borrowing in different seasons.

. . .Synthesizing buildings, hillocks, pools, flowers, and trees into an organic whole is critically important in the art of gardening. When a pavilion or two-story pavilion is built atop a hillock, it should be relatively small and delicately shaped. With trees and plants as a foil, it would look natural and lively. Moreover, due to its high elevation, it can always serve as an important spot for observing scenery, whether one gazes downward at the scenery inside the garden or looks afar at the scenic objects beyond the garden limits. . .

To attain harmony with the water surface, a building beside a pool usually is spacious and low. Fitted with white walls and tracery windows, and surrounded by one or two tall trees, the building's inverted image is vividly reflected in the water. . . .

Buildings in gardens are also designed to match the flowers and trees. Not only can flowers and trees form scenery in a small courtyard, but their shapes and locations can play an important part in a building's overall design. There are many examples of buildings planned to match a delightful garden scenery or flowers and trees, especially trees having many long years' growth. Including old trees in garden planning is traditional.

THOMAS D. CHURCH
HARD SURFACES (1955)

Pioneer of the California Style, Church (1902–1978) utilized in his garden designs asymmetrical plans, raised beds, seat walls, paving, and broad timber decks. His best-known commission, the El Novillero garden at Sonoma, California (1947–49), has become an icon of twentieth-century landscape architecture. Church described his view of garden design in his first book, *Gardens Are for People*, from which the following text is excerpted.

PAVING

Paving—something hard and convenient under foot—has been man's concern ever since he came down out of the trees.

Paving to keep his feet dry—paving to pull his chariots over—paving to accommodate mobs of people—paving to walk on in a garden.

The cobblestones of Europe represent centuries of labor by men determined to pull themselves out of the mud of the Middle Ages. Their patterns, from the bold cobblestones of the Paris streets to the pebble mosaics of Spain, have been an inspiration to all garden designers.

Paving must be sympathetic with the grass, trees, and flowers upon whose domain it has encroached and must set them off to their best advantage. They will in turn enhance the paving by softening its outlines and casting shadows across it.

Paving leaves less area for planting, and since there are fewer plants, they should be selected with more care and cared for with more enthusiasm.

If complicated paving patterns and colors are introduced into an already exciting composition, the resulting confusion, rivaling Joseph's coat, may be a constant irritation.

It may be the role of paving to remain calm, to be the common denominator and a foil for the excitement created by fences, steps,

following spread:
ROBERTO BURLE MARX HOME AND
GARDEN (1949–94)
Rio de Janeiro, Brazil
Farrell Grehan/CORBIS

PORCH
Royalty Free/CORBIS

grass forms, brilliant flower combinations, foliage textures, and distant views…

Paving cannot substitute for the expanse of open lawn on a large property, but the relative proportion of paving to grass can often be increased with good results. In hot or subtropical climates, large paved areas will radiate too much heat unless shaded; but for the average house on a small lot the amount of paving can be greatly increased without robbing us of the fundamental pleasures of a garden.

STEPS IN DESIGN

When a broad flight of steps can also retain a change in grade, the question of whether it should be curved or straight may come up.

There is no rule to determine this other than the overall garden design. It's a matter of creating contrast in the composition. A curve seems more so if it has contrast to the strength of a straight line. The interplay of curving and linear forms adds zest to the pattern. It is the prerogative of the designer to decide where the emphasis should be placed.

Once the question of design is settled, there are practical precedents as to use of materials. Brick or stone, being modular, is easy for building curved flights. A straight run may be of brick, stone, concrete, or wood. The choice again reverts back to the need for using materials harmonious with each other, with the architecture, and with the mood of the garden.

Steps can be much more than a connection between two levels. They can have strength and crispness of line. They can steady the composition, point the direction, and ornament the scene.

They may be used to express the mood and tempo of the garden. They can put you in a leisurely mood, make you hurry, or arouse your curiosity.

Use them with care and forethought.

MOWING STRIPS

Narrow bands of hard paving, level with and at the edges of a lawn, provide a track for one wheel of the mower, minimize hand trimming, and keep the grass shape intact and free from encroaching plants. They provide a decorative, permanent border and strengthen the garden pattern where a crisp, neat line is desired.

THE TERRACE MAY BE FLOWING OR FORMAL IN OUTLINE

Today's terrace is no longer thought of as a small rectangle directly off the living room; it may go around the house or wander over a large portion of the property.

It may reach out some distance and at seemingly odd and unpredictable angles, seeking a tree for shade, securing a vantage point for a view, or avoiding rough topography.

It can be generous in extent or intimate in feeling; not so big that it looks like a corporation yard nor so small that one is pushed into the flower beds. It can encompass grass plots, flower beds, potted plants, arbors, sun platforms, windscreens, sand for the children, and a drinking fountain for the dog.

It should have comfortable furniture with convenient storage and easy access to the living room and kitchen. The terrace should do all these things, as well as put some people in the sun, some in the shade, and others out of a draft.

The problems of design, orientation, and materials vary enormously in different parts of the country. In some sections the garden and terrace may be 90 percent paved and be a logical solution. In others the lawn may be the terrace.

The problem may be protection from wind in San Francisco or reaching out for a breeze in St. Louis. The terrace may be designed largely for use at night in Texas or require screening in the mosquito belt. It may need shade most of the time or sun most of the time (the terrace large enough for both is ideal.)

A TERRACE MAY BE AWAY FROM THE HOUSE

When possible, a part of the terrace should be far enough away so that the view back to the house is pleasant. The areas around it compose best only from a certain distance. If your terrace is small

and you sit with your back to your own house, you may look only at your neighbor's.

If your neighbor's house is better looking than yours, don't read any farther.

Try walking around your house. In some places you will walk fast, but sooner or later you will reach a spot where you feel in repose. It may be the lines of the house or the position of trees, or you may never know why; but it could be the place for your terrace.

DECKS

The wooden balconies of eighteenth-century European design were forerunners, and the spacious front porches and verandas of English and American architecture during the Victorian era were ancestors. But porches have become detached from houses and wander freely around the property—sometimes jutting out over it, providing the illusion of level spaciousness on a sloping hillside lot. These wandering porches, which, in one form or another, have been with us for a long time, are now what we call decks.

As the deck becomes more and more important to us for both aesthetic and practical reasons, we are more and more aware of its varied uses; the dominant line of a fill may be broken and consequently softened, the shade of a tree may be welcomed in a sitting area, the last hour of sun may be relished; the house may be viewed from a certain distance so that it is seen in the full round instead of in profile.

For the home owner on a budget—and name one that isn't— a deck can serve as the ideal compromise, using natural materials in an outdoor setting but retaining the low-maintenance attractions of a practical space paved in concrete.

The creation of flat terraces around trees already growing on slopes is inexcusable. When the normal breathing and drainage are disturbed, trees become sickly and die, and sooner or later the sitting area is no longer under an inviting canopy of green. Drainage and aeration may prevent such a calamity, but why take a chance when decks offer a safe alternative?

Decks are at home among the tree trunks, and people are happy when they are among the trees....

GARRETT ECKBO
SHELTER ELEMENTS (1950)

An American landscape architect, Eckbo (1910–2000) studied landscape architecture at University of California, Berkeley, and Harvard University, where he developed friendships with Dan Kiley and James Rose. In 1938 Eckbo returned to California and worked briefly for Thomas Church. He joined forces with Royston and Williams and designed hundreds of American gardens. Eckbo became chairman of the Berkeley Department of Landscape Architecture in 1963. Founded in 1964, The EDAW practice (Eckbo Dean Austin and Williams) undertook a wide range of large-scale landscape architecture projects. This passage originally appeared in Eckbo's first book, *Landscape for Living*. It showed a fresh new "California" approach to the modern garden.

SHELTER

We normally think of the garden as unroofed living space, open to the sky, by contrast with the complete enclosure of the house. This is the main reason for the emphasis on the quality of the side enclosure.

We have found, however, that there is no sharp break necessary between living inside the house and living outside. The two tend to overlap in the area immediately around the house. Here we are apt to find a need for an extension of the shelter function of the house roof. This will give partial or complete overhead protection to the primary outdoor living spaces, and also help to protect the house from climatic extremes. This is important in the control of such elemental forces as sun, rain, wind, snow, heat, glare, dust, noise, insects. Such supplementary shelter may be supplied by structures, vines on structures, or trees.

Shelter elements are at the same scale and have the same importance in the landscape as houses. If structures, they supplement the house, extending it into the garden, making it feel bigger, easing and strengthening the connection with the garden. Trees complement the house, balancing it with landscape elements of the same importance, framing it and settling it down on the land, and at neighborhood scale establishing a natural structural pattern which can integrate a collection of miscellaneous houses and unify the neighborhood landscape.

These shelter elements are of relatively greater architectural importance in the garden scheme than surfacing, which is primarily a ground pattern, or enclosure, which is generally at direct human scale, on the eye level rather than above it. Garden shelter may be provided with the original house, as porch, lanai, lath, or arbor extensions. Or it may be added when the garden is designed, either joined directly to the house or as an independent structure; or it may consist of trees in the garden. . . .

WEATHER CONTROL

Sun, heat, and glare are usually best controlled by filtering through *open patterns* such as vegetation, lath, treillage, or netting, or through *translucent materials* such as canvas, plastics, or glass. The former give greater control, or allow greater reduction in quantity of sun, than most of the latter. The open pattern controls also allow greater circulation of air, which is usually an essential partner in the reduction of sun, heat, and glare.

Translucent materials are useful for light shade where summers are mild, and they do have the virtue of diffusing light evenly. The dappled light of the open pattern materials is sometimes hard on the eyes. The primary usefulness of the translucent materials is for shedding precipitation (rain and dew) without losing much light. They provide outdoor skylights and give warm shade, useful in cool, bright weather.

Rain, Snow, and Wind Control. Protection from rain and snow requires, of course, a solid and leakproof roof equal to that on the house. The solid shade of such a roof may be very welcome in hot weather, if provided by a structure of open sides which allow breezes to blow through. In cool regions where we want to escape from the wind or protect ourselves from it, both solid and open shelters will function with enclosure structures to increase the windbreak area and extend the quiet zone produced by it. The function of slanting shelters in diverting wind should not be overlooked. . . .

SHELTER DETAILS

The detailed design of shelter elements is as variable as the detailed design of houses and their planting arrangements. Structural shelter, since it is supplementary to the house, must partake in some manner of the character of the house in order to be harmonious with it. This does not mean that, if we happen to have a Georgian or Colonial house, we must make a frenzied search of the history books to find "appropriate" historical shelter forms to copy. It does mean that we must examine the house as a physical reality of specific materials and details.

These can be reflected in a specific and realistic way in the design of additional shelter elements, without being either "modern" or "traditional." Bearing in mind the great potential variability in the design of shelter elements stemming from current combinations of ingenuity, imagination, new materials, old forms, and new ways of looking at old problems, we can classify the possibilities into generalized types of structures.

Wood Structures. Structural shelters may be open, ranging from simple post-and-beam pergolas and arbors to the 50 per cent or more enclosure of lath houses and more elaborate treillage structures. These have many uses, including the extension of houses into their gardens, the connection of houses with other structures, the support of climbing roses and other flowering vines, the provision of filtered light for shade-loving plants and people. These are usually thought of as landscape structures: posts may be set in the ground for simple bracing, and there is a general tendency to make them somewhat too careless, rustic, or flimsy. Even with the simplest arbor there is no substitute for the use of members of adequate size for the loads and spans they must carry; for vertical posts set solidly in the ground or on footings; for horizontal or accurately sloped beams; for proper, strong, clean connections between members; and for proper finish with paint or stain.

Metal Structures. Traditionally the material for these open garden structures has been wood, but metal, in all its many structural forms, has great possibilities for frames which are lighter and stronger than wood.

The techniques are primarily those of plumbing and welding, and these are generally available. The parts are usually best made up completely in the shop, which means that they must be more carefully designed beforehand. Metal is not so flexible as wood on the job. Iron and steel must be finished very carefully with paint or galvanizing to avoid rusting. Rust-proof aluminum is now generally available.

Frameworks of both wood and metal must be designed both for their own appearance, and for the lath, siding, plywood, or other panel material, or glass, plastic, wire screen, or fiber netting, which may be added to them. Metal will cost more than wood, therefore is apt to be used only where extra strength or thinner members are worth the extra cost. Open shelter structures are most flexible and open to imaginative development. These overhead patterns are both practical and esthetic in the garden.

Extending House Structure. Structural shelters may be closed either at top only, with solid roofs for complete shelter, or at some or all sides as well, to provide garden rooms, barbecue rooms, play and rumpus rooms, tea houses, screened porches, pavilions, casinos, cabanas, bathhouse-dressing rooms, work and storage spaces, and the like. With such structures we begin to do serious building comparable to the house. The quality of construction should be at least as good as that in the house; the same building code will apply to both. Some of these elements may be portions of the house opening to the garden, some of them may be built independently in the garden....

Vines and Structures. Planted shelter is of two kinds: vines on open structures, and trees. Vines are widely misunderstood and misused plants. They provide more show and interest from less ground space, and are more flexible in tight spaces, than any other plant forms. However, these possibilities can be realized only by careful study of the characteristics of the various kinds of vines...

Vines on open structures are intermediate in usefulness between structural shelters and trees. You get partial shelter sooner than with trees of economical size. The cost is less than that of more complete structural shelter, but more than that of ordinary trees. With deciduous vines you may get a more flexible shelter, if their dormant period coincides with the season in which you do not need shade. Old favorites, such as grapes, honeysuckle, wistaria, or climbing roses may be able to play a structural role in your garden. This is the most direct and balanced combination of the precision and order of good construction and the wayward charm of vegetation.

On the other hand, vines are very apt to be messy in tight spots, to build up mounds of dead wood which are very difficult to clear out, to rot, distort, or undermine construction, cause leaks in the roof, and so on. This is the reason for emphasizing the need for very careful study before a specific vine is planted on a specific structure.

TREES

...Definition of tree forms as those spreading foliage over our heads is a landscape classification, based on the function of plants in shaping our living spaces. Shrubs give enclosure at the *sides* of garden or park spaces, to any height, and with any degree of thickness or thinness. Trees give additional enclosure, or shelter, *overhead.*

As Fitch says:

> The scientific use of . . . trees will accomplish any or all of the
> following:
> Deflect, absorb and reduce the heat radiation . . .
> Reduce the free air temperatures . . .
> Filter the atmosphere . . .
> Reduce intensities and glare . . .
> Increase visual privacy . . .
> Reduce the transmission of airborne sound . . . .

Deciduous trees have a specific functional value, in that they provide shade in the summer when it is needed, and let in the sun
in winter when it is needed. This simple fact makes deciduous
trees (sycamores, elms, maples) the most relevant large trees for
use anywhere close to buildings, or over garden spaces which
are to receive fairly intensive use. In the cooler northern half of
the country, the space beneath the big evergreen trees, cool and
breezy in the hot summer, becomes dank and forbidding during
cold and wet winter months.

9

WATER

For fountains, they are a great beauty and refreshment; but pools mar all, and make the garden unwholesome, and full of flies and frogs. Fountains I intend to be of two natures: the one that sprinkleth or spouteth water; the other a fair receipt of water, of some thirty or forty foot square, but without fish, or slime, or mud. For the first, the ornaments of gilt, or of marble, which are in use, do well: but the main matter is to convey the water, as it never stay, either in the bowls or in the cistern; that the water be never by rest discoloured, green or red or the like; or gather any mossiness or putrefaction. Besides that, it is to be cleansed every day by the hand.

Francis Bacon (1561–1626), English philosopher, essayist, jurist, and statesman

At the beginning of this year (329/940), al-Nasir finished the construction of the extraordinary man-made aqueduct that brought fresh water from the mountains to the Qasr al-Naura on the west side of Cordoba. Water flowed through fabricated channels on a fantastic arrangement of connecting arches, emptying into a large pool at the edge of which was a lion enormous in size, unique in design, and fearful in appearance.... It was plated with gold and its eyes were two brilliantly sparking jewels, Water entered through the rear of the lion and was spewed into the pool. It was dazzling to behold in its splendor and magnificence and its copious outpouring, and the palace's entire range of gardens were irrigated by its juices which flowed over the grounds and surrounding area.

al-Maqqari (c. 1591–1632), Arabic historian

What a watercourse! Gem of the river, ornament of the garden. No, I am mistaken: it is the soul of the garden's body.

Kalim of Kashan (died 1651), Persian poet laureate of Shahjahan

These Gliding Streams refrigerate the Air in a Summer evening, and render their banks so pleasant, that they become resistless Charms to your Senses, by the murmuring Noise, the Undulation of the Water, the verdant Banks and Shades over them, the Sporting Fish confin'd within your own limits, the beautiful Swans, and by the pleasant notes of singing Birds, that delight in Groves on the Banks of such Rivulets.

John Woolridge (Worlidge) (1669–1698), English garden writer

ATTRIBUTED TO TACHIBANA NO TOSHITSUNA
PONDS, ISLANDS, AND STREAMS (c. 1050)

Scholars have attributed the text of the classic Japanese garden treatise *Sakuteiki* to Tachibana no Toshitsuna (1028–1094). One of the Four Great Families during the Heian period, the Tachibana family enjoyed grand palaces and gardens. Toshitsuna gained knowledge of garden design through his exposure to these properties and headed a government office responsible for construction and repair of imperial estates. This excerpt is taken from a translation by Jiro Takei and Marc P. Keane.

PONDS AND ISLANDS

Since it is not possible to fill ponds with water before they are built, prior to the construction of a pond and its islands, a Water Level must be set up. The surface of a pond should be twelve to fifteen centimeters beneath the bottom edge of the veranda of the Fishing Pavilion. Stakes should be placed where a pond will be built and marked with this height. In this way one can determine exactly how much a given stone will be covered with water and how much will be exposed. The soil base underneath stones set in a pond must be reinforced with Foundation Stones. If this is done, even though many years might pass, the stones will not collapse and, moreover, even if the pond is drained of water, the stones will look as if they are well set.

If an island in the pond is constructed to the exact shape that it is planned to be and then lined with stones along its edges, the stones will not hold when the pond is filled with water. It is better to dig out the shape of the pond in a more general way and then after setting stones on the island edge, gradually determine the shape of the islands.

The waters of the pond and Garden Streams should flow out of the garden to the southwest, because the waters of the Blue Dragon should be made to flow in the direction of the White Tiger. A horizontal stone should be set at the outflow of the pond, its top set at twelve to fifteen centimeters below the bottom side of the Fishing Pavilion's veranda. When the pond is completely filled with water, the excess will flow out over this stone, thereby establishing the water level in the pond.

GARDEN STREAMS

First, the direction of the stream source must be determined. According to the scriptures the proper route for water to flow is from east to south and then toward the west. Flowing from west to east is considered a reverse flow, thus a flow from east to west is standard practice. In addition, bringing water out from the east, causing it to flow under the residence halls, and then sending it off to the southwest is considered the most felicitous. This is because the waters from the Blue Dragon will wash all manner of evil off to the Great Path of the White Tiger. The master of a household who does this will avoid sickness and tumors, be of sound health, and lead a long and happy life.

When one is trying to select a site with correct geomantic conditions, remember that the place on the left side where water runs from is called the Land of the Blue Dragon. Similarly, water should run from the east of the Main Hall or outer buildings, then turn south and finally flow out to the west. In the case of water that flows from the north, the stream should first be brought around to the east and then caused to flow to the southwest.

According to scriptures, the inner curve of the Garden Stream is considered to be the belly of the dragon, and it is considered felicitous to build one's home there. Conversely, the outside of the curve—the dragon's back—is considered to be unlucky. There is also a theory of sending water from north to south because north is the Water direction while south is that of Fire. In other words one should send *Yin* in the direction of *Yang,* and thus by facing the two forces against each other, create a state of harmony. Considered in this way, the notion of sending water from north to south is not without merit indeed. . . .

It has been said that when making a garden, deep spiritual concentration is required. Earth is lord, water servant. If earth permits it, water will flow, but if earth prevents it, it will not. Seen another way, mountain is lord and water the servant, while stones are the lord's counselors. Water thus flows in accordance with the nature of the mountain. However, if the mountain is weak, it will be destroyed by water without fail, like a servant opposing a lord. The mountain is weak where there are no stones to lend it support, just as the lord is weak when he lacks supporters. Therefore, the mountain is complete when it contains stones, even as the lord rules by the support of his servants. That is why stones are imperative when making a garden.

With regard to the slope of a waterway and the manner in which water will be made to flow, a fall of nine millimeters over thirty centimeters, nine centimeters over three meters, or ninety centimeters over thirty meters will make for a murmuring stream that flows without stopping. At the end of such a stream, where the land turns flat, the water will be pushed by the force of the incoming stream above it and continue to flow forward. Since the slope of the stream is difficult to perceive while it is under construction, place a length of bamboo that has been split in half lengthways on the ground and fill it with water in order to determine the slope of the ground. Building a home without having performed these studies is the act of an unrefined man. In the case of property that has a natural water source in a high place there is little need to consider such matters, making such places ideal for garden building.

No matter which direction the source of the water is in, a stream should not be made to appear contrived, but rather it should flow this way and that, from the edge of one hill to the edge of another. Dig the water channel in such a way as to create a stream that flows in a captivating manner.

Garden Streams that enter Southern Courts flow most com-

monly out from under the Breezeway then turn to the west. Similarly, streams are often constructed in order to flow from beneath the Northern Annex Hall, between the Twin Halls, then under the Breezeway before passing in front of the Middle Gate and entering the pond.

Regarding stones in the Garden Stream stones should not all be set in a similar manner and crammed together. The same can be said for stones placed in a stream where it flows out from under the Breezeway, turns about the bluff of a hill, enters the pond, or flows back upon itself sharply. In any of these places, first set one stone. Any other stones set there, without regard to their number, should be set according to the request of this first stone.

The first place to set a stone in the Garden Stream is where the flow bends sharply. In nature, water bends because there is a stone in the way that the stream cannot destroy. Where the water flows out of a bend, it flows with great force. As it runs diagonally, consider where the water would strike an obstacle most powerfully, and at that point set a Turning Stone. The same should follow for stones set downstream as well. Other stones should be set without affectation or pretense in the places that require them. In most cases, if too many stones are set at the point where a stream curves, although it may appear acceptable when seen up close, from a distance it simply appears as if there are too many stones. It is uncommon to see these stones up close, so preference should be given to how they are seen from a distance.

The types of stones to set in a Garden Stream are Bottom Stones, Water-Splitting Stones, Foundation Stones, Crosswise Stones, and Spillway Stones. All of these must be set deeply into the riverbed. Crosswise Stones are those that are set diagonally in the water. They should be long, and somewhat rounded. It is most attractive when water flows around both ends of the stone and more so if the water is caused to fall evenly over the whole surface of the stone.

The style of Garden Stream called Valley Stream is one where the water runs full force from between the narrow confines of two hills. Where water flows over stones in the stream, if it falls off to the left side of stone, then next it should be made to fall to the right. The flow of water should alternate this way and that, left and right, splashing white froth as it goes. Where the stream widens, there should be a Middle Stone that is somewhat tall, and, on both sides of that, Crosswise Stones should be placed, forcing the stream to flow quickly about the upright Middle Stone. If another stone is placed in the midst of this accelerated stream, then the water will foam white as it passes over it, making for a most pleasing site. . . .

ATTRIBUTED TO ZOEN
EXCAVATING THE POND (1466)

The two oldest extant Japanese garden manuals to have been translated into English are *Sakuteiki* **(Notes on Garden Making, c. 1050) and** *Senzui narabi ni yagyo no zu* **(Illustrations for Designing Mountain, Water, and Hillside Field Landscapes, c. 1466). The basis for the text of the latter is a Kyoto temple scroll that bears the name of the priest Zoen as its compiler, although the attribution of the text is dubious. David A. Slawson translated, in his book** *Secret Teachings in the Art of Japanese Gardens,* **the text from which this excerpt is taken.**

In the design of the pond, you may take as your model the shore-lines of an ocean, or you may model it after the configuration of a river flowing out into a bay. You need not make the pond very deep; the depth will depend on the size of the pond. Excavate the pond so that the contour from the edge to the bottom of the pond is shaped like a druggist's mortar. Then, even when the water level is low, the surface of the water will retain the shape of the original pond. If fish are to be put into the pond, there is no problem in its being a little deeper than ordinary. For a pond where such fish as

cyprinin carp are to be raised, you generally make a small pond alongside the main pond, with a corresponding shape. Construct it by laying up rocks in an interlocking fashion so that they will not collapse into the pond. Set the rocks so that those at the top retain the earth and look like mountains along a shore, while those toward the bottom obscure the pond from view. If in this way you prepare a place for the fish to spawn, they will naturally give birth to their young, and they will thrive. You can conceal from above the channel through which the fish enter and exit, by arranging rocks in an interesting and natural way. If around one pond you create two or three such places for the fish to seek shelter, they will flourish. For a pond to be stocked with crucian carp, you need not make the special ponds to provide cover such as you do for a pond in which cyprinin carp are to be released. You need only prepare two or three places with an interesting and natural quality so that the crucian carp can find cover within the main pond, and they will thrive. Furthermore, if a pond to be stocked with water birds is constructed in this way, the fish will be able to take cover. They will neither be caught by the birds nor leap out of the pond when frightened, and thus will thrive. When the pond is stocked with water birds, they may be harmed by a fox that lies in prey along the shore. So, while you are closely interweaving scenic rocks to create a pleasing effect along the shore, set some commonplace rocks just offshore to create the impression of frolicking birds.

There is also the marsh-pond, which has the feeling of just an ordinary pond. The scenic effect of a marsh-pond is achieved by composing plantings of sweet flag, rabbit-ear iris, eurya, kerria, azalea, wisteria, and gromwell along the shore of the pond so as to create an interesting ambience. Rocks must be visible only here and there. Or you must set them to produce an effect where they are not even noticed.

Another type of shoreline scenery is the ebb-tide beach, which has no striking features but simply creates the impression of the tide constantly ebbing and flowing. Here, if just by spreading fine and coarse grades of sand and without setting any rocks you can

NINOMARU GARDEN (early 17th century)
at NIJOJO CASTLE
Kyoto, Japan
Archivo Iconografico, S.A./CORBIS

visually re-create a single scenic ambience—that of a beach rising
to a knoll where a pine or some such tree alternately appears at high
tide to be out in the middle of the sea, and at ebb tide to tower as
if suddenly borne high above the beach that is now exposed so far
into the distance that one cannot tell where it ends and the sea
begins—you have nothing more to learn. The visual impression of
an ebb-tide beach is produced simply by the way the tree is planted
and the way the fine and coarse grades of sand are spread. . . .

On the seashore, one should not find such plants as sweet
flag, rabbit-ear iris, and kerria. It is common practice nowadays to
use such plants when creating the scenic effects of the seashore,
but this matter should be taken more seriously. People who are
discerning with regard to this type of scenery are rare. It is all the
more important, therefore, that you view the garden with a discerning eye, always bearing in mind that a mountain is a mountain,
an ocean is an ocean, and a stream is a stream. . . .

The term "stream valley" merely refers to the scenic effect of
foothills running along a stream valley. For this effect, you must
not set rocks too conspicuously, but rather, principally by planting
trees and herbs, you must aim at creating the scenic atmosphere
of hills and fields. You should simply make the stream valley ever
so gently rolling and utterly ordinary. . . .

If there is a pond in the garden, such birds as the white egret
may naturally alight on the roof and eaves with the intention of
feeding on the fish, without cause for concern. However, in the
event that they are perched on the roof where no pond exists, an
exorcism must immediately be performed.

SHALAMAR GARDENS (1633–42)
Lahore, Pakistan
Royalty Free/CORBIS

MUHAMMAD SALEH KAMBOH
STREAMS, CHADARS, AND FOUNTAINS (1646)

An Indian court historian, Kamboh (born c. 1610) was raised by Sheikh Anaiyat Ullah, a prominent literary figure and historian of the time. Kamboh served as the diwan of the province of Lahore and composed in two books the unofficial history of Shah Jahan. His second book, *Bahar-e-Sukhan*, provides a clear understanding of the concept, meaning, and form of Mughal gardens. The following text is a passage from the translation from Persian by Abdul Rehman.

I am paying tribute to the dust of this garden [Shalamar Garden, Lahore] so that I could give a new life to my writings. The beauty of this garden is heavenly. It has given freshness to each and every thing with the help of spring. This freshness has given bounty and liberality to its greenery. One can find fate, happiness, and success in its dust. The nightingale has also started scattering melodies there. Its fragrant air takes off the veil from the beauty of the garden. . . .

The plant of life is being raised at the bank of its stream because God has nurtured this flowered earth with the mercury water of heaven. The sunflower is being washed with rose water. God has filtered its dust with heavenly sieve. Its beds are full of flowers and give an impression that galaxy of stars are knit together. . . .

This fragrance seems like the soul of pious people. Its lawns are full of tulip flowers. The gardens of paradise feel depressed to see the greenery of its grassy plots. The nightingale is surprised at this perception. The intoxication of its narcissus has worked in such a way that morning breeze is being distressed in search of this condition. Due to the beauty and quality of its atmosphere, the rose bud has taken off the veil from itself without the help of morning breeze. . . .

Its plants are themselves rooted in each heart due to their well-balanced, symmetrical, and rhythmical beauty and elegance.

The hyacinth flower has flawless fragrance and its gilly flower has lowered down the value of perfume. God has put a black mole on the face of its tulip to keep it away from an evil eye. The gardener of the wild rose has won the competition of flower arrangement from the galaxies of stars. The breeze of heaven comes to make circuit of its garden before the sun rises. These qualities are so strong that it is justified to be called Farah Bakhsh. . . .

In the center of this earthly paradise a sacred stream is flowing gently with its full elegance and sweetness. The stream flows with its charming, fascinating and exhilarating nature and passes through the garden by irrigating the flower beds. Its smile is like the smile of the sun. It gives so much freshness that the ringlet of its waves, in order to deceive the bridle of the garden, has tightened the bouquet with the string of the sun in an elegant manner. The moon which is the source of illumination in the dark gets light for its sword from the water of this stream. Its water is beautiful like greenery. The divine mercy is clearly apparent from its existence. The vast stream is just like clouds pouring rain and opens the doors of divine mercy. Its chevron patterns are like an institution of worship where the hearts of believers are enlightened. . . .

Its fountains are apparent like opportune meanings. Thousands of camphorated lamps are burning face to face to light the sky. The garden has permanent light due to their luster. They have opened their lips in the praise of Almighty Allah. . . .

This stream, which has a quality of freshness and dampness, has fountains in its surroundings. These fountains always emit beads from their mouth. The vast greenery is like the color of emerald. The abundance of red roses which are blooming there has brought the meaning closer to the reader. . . .

In the center of this garden extraordinary, curious, and tall trees of cypress are decorating the beauty of garden. On one side the cypress trees with their luster have increased its charm in the courtyard, and on the other side fountains with their musical sound have awakened the dead people without the trumpet of Israfil. . . .

MARIE ANTOINETTE'S HAMLET
(designed in 1783 by Richard Mique)
Versailles, France
Adam Woolfitt/CORBIS

Sometimes tears come out of the eyes of fountains because of the scene of the cypress trees. Sometimes sweet melodies of fountains surprise the cypress trees. It seems as though two deep lovers in this beautiful courtyard are picking the flower of love and relationship. Glory be to Allah! What a fascinating scene is this. The rose is twisting and twining due to the beauty of this scene. Its courtyard is clean from every darkness and impurity like the heart of pious people. Its door is scattering unlimited happiness and love like the door of heaven. . . .

What a beautiful pavilion is this. The eye concentrates on its walls portraying the painting of gardens. Its door is like the door of heaven which spreads unlimited happiness. The floral decorations on the walls and ceilings are like the pleasant atmosphere. The pious people feel extremely satisfied with the culmination of water and color. Its coloured pillars become closer to the heart like the beloved. The palace of heaven provides an opportunity to people to see the unlimited beauties of paradise on the earth. Its high pavilion is a place from which the divine light rises every morning. It is like the residence of heaven which is willingly spreading eternal generosity. Its high *jharoka* is the place of the rising sun and opens the doors of fortune and happiness on the world like the breaking of dawn. We feel proud of its crystal clear tank. God's blessings are lying in its heart as beads in the hollow of a shell. Generosity has been contained in its nature like sweetness in a cup of sugar candy. The sky has its face enlightened with the reflection of its tank. In this tank thousands of delicate fish are mingled and composed as suitable lines in a verse. . . .

RENÉ RAPIN
STREAMS AND FOUNTAINS (1664)

In 1639 René Rapin (1621–1687) entered the Jesuit order, where he taught rhetoric and wrote extensively in verse and prose. His long poem *Of Gardens* (Paris, 1664) was written in Latin and entitled *Hortatorum libri IV*; it became quite popular and was translated in 1673 by noted English garden designer and writer John Evelyn. The poem was "English'd by Mr. Gardiner in London and Printed by W. Bowyer for Bernard Lintott in 1728." The following excerpts come from that translation.

But let your Water Searcher try in vain,
(For many by the Earth deceiv'd have been)
The Tokens of a secret Spring I'll show,
Such the cold Ground where Flags and Rushes grow,
Where Graves sink in, or swelling Hillocks rise,
Where slimy Ooze on the soft Surface lies:
Thick Weeds and Tracts of bushy Sedge produce
Undoubted Tokens of the latent Juice,
And Moss, with which the watry Soil's o'erspread,
And Fleabane blooming in his Oozy Bed:
Nor with less Certainty of Springs we guess,
From Crainsbill, Calamint, and Water-Cress.

So when from various Quarters of the Hill,
You've drawn together ev'ry wandring Rill,
Thence to the neighb'ring Garden next prepare
To bring them down, and sev'ral Ways there are.
Sometimes inclos'd in Lead, and harden'd Clay,
To Vales beneath you may the Streams convey,
If easy the Descent, and short the Way.
Chiefly if larger Stores the Hills produce,
And in full Tides send down the rolling Juice;

If from the Hills your Waters rise but slow,
And to the neighb'ring Vale Supplies you owe,
Within the Ground a stony Channel build,
Which will with Rain and falling Show'rs be fill'd,
Into this Duct of the Countrey's Stores may glide,
And crouded, pour at last a rolling Tide:
Yet lest the running Water chance to pass
Through many foul and miry Passages,
Or from its Mixture with the Earth may get
Much Filth, at certain Distances, 'tis fit,
Along the watry Course you sink a Pit;
In whose deep Bottom all the Mud may stay,
Which by an even Stream is born away;
Nor can the Slime from thence a Passage find,
Stop'd in its Course, and left in Drains behind;
But tho' your Pits below the Earth descend,
Let lofty Grates all their wide Mouths defend,
By which the troubled Waters may be clear'd,
And all the Mud that from the Bottom rear'd,
Ran in the Channel, be supprest again,
And so the Stream flow free from ev'ry Stain....

But if you can with no such Riv'let meet,
Near to your Garden sink a spacious Pit,
That gath'ring Waters round may settle there,
And in vast Concourse from the Hills repair:
But first white Marle in the deep Bottom lay;
For Marle will best the sinking Waters stay.

Then how through all the Garden to contrive
The Fountains and the Ducts, some Rules I'll give,
The Motions of the Streams to rule I'll show,
All which the skilful Gard'ner ought to know;
A thousand Ways the wand'ring Streams will move,
And in a thousand various Figures rove.

In a near Valley let the Water pent,
In leaden Pipes be through the Garden sent,
There prest within the narrow Pass remain,
That it may higher mount from forth the Vein.
Some brazen Pipes will use, that Streams may pass,
With forceful Fury through the sounding Brass,
And so rise high'r; but lest th' unruly Wind,
Within the lead, or stronger Brass confin'd,
Should burst the Pipes, and range the hollow Cell,
Break ev'ry Bond, and make the Water swell;
You breathing Holes along the Pipes should bore,
And thence the Wind to open Air restore.
As when new cask'd *Falernian* Wines ferment,
The Artist straight gives foaming *Bacchus* Vent,
Lest in his Heat he force the Cask to fly,
And bursting through, unloosen ev'ry Tye.

That Streams, collected thus from ev'ry Side,
You through the Garden rightly may divide,
First in the middle of the Garden lay
A spacious Fountain, where the Waters may
Roll in, and through a narrow Tunnel rise
In spouting Streams, and dash the Winds and Skies.
The Fountain's Bottom, and the Brim inclose,
With polish'd Marble or soft Turfs of Moss;
Instead of Tubes, some Men their Fountains grace
With Sea-calves, or with *Scylla*'s dubious Race,
Or with wild *Tritons* cast in molten Brass.
Thus a proud *Triton* on his Dolphin rides
At Luxenburgh, and spouting Waters guides;
This Fountain is with Marble beautify'd,
And from *Arcueil* with Water well supply'd:
Yet as *St. Clou* the Fountain more demands
Our Praise, where the fam'd Seat of *Philip* stands,
Proud with its noble Groves and murm'ring Springs,

And boasts it self the Royal Seat of Kings;
First in the King's and People's just Esteem,
And stands a Pattern for your spouting Stream;
With this no Fountain can in *France* compare,
To flow, or mount aloft in open Air. . . .

Lakes of whatever Shape great Pleasure give,
(Tho' Gardens best the circling Form receive)
If Trees too with their shining Scenes shall crown
The verdant Banks, and bend their Branches down,
O'er Beds of Grass, or Seats of living Stone;
Whether your stagnant Waters sleep, or move
With flowing Tides, adorn them with a Grove,
Whose twining Boughs on ev'ry side may lean,
With Shade and Coolness to refresh the Scene:
'Twixt Groves and Fountains mutual Friendship's made,
The murm'ring Stream still courts the cooling Shade.
But hence be sure to drive the croaking Race,
Nor let their hoarser Sounds offend the Place,
The noxious Rout will raise the sordid Mud,
And with their Sports disturb the crystal Flood.

CLAUDE-HENRI WATELET
A RIVER GARDEN (1774)

French painter, poet, playwright, and theoretician, Watelet (1718–1786) designed the famous gardens at Moulin Joli. In 1774 he wrote his *Essay on Gardens,* which reveals the shift in French garden design from a formal style to a more simple and natural presentation. The selection is from the recent translation by Samuel Danon.

THE GARDEN OF MR. WATELET NEAR PARIS

To the west, an hour's distance from the city, the river irrigates lovely meadowlands as it divides into many branches and forms a number of islands shaded by thick willows and tall poplars. The banks of these winding canals offer continuous shade and greenery that is preserved by the coolness of the water. The eye delights in the picturesque vistas on all sides and the distant expanses adorned with villages and castles. Finally, in this rather limited space, the variety of perspectives, the irregularity of the terrain, the windings of the riverbanks, the asymmetrical placement of the trees, slopes, islands, and of the dikes connecting them, all produce such a charming diversity that you have no desire to leave. In this small enclosure you feel protected, not confined, whether by a hawthorn hedge or by the banks of the various waterways.

This unusual site had long been neglected. Its potential for beauty existed only in the possibility of being realized when, one day in spring some twenty years ago, I discovered this charming location. I was crossing the river in a ferryboat on my way to the city, calmly preoccupied with thoughts of my friends and of the Arts, two subjects so agreeable to me that, as you know, I have allowed them to dominate all others. I let my gaze wander. The grove whose description I just sketched for you attracted my eye. An eighth of a league in the distance, it offered such a lovely view that I wished to enjoy it more fully. A meadow, flowing waters, shade! There, I told myself, away from the tiresome and sterile bustle of society, away from the childish and gloomy anxiety of those who search in vain for happiness while running away from it, this is where, in tranquility, one may taste both the delights of study and the beauties of nature.

I did not resist this first impression. Hardly had I disembarked when I proceeded toward a place that lured me by some kind of secret affinity. Walking along a narrow path through a meadow covered with flowers, I followed the riverbanks which here, far from being steep, descend in a gentle slope toward the water's edge. This path took me to a road lined with linden trees. Suddenly,

GARDEN POND (design begun in 1890 by
Claude Monet)
Giverny, France
Robert Holmes/CORBIS

islands shaded by old willows appeared before me, and the sight
of a small country house confirmed what I was already thinking.
The dwelling that rose on the side of the meadow resembled, in
its simplicity, the vicarage of a parish priest. Near the house, a quin-
cunx of tall poplars and lindens provided, as they still do, shade
that the most brilliant rays of the sun cannot penetrate. And this
cover continues all the way to the edge of a natural canal formed
by islands and small half-broken levees against which the flow
of water still breaks and bubbles as it rushes through, offering
landscape painters surprises that must certainly interest them.
The house, which stands on the flower-covered meadow as if on
a magnificent carpet, was surrounded by a small orchard, and
toward the river there were four rows of lindens, neglected but
still providing abundant shade, giving the impression of a paved
avenue that until then no one had considered using. As for the
vistas, when I looked in a southwesterly direction, they offered
me the most expansive perspective....

I did not go long without exploring my happy find. Shortly
after being enchanted with the sight, I made plans to share its
enjoyment with friends; I took them to visit it, shared my impressions with them, and eventually became, in their company, both
the owner and a resident of the place....

But let us retrace our steps.... A barren island rises in the near
distance ... and our gaze extends beyond [the adjacent island] to
rest on some buildings.... Among these structures, there is one
taller than the others and therefore more imposing. In itself it is
not very remarkable, but Héloïse lived there. Upon hearing this
name, who would not stop to reflect! Who would not take a
moment to talk about that frail and all-too-unhappy lover! After
her tragic adventure she withdrew to a monastery whose abbot
was the wise, troubled, severe, and jealous Abélard. What you see
here is that very monastery....

As you leave this pleasant setting, you may choose among
many roads leading out of the forest of willows and down to the
vast riverbed. Here the prospects are too exposed to encourage

meditation and poetry. For as the view expands, so does the soul
which truly, if vaguely, relishes even those beauties that lead it
astray. To be inspired, the soul must be more closely contained;
it must experience without distractions and in an undisturbed
reverie the pleasure of recognizing familiar sensations.

I shall therefore quicken my step as I take you along a terrace
road several fathoms long which follows the contour of the island
alongside the navigable canal. This magnificent scene is enlivened
by ships that constantly sail from the maritime provinces. But it
only inspires admiration, so it is best to leave it behind and return
to the interior canals and walks, crossed by a wooden bridge of
considerable span. Because of the disposition of the three islands
situated below the rest of the terrain, the bridge rises up to the tree-
tops, the highest branches providing the shade that transforms
this passageway into a covered allée. Here you can walk without
fearing the intensity of the sun, and as you move from one place to
the next you can see, thanks to the gradual widening of the various
canals, prospects made all the more picturesque for being perceived from this rare setting. Moreover, the bridge widens above
the canals at regular intervals, thereby making space for seats
where one may rest, enjoy the coolness of the place, and delight
in the pleasures of the eye.

From here you may discover in greater detail the appealing
meanderings of the water as well as the charming reflections of
various objects painted clearly upon its surface....

At one end of the bridge a mill comes into view. The sight of it
rarely fails to attract those who have seldom seen such machinery
close at hand. As you approach, you find yourself looking down
at the wheel. The sound it produces, its rhythmic beat, its steady,
repeated movement, all induce a few moments' reverie. You watch
with growing intentness as the paddles emerge from the current
one after another, slowly rising to the highest point of their orbit,
only to start down again, plunge into the water, and disappear.
The wheel naturally inspires contemplation, but reflections of too

somber a hue would not match the shadings of the scene as well
as this:

> Oh, don't ignore the worth of time,
> For while the water rushes forth
> And the wheel meets its rapid beat
> Your day's spindle is rolling on
> Enjoy, enjoy your allotted time.

REGINALD J. FARRAR
DON'T BUILD A WATER GARDEN (1908)

**Botanist, plant-hunter, and influential gardener, Farrer (1880–1920)
put his garden theories into practice at his ancestral home of
Ingleborough House in Clapham, West Yorkshire, England. Yet
Farrer spent much of his life in East Asia collecting plants. He
wrote numerous books, including *The English Rock Garden* (1928),
Alpines and Bog Plants (1908), and *On the Eaves of the World* (1916).
The excerpt comes from *Alpines and Bog Plants*.**

Advice to those about to build a Water-garden—DON'T. Not that
the Water-garden is not a joy and a glory; but that it is cruelly hard
to keep in order and control unless you are a master of millions
and broad ample acres of pool and pond. Water, like fire, is a good
servant, perhaps, but is painfully liable to develop into a master. . . .
How many little ponds are unguardedly built, only to become
mere basins of slime and duckweed? How many larger pools are
made, only to fill with *Chara, Potamogeton,* and the other noxious
growths that make its depths a clogged, waving forest of dull
brown verdure? The fact is, a pool—not an easy thing to build and
set going—is of all things in the garden the hardest of all to keep
in decent order. Some of its choice inmates devour and despoil the
smaller ones; water weeds increase and multiply at a prodigious

rate; dead leaves drift thick upon it in autumn, slime and green
horrors make a film across it in summer.

Contrast with this grim picture the water-garden as it glistens
before the sanguine eye of him who contemplates possessing
one—that crystal expanse, starred with goblets of *Nymphaea,*
those neat yet luxuriant shores aglow with every glorious plant
of the marsh. But the ideal water-garden I need not draw from my
own words. The ideal water garden has been described, once and
for all, in the Parable that tells how Brahmadatta the King made
and adorned a marvelous lake to allure the Most Perfect One, Our
Lord Buddha. You will find the tale in the Swan-Birth Story of the
Blessed One. . . .

Beautiful though we may build our ponds and keep them,
I fear it is not likely we shall ever allure a Bodhisattva. Nearest
approach to a divine swan will be a very worldly heron, filled with
belly-thoughts and murder, who will come to take toll of any
little frogs and fishes that may be enjoying our waters. Nor are
saintly herons, I believe, so common that the prayer of frog or fish
may turn their hearts to kindness; therefore if you want to nourish
goldfish in your pools, see to it that the water be deep enough to
guarantee them from the heron's marauding bill. Indeed, the too
common fault in pond-building is shallowness, which fosters
slime and water-weed to an intolerable extent, and makes more
disastrous the silting up of dead leaves in autumn and winter. A
shallow pond must needs be exhaustively cleaned out each season,
and even so the job will never be satisfactory for more than a
month. Intolerable sight, a shallow little basin all a muck of weeds
and autumn wreckage; not to mention that water-weed clogs and
ultimately conquers even the most stalwart Nymphaeas. Therefore I would prescribe no less a depth than four feet for the pond,
and will now begin at last to prescribe for those who refuse to be
daunted by my jeremiads, and insist on having a water-garden.
And, first of all, let me say that if the water-garden be hard to keep
in order, yet, if kept in order, dainty and clean, it is the very jewel
and eye and omphalos of the rock-garden, doubling its own beauty

by the neighbourhood of grey stone, and doubling the beauty of "the stone by its own limpid light. Pray, then, and make offering to the high gods that you may have running water in abundance at your disposal. So you shall have a little mountain stream to bubble and splash through the rock-garden, trickling dispersedly down over the shoulder of the Alpine bog, and so to leap like Niagara into a bright sparkling little lake below.

In planning your lake, be very careful of its curves. Map and scheme with the utmost deliberation. Unfortunately, this is not a question for general law-giving, as the lie of each piece of ground must determine the proper shape of any piece of water. But a misplaced bay or promontory will be as fatal to the harmony of your design as a duly, tactfully placed one will be satisfying and completing. Therefore go at the shaping of your pond with pains, and don't rest content with a mere circle or oval, like the bed of some great pie or pudding. Excavate, then, to four feet and a half at one end—for I advise a kidney shape, with many variants, as the best general design for the pond—and at the lower end have a lesser depth—say about three feet to three feet and a half. For remember that this is not your depth as you will have it, since the concrete bottom will swallow up at least six inches if you wish to be quite safe against any possible shiftings, frosts, and other disasters. This, with a superimposed six inches of soil, will leave you, at your deepest, three feet and a half of water at the deeper end, and two and a half at the shallower. If you delve any deeper, you may have too much water for some of the frailer Nymphaeas; if you spare trouble and make the pond shallower, you run the risk, in hard winters, of having the pond frozen solid, so that the cement, unable to contain the expanded mass, cracks, and bursts.

You will add a notable advantage and beauty if you give the pond a false wall. That is to say, make it a solid tank of concrete, with four sides and bottom, quite simple. Then, in brick, build an inner wall, rising to within an inch or so of water-level. If the narrow trench thus formed—it need not be more than eight inches wide—be filled with rich soil on a rubble base of two feet or so,

it will give you a most lovely ring of bog-plants round your lake, being perpetually wet with the water that just overtaps the false inner wall, and for ever percolates into the soil. There is, of course, no need to have this all round, if you do not want it, but one of the loveliest pools I know sits high on a Surrey down, and owes half its beauty to its complete girdle of Iris, Spiraea, and fen-plants generally.

Again, nothing looks better than to diversify your bank here and there with some bold feature. Here and there round my two ponds I have immense boulders of water-worn mountain limestone, specially selected blocks, hollowed by wind and weather, in which I grow waving masses of Saxifrage and Dianthus over the water; or, yet again, you may very effectively bring the line of your lake round under some dominant cliff of the rockwork. I have done this at one point of my New Garden, with the most commanding effect. The one drawback is that the walk round the pond—an indispensable feature—is narrowed, at this point, to an irreducible minimum of about six inches. So that if, for instance, one wants to photograph any plant on the promontory, one runs the risk, in the course of the photographer's manoeuvres, of walking innocently backwards into four feet of water.

And, for a last word on shape. I can give one very definite and valuable piece of advice. Wherever you make your ponds, never let any consideration seduce you into allowing straight lines or anything approaching to a square or rectangle. . . .

VITA SACKVILLE-WEST
WATER IS THE MAKING OF A GARDEN (1953)

A renowned English literary figure, Sackville-West (1892–1962) produced eight novels and five plays between 1906 and 1910. In 1913 she married the diplomat and critic Harold Nicolson, with whom she eventually purchased the Sissinghurst Castle in Kent. She is remembered for her novels, but her most enduring work was perhaps the garden at Sissinghurst Castle. She wrote numerous articles and books about gardening, including *In Your Garden Again,* from which this selection is taken.

It sometimes happens that people inherit, or acquire, an old dwelling house or cottage with a pool or even with the remains of a moat. Presumably, such surroundings are highly picturesque, and the fortunate owner wants to make the most of them. Let us assume also that no previous owner has bothered about suitable planting, and has left the waterside to ramp away into a terrible mess of unworthy weeds.

Water is the making of a garden. It gives a rare chance to the gardener. He can grow things *in* the water, and *beside* the water, and even *on* the water—a triple pleasure, far more agreeable than the filling up of triplicate forms. I will take *in* and *on* the water first.

Waterlilies come first to mind: and apart from the white and yellow ones, there are hybrids in pink, red, and primrose. Twelve to eighteen inches of water-depth is a safe rough guide, and full sun. The usual method is to sink the plants in an old basket, when they will root through the basket into the bottom mud; but they can also be tied between two turfs and sunk (the right way up). Late May or early June is the time. If you think the leaves of waterlilies too large for a small pond, there is the bog bean with small white flowers, floating; or *Pontederia cordata,* like a pale blue arum. For the edges, where the water is not so deep, our yellow flag iris is both lovely and reliable; the flowering rush, *Butomus umbellatus,*

is an arrowy grower three or four feet high with rosy flowers; it looks exotic, but is in fact to be found wild in Britain. *Sagittaria,* the true arrowhead, white flowers, associates well with this rather spiky group.

For something lower in stature on the boggy margin the water forget-me-not, *Myosotis palustris,* is a great spreader of a china blue, paler than the garden varieties. The king cup or marsh marigold will grow either in sun or shade, which is obliging of it.

Finally, the very brave could experiment with the ordinary white arum, the lily of the Nile, which, if planted deep enough, should survive an average winter in the south. But if you want to grow arums out of doors in water, the bog arum, *Calla palustris,* is a less risky investment.

In choosing plants for the waterside, I think it is important to remember that their beauty will be doubled if you can arrange for them to be reflected in the water. If the water is covered by floating plants, such as water-lilies, this will not be possible, though one can usually contrive to keep a bare zone round the outside to serve as a mirror. Much will depend, of course, on whether the pond has banked-up sides, or fades away into a swampy level; these are differences which can only be considered on the spot.

For the marshy swamp, I would suggest a drift of the moisture-loving primulas: *P. Japonica, chionantha, bulleyana, helodoxa,* known as the glory of the marsh. If economy is a consideration, as it usually is, these primulas are all easily raised from seed. The tall clematis-like Japanese irises, *I. kaempferi,* look most beautiful growing amongst them, but I always think their requirements are a little awkward to manage—wet in summer, dry in winter. Nature's water supply usually works the other way around. The blue *Iris laevigata,* on the other hand, does not mind boggy conditions all the year through. *Iris sibirica,* less large and handsome than the Japanese, is exceedingly graceful and pretty and most accommodating, though it does not like being too deeply drowned. *Iris delvayi* resembles it, and is useful because it flowers later,

VIZCAYA, JAMES DEERING ESTATE
(designed by F. Burrall Hoffman and Paul
Chalfin) and GARDEN (1912, Diego Suarez)
Miami, Florida
Scott J. Tilden

when *sibirica* is over. The richer the soil, the better for all these irises, even to a mulch of rotted manure.

These are all tall-growing, but if you can spare a special corner, marking it off with a ring of rough stones, do try the little almost-black gold-veined *I. chrysographes,* a real gem; and *I. fulva,* a coppery red.

So much for the waterside irises, but coming higher up on the bank, assuming that there is a bank, and that it is dry, I think one might plant the scarlet dogwood, *Cornus alba.* Do not be misled by the name; *alba* in this case refers only to the flowers, which are silly, contemptible little things in summer. The glory of this plant is the red bark of its bare stems throughout the winter. Caught by the light of the sinking sun, reflected in water, it is as warming to the heart as a log-fire on the hearth after a cold day.

KINSAKU NAKANE
STREAMS IN A JAPANESE GARDEN (1965)

The Japanese landscape architect Kinsaku Nakane (1917–2002) designed Japanese gardens throughout the world. He also restored gardens in Japan at Jonangu, Rakuseien, Korin'in, and Taizo-in. He designed gardens in the United States at the Jimmy Carter Library; the Museum of Fine Arts, Boston; and Lili'uokalani Park, Hilo, Hawaii. He served as a professor at Kyoto University and president of Osaka University of Arts. This essay comes from Nakane's book *Kyoto Gardens,* translated by Money L. Hickman and Kaichi Minobe.

Kyoto is situated on a gently inclined plane, enclosed by a horseshoe-shaped perimeter of low mountains, open only on the south. From a climatic standpoint, it is far from ideal, for the surrounding mountains cut off the winds in summer, resulting in a high, constant humidity, and act to preserve the penetrating cold which marks the long winter season. During the summer, when the humidity continues through the night, the climate is particularly enervating, a condition which has given rise to the practice of utilizing water in a variety of ways to mitigate the heat. Thus, networks of canals have been constructed in various parts of the city (a testimony to the copious supply of water in the area), and it has been customary in Kyoto since Heian times to channel water from rivers and springs, and direct its flow through gardens, close to dwellings. This practice, known as "yari-mizu," creates an atmosphere of coolness by its sound, as well as actually relieving the humidity through the presence of running water, and there are frequent references to it in the *Tale of Genji* and *Makura-no-Sôshi,* literary works of the Heian period. Such artificial streams were installed in the gardens laid out in conjunction with the splendid residences of the nobility, the buildings of which were erected in an architectural style known as "shinden-zukuri," a distinctive form of single-storied, unpainted construction, with shingled roofs. The ground plans for such buildings varied, and different subsidiary structures were connected to the oblong main building by veranda corridors. Orientation was invariably toward the south, facing a broad garden which had running water as an integral feature.

Standard practice seems to have been to draw water from a source on the north side of the complex, direct its flow under the raised veranda-corridor leading from the main building to subsidiary living quarters on the east, and then have it run in a meandering course past the main chamber, finally to empty into a spacious pond. Unlike the practice in earlier times, rocks were used sparingly, and set up only at those few locations along the course of the stream where they were thought to be necessary as points of visual emphasis. In laying out such gardens, the main objective was to reproduce the atmosphere of natural fields, and the stream usually flowed in a circuitous, dilatory manner between gentle knolls covered with pampas grass and wild flowers. During Heian times, the fresh green moors of Murasaki-no and Saga lay close by the outskirts of the city, and their beauty provided an ever-present source of inspiration for garden design. The nobility of the period enjoyed frequent excursions to the surrounding countryside, where they delighted in listening to the pleasant sounds of birds and insects, and searching for wild flowers. Their fondness for this sylvan atmosphere is clearly revealed in their preoccupation with accurately reproducing it in their gardens.

In addition to utilizing fashioned streams ("yari-mizu") to alleviate the enervating humidity characteristic of Kyoto summers, it was only natural that the many springs and natural ponds in the area constituted attractive locations where one might find some relief from the stifling heat. Consequently, it is not surprising that the nobles of Heian times appropriated the best of these sites for certain of their residences....

No point of visual focus is more important in the organization of a traditional garden than the waterfall, and an interesting Heian period document, the *Sakutei-ki* (Notes on Garden Design) lists ten different varieties, additional evidence of the considerable repertoire of arrangement features developed by garden designers during Heian times. The notable progress made in constructing waterfalls and channeling water in this period may be explained in large part as representing the influence of the topography of the Kyoto basin, for the close contiguity of low mountains on three sides provided the natural features essential for this development.

Among early garden waterfalls, two noted works should be mentioned: the one built in connection with the Hôkongo-in, which was completed in 1130 in the Hanazono area, and another fashioned in a hillside behind the garden of the Kitayamatei villa of Saionji Kintsune, which was described by a contemporary poet, Sadaie, as being forty-five feet in height. It is obvious that great care was always exercised in arranging a waterfall and its associated boulders because of its importance as a primary point of focus in garden composition. The finest stones were selected for the rock formation bordering the fall, and considerable time and effort were devoted to studying the most appropriate manner for the water to

descend. Thus the categories of falls mentioned in the *Sakutei-ki* are differentiated on the basis of the manner in which water actually falls—in a broad torrent, like a thin thread, laterally, or divided into two streams. Furthermore, the sounds of falls were subject to particular scrutiny, and the rocks at the bottom were chosen so that the impact of the water on them created an acoustic quality in harmony with the total composition....

The plenitude of hills, knolls, and rocky promontories which surround Kyoto provided a fine choice of inclines and cliffs for the construction of waterfalls, and it is not surprising that this aspect of garden layout reached an impressive level of achievement locally, and has exerted a continual influence on garden composition in other regions of Japan since Heian times.

In traditional garden design, two factors were always given basic consideration: the use of the best natural features and topographical variations of the site, and the most effective utilization of scenery in the distance so that it might be drawn into, and employed successfully in the total composition of the garden.

KENROKUEN PARK (late 18th–early
19th century)
Kanazawa, Japan
Michael S. Yamashita/CORBIS

CHRISTOPHE GIROT

ACCEPTING THE LANDSCAPE (2004)

Born in Paris in 1957, Girot has been professor and chair of landscape architecture at the ETH Zurich since 2001. He studied environmental planning and management at the University of California in Davis from 1979 to 1981, and from 1982 to 1988 he studied architecture and landscape architecture at the University of California, Berkeley, where he also taught. Upon his return to France in 1989, Girot first became professor and then chairman of the Landscape Design Department at Ecole Nationale Supérieure du Paysage at Versailles. After serving as a partner with VUES SA in Zurich, he recently established his own design studio there.

"Accepting" in the Oxford dictionary gives us the following definition: "Consent to receive; to regard with favour; allow the truth of; believe."

To make a form is to consent, to regard with favor a series of ideas. This process allows us to better understand the act of creating and the form that results. Through the history of landscape, this process of apprehending the nature around us could be generally called the act of mise-en-scène or "scenography": it is an act that transforms the natural subject into something understandable to us, namely into culture.

The relationship between landscape and scenography is one that merits reflection. The play between landscape and scenography arches back to the beginning of our history; to a place where the sacred and the ritual extracted their substance through the juxtaposition of man-made culture to a natural backdrop. Over the history of theatre, the natural backdrop gradually became increasingly internal and artificial. Bringing us today to the absolute theatricalization of nature where nature can be reduced to complete abstraction and metaphor. What can we learn from this gradual shift to help elucidate us on our contemporary landscape practice?

One way to shed some light on this topic is to read the landscape, in order to better apprehend the richness and the complexity of the relationship between landscape and the scenographic mode. The following examples represent and affirm the landscape. These are each emblematic, with not only an incredible capacity to move us and to awaken the senses; but also a capacity to reinvent combinations of the relationship between landscape and its mise-en-scène. The examples chosen today correspond to three well-established logics, three modes of reading—these are mainly: Irony, Pathos, and Comedy.

IRONY

The first scenographic mode of reading the landscape is Irony. Irony is very complex, because among many differing niveaus, the sense of a subject becomes amplified by its opposite. Irony comes from the Greek word *eironeia,* which signifies literally to simulate ignorance. In the case of landscape, the ironic mode would be then to produce and underline an idea of nature by making use of its extreme opposite. Such inversion is a phenomenon which has existed in landscape and scenography since the Renaissance, where the art of creating from scratch fake old ruins were juxtaposed to a natural context in order to amplify the sense of a rustic nature by connoting to the visitor notions of chaos and abandonment. There is however a deep gap of usage and meaning between the eighteenth-century follies and the following contemporary examples. Whereas the eighteenth-century follies are an exaltation of the artifice of the ruin, the contemporary examples are concerned with literal ruins, sometimes even stigmatized ruins, that are transformed into positive elements of the landscape they stood in.

As stated before, Irony operates a transformation of the meaning and acceptance of an object at radical opposites of its original and implicit raison d'être. The opening to the public of Gas Works Park on the small island in Puget Sound at Seattle in 1975 marked a decisive moment in the then-contemporary landscape theory. This project refutes all rules of good taste and opinion of the epoch by marrying in an as yet unconceivable manner two great opposites. Gas Works Park announces a genre of a new nature: a nature that allies itself to its worst enemies, the gas industry, to offer neighboring families a place to relax and play. The project is the old, dirty, obsolete gas plant. The reality of the object is in no way hidden or distorted, the modifications remaining in fact minimal. The realization of the project was quite summary, the finishing details are almost absent, but the streak of genius of this project lies in the invention of a new genre of landscape—radical and ironic—mixing nature and hard core industry. Many projects of this sort followed in the footsteps of Gas Works Park, each one going further in the sophistication of detail and sublime beautification of what was once prohibited ground to the public.

Another example of a landscape of Irony brings us to Berlin on the abandoned train tracks of postwar Germany. The old site of the Schöneberg Sudgelander, situated in the heart of the city, has focused its energy in the protection and proliferation of indigenous plants that have cropped up among the remnants of the tracks since 1952. Going fully against the previous practices of using chemicals to maintain the train tracks free of any sign of nature, a new ecological pact was made and scrupulously followed. In a few seasons, could the site be transformed into a perfect example of an anarchic botanical renaissance where each fledgling was noted and entered into maps and statistics? This site and its new nature were declared off limits to the public. This idealization of a spontaneous and undisturbed nature was fully in echo of the West Germans' postwar rigid, moralist stance. How else to explain a fervent desire to generate a natural reserve in the middle of the city and at the same time of the drama of the Berlin Wall being built? Irony supposes that two extremes rally together to generate a completely new sense of place. Forty years of this *laissez la nature faire* approach left the remnants of the train tracks hardly visible. With the fall of the Wall, the very essence of this natural reserve and its inaccessibility to the city dwellers came into question. In 1995, the city decided to take the project further by transforming it into a city park. A series of artists were invited to design a series of wooden walkways above this land upon which one may cross and visit the park without disturbing the nature below. This surprising scenography reconciled the histories of this site with the contemporary city. People are now walking above the grids of the train tracks, and upon the haphazard nature that followed. The juxtaposition of two diametrically opposed ideas—nature and technology/industry—becomes the motor for this landscape project. It is the fruit of a deep inversion in the moral order of things, making it thus a place where wild ecology becomes ironically cultural.

PATHOS

The second mode of scenographic reading is Pathos. It has nothing to do with Irony, where the new symbolic charge inverts the previous meaning of a place. Pathos, on the contrary, plays upon the idea of resonating the physical and emotional state of the visitor, in order to create an upheaved landscape and experience. In a landscape of Pathos, the given form of the terrain, or more precisely, the scenography of the intrinsic substance of a place, generally provokes a sentiment of sadness or discomfort. In most cases, we are speaking of a place where the historical weight of the events that took place there provokes emotions in us. The question is how to narrate such sentiments without falling into a too pathetic or too narrative landscape. The respect of memory does not in any sense guarantee the success of such a project. In fact, Pathos is probably the most difficult genre of landscape to master and express. A landscape of Pathos relies mostly on a scenography of the impalpable,

a scenography that moves us, in some sense, conjuring, through memory, another time and place.

The first example of such a landscape that resoundingly succeeds in this object is, without a doubt, the project of the National Vietnam War Memorial that stands on the large grass lawn, the National Mall, in Washington D.C. When one approaches this large grass field one does not expect anything because nothing alerts one to the Memorial's presence. The Memorial is a landscape that digs into ground level, pulling us very subtly and gradually into the metaphor of burial and bereavement. No visitor remains insensible to the path's very subtle slope, which draws the visitor toward the point of the V submerged in the lawn. At this point, a person stands only a few centimeters below ground level. Here is a literal and ritual burial that operates on the public by the mere gravitational force, provoking in us a very clear physical and psychic feeling of Pathos.

This project, chosen out of 1,421 final competition entries, is the work of a woman, Maya Lin, then a twenty-two-year-old architecture student at Yale University. This memorial is a place simultaneously opened and closed, depending on your approach and viewpoint. Open to the sky, generously open to the large lawn, this landscape confers an immense feeling of calm and liberty. On the contrary, on the side of the vertical wall that defines the trench, the feeling of enclosure becomes real and oppressive. "I thought about what death is, what a loss is. A sharp pain that lessens with time but can't quite heal over. A scar. The idea occurred to me on the site. Take a knife and cut open the earth, and with time the grass would heal it. As if you cut open the rock and polished it . . . " Streets and skylines disappear to leave you alone in front of a series of steles in black polished granite upon which are inscribed in chronological order the 58,175 servicemen and women who perished from 1959 to 1975. The viewer recognizes the singularity of each name, while also having a clear sense of the huge number of names making up the whole list. ". . . I wanted the names in chronological order because to honor the living as well as the dead, it had to be sequenced in time . . . " The strict minimalism of this work confers a very strong force and singularity. This landscape, emblematic of our epoch, also aroused deep controversy and provoked profound feelings about grief and the Vietnam War in general. The play of the topographic and gravitational force, so physical and simple, allows the visitor to engage himself body and soul in the act of remembering the dead buried so far away from this site.

The second example of a landscape of Pathos is the Memorial to Walter Benjamin. It is located next to the local cemetery of Port Bou, a small Spanish port next to France. The tragic suicide of this writer trying to escape in 1944 from the Nazis and to emigrate to America incarnates a whole part of an epoch. As in the first example, this memorial does not correspond to the exact place of death. It is a project that again depends on strong scenography and the mastering of inherent physical forces of the site. Dani Karravan chose here to work on the metaphor of the fall and the abyss. The project forces the visitor to transpose his physical sensation of vertigo into the sentiment of loss and death. The natural elements of the site—the sky, the sunlight, the precipitous rocks of the coastline, the open horizon, and of course the sea with its sea floor—are juxtaposed to an almost sculpture-like steel structure. In the dark metal corridor entrance, the strong natural elements immediately vanish, leaving us only the light emanating from the sea floor visible at the end of the vertiginous stairway that stands in front of us. We are literally pulled towards a descent, that is neither easy nor comfortable, towards a brilliant blue light that becomes, gradually, the rocks and the plants under water moving with the sea's constant undercurrents. Our only protection from continuing the descent is a glass wall upon which is engraved a fragile quote from the writer. Here is a scenography of the pathetic trajectory of the absurd and of the horror, a trajectory where the physical force of the site, the irresistible attraction toward the physical fall as well as the fall into memory and history, becomes the catalyst for many emotions and questions. The climb back up is as difficult as the descent, but this time oriented towards the sky, where the blue is no longer blue, but just a blinding light, pure and strong, belonging to the outside world.

COMEDY

The third and last scenographic mode is simpler and in appearance lighter. It is the landscape of Comedy. With Comedy, the goal is not to take a respectful stance toward the past, but rather to underscore the capacity of a landscape to be completely ingrained in the present, regardless of what its history is or was. With Comedy, we are immersed in a resolutely contemporary nature, where scenography and technology allow us to arrange new events, to invent a new form of nature, and to create a new memory of a place. Comedy permits new rituals, even contradictory ones, to install themselves upon a landscape so that a new form of society can evolve. In this mode, we are talking of nature in the service of man, nature full of surprises, playfulness, and discovery. Through Comedy, nature becomes a social and historical lubricant of sorts, a landscape of potentialities and possibilities, in other words, a place of hope for contemporary man and culture.

My choice of the first example may surprise more than one reader. However, this project of landscape architecture born in the fervor of the

Third Reich becomes after the war a perfect space for a large range of human activities—raging from car races to huge music festivals. The idea here is not to efface the shame and weight of one of the most emblematic sites of Nazi Germany, but to understand how a satirical view of such a site permits it over time to transcend, should we say exorcise, its frightening origins. This precise example of human Comedy shows us, whether we like it or not, that a site adapts itself through time. Landscapes of Comedy generate antinomic ambiances that actually force the form and historical dimension of a site, to transgress itself. One can hardly confuse a hippie smoking hash at a Bob Dylan concert in 1969 with the fanaticism of Hitler youth that danced, just as entranced as our hippie, upon the same earth a mere 30 years before. It is not the site that changes, but rather this new and shocking usage transfigures the physicality and raison d'être of Zeppelin Feld. Nature in this example is reduced to a space of possibilities. As we know, Comedy is not synonymous with happiness. It is precisely this playing with the pathos of memory that procures this seductive insolence. Perhaps for this reason alone, we should dig in our historical heritage in order to understand the regenerating force of human Comedy in our domain of work.

My second and last example concerns an ephemeral project that has taken place for the last two summers in Paris. The right bank of the river Seine, usually an overflowing car boulevard, is closed to automobiles for an entire month and transformed into a river boardwalk. Real sand beaches, changing booths, palm trees, hammocks, lounge chairs, lawns, and endless sport and cultural events are provided. Here we find a completely artificial nature, installed like a stage set in a minimum of time, ages away from the traffic jams and the polluted image of the Seine. Paris Plage is a nature dedicated to human events that are imagined and organized day and night. It is a landscape where that sometimes ridiculous beach culture of Deauville and the South of France becomes a tangible reality in the middle of Paris. Tons of sand and grass cover what normally are kilometers of asphalt, to allow a city dweller the luxury of a real sun bath—the supreme privilege of the summer.

No one forgets that one lies in the heart of the city, in front of L'Ile de la Cité, but everyone revels in the surrealism of the Paris Plage and reinvents each day their metropolis. Immense crowds come from the outskirts each day to see the unthinkable and live a piece of this surrealist moment. The project evolves each year, and this summer, the surrealism will go further with a planned 200-meter swimming pool in the Seine, providing a bathing spot for 50,000 swimmers in waters that have long been considered taboo and dangerous. Since its opening day, Paris Plage has been a resounding success (with 600,000 visitors on opening day), and an incredible marketing feat for the city mayor. This is a landscape of people that come to see and be seen. It is in some way a Brecht theatre set at the natural scale where the right bank of this river becomes a continuous Comedy day and night that vacillates with each human event taking place there. This example should serve us, not as a project to copy, but as an operating mode for contemporary urban landscapes. Intervention here is reduced to its strict minimum, a few palm trees, and carpets of lawn do the job. It is the natural elements that are the essential actors, the wind, the water, the sky, and mankind. The human Comedy plays against the unchangeable urban character of a place and depends on the human element to effect a transformation. Comedy here has presented a successful example, where even the most ephemeral event can mark forever the spirit and memory of a city.

The three modes of reading the landscape, presented here, show us how thinking about landscapes permits us to question their role in our contemporary society. We are very far from the art of the garden where the mastering of nature represented an accepted vision of our cultures. What is common to these three distinct modes is the reduction of natural expression. This means in no way that these modes lack expression; on the contrary, I would argue that these situations generate new and different natures. There is the Ironic nature of the buried train tracks, the Pathetic nature of a simple inclined lawn, and the Comic nature of an event completely out of context. It is however difficult to confuse Irony with Pathos, Pathos with Comedy and Comedy with Irony, because each plays with a different transformation of our idea of nature. Contemporary landscape is therefore before all the product of differing juxtapositions and convergences. It is up to us as designers and then to all of us as users to recognize and decode this potential. In our contemporary landscapes it is much less the allusion to a lost paradise that is key than to refer ourselves to and accept the intrinsic characters of our civilization in order to elevate the landscapes around us by imbuing them with a richer cultural sense.

SCHÖNEBERG SUDGELANDER
(designed in 1985)
Berlin, Germany
Thilo Folkert, Professor Christophe Girot,
ILA ETH Zurich

BIBLIOGRAPHY

Addison, Joseph. "The Spectator 477." In C. C. L. Hirschfeld, *Theory of Garden Art*, p. 123, Edited and translated by Linda B. Parshall. Philadelphia: University of Pennsylvania Press, 2001.

Alberti, Leon Battista. *On the Art of Building in Ten Books*, pp. 9, 11, 13, 15, 140. Translated from Italian by Joseph Rykwert, Neil Leach, and Robert Tavernor. Cambridge, Mass.: MIT Press, 1988.

Bacon, Francis. *Selected Writings*, pp. 118, 121. New York: Modern Library, 1955.

Baraudiere, Jacques Boyceau de la. Quoted in *The World of André Le Nôtre* by Thierry Mariage, p. 52. Translated from French by Graham Larkin. Philadelphia: University of Pennsylvania Press, 1999.

Baridon, Michel. *Les Jardins: Paysagistes-Jardiniers-Poètes*. Paris: Robert Laffont, 1998.

Barragan, Luis. "1980 Acceptance Speech." The Pritzker Architecture Prize Web site: http://www.pritzkerprize.com/main.htm.

Beales, Peter. *Classic Roses*. New York: Henry Holt, 1997.

Blomfield, Reginald and F. Inigo Thomas. *The Formal Garden in England*, pp. 1–4, 10–11. London: Macmillan, 1892.

Bridgeman, Thomas. *The Florist's Guide*. New York: Author, 1844.

Brookes, John. *Gardens of Paradise: the History and Design of the Great Islamic Gardens*. London: Weidenfield and Nicholson, 1987.

Brown, Lancelot (Capability). Quoted in Roger Turner, *Capability Brown and the Eighteenth-Century English Landscape*, pp. 78–79. New York: Rizzoli International Publications, 1985.

Browne, Thomas. *Hydriotaphia (Urn Burial) and the Garden of Cyrus*. New York: Appleton-Century-Crofts, 1966.

Burke, Edmund. *A Philosophical Enquiry into the Origin of Our Ideas of The Sublime and Beautiful*. Oxford: Oxford University Press, 1990.

Burle Marx, Roberto. *Christian Science Monitor*, August 12, 1986.

Caruncho, Fernando. "Dialogue with a Gardener." In Guy Cooper, *Mirrors of Paradise: The Gardens of Fernando Caruncho*, pp. 22, 23, 25–27. New York: Monacelli Press, 2000.

Chevreul, Michel Eugène, *The Laws of Contrast of Colors and Their Application to the Arts*, p. 180. Translated from French by John Spanton. London: Routledge, Warnes, and Routledge, 1859.

Chevreul, Michel Eugène, *The Principles of Harmony and Contrast of Colors*. New York: Van Nostrand Reinhold, 1967.

Church, Thomas. *Gardens Are for People*, pp. 31–34, 40, 44, 50, 79, 86, 120, 122. New York: McGraw-Hill, 1983.

Clunas, Craig. *Fruitful Sites: Garden Culture in Ming Dynasty China*. Durham, N.C.: Duke University Press, 1996.

Cobbett, William. *American Gardener*, pp. 13–14. New York: Modern Library, 2003.

Colonna, Francesco. *Hypnerotomachia Poliphili: The Strife of Love in a Dream*. Translated by Joscelyn Godwin. London and New York: Thames & Hudson, 1999.

Comito, Terry. *The Idea of the Garden in the Renaissance*. New Brunswick, N.J.: Rutgers University Press, 1978.

Conder, Josiah. *Landscape Gardening in Japan*, pp. 128–32. New York: Dover Publications, 1964.

Corbusier, Le. *The City of Tomorrow and its Planning*, p. 17. New York: Dover Publications, 1987.

Crescenzi, Piero. "Tradition and Transformation: The Pleasure Garden in Piero de' Crescenzi's *Liber Ruralium Commodorum*." Translated from Italian by Johanna Bauman. *Studies in the History of Gardens & Designed Landscapes*, 22, no. 3 (2003): 100–103.

Crowe, Sylvia. *Garden Design*, pp. 81–87. London: Country Life, 1958.

Danby, Hope. *The Garden of Perfect Brightness: The History of the Yüan Ming Yüan and of the Emperors Who Lived There*. London: Williams and Norgate, 1950.

Darke, Rick. *The American Woodland Garden: Capturing the Spirit of the Deciduous Forest*, pp. 107–8, 115, 130, 133, 140, 142, 144, 147–48, 152–53, 160. Portland, Ore.: Timber Press 2002.

Darwin, Charles. *The Formation of Vegetable Mould through the Action of Worms with Observations of their Habits*, pp. 113, 115. Whitefish, Mont.: Kessinger Publishing Company, 2004.

Dash, Robert. *Notes from Madoo: Making a Garden in the Hamptons*, pp. 11–15. Boston: Houghton Mifflin, 2000.

Dezallier d'Argenville, Antoine-Joseph. *The Theory and Practice of Gardening*, pp. 15, 17–20. Translated from French by John James. London: George James, 1712.

Downing, Andrew Jackson. *A Treatise on the Theory and Practice of Landscape Gardening*, pp. 63–67. Little Compton, R.I.: Theophrastus Publishers, 1977.

Eckbo, Garrett. *The Art of Home Landscaping*, pp. 169–80. New York: F.W. Dodge, 1956.

Ettinghausen, Richard. *The Islamic Garden*. Washington, D.C.: Dumbarton Oaks, 1976.

Farrer, Reginald. *Alpines and Bog-Plants*, pp. 259–60, 263–66. London: Edward Arnold, 1908.

Farrer, Reginald. *In a Yorkshire Garden*, pp. 25–27, 29. London: Edward Arnold: 1909.

Foerster, Karl. *Rock Gardens Through the Years*, pp. 10–12, 16–18. Translated from German by Kenneth A. Beckett. New York: Sterling Publishing, 1987.

Forestier, J. C. N. *Gardens: A Notebook of Plans and Sketches*, pp. 49–54. New York: Charles Scribner's Sons, 1928.

Frederick, William H., Jr. "The Artist in his Garden." In Denise Magnani, *The Winterthur Garden: Henry Francis duPont's Romance with the Land*, pp. 31–35. New York: Harry N. Abrams, 1995.

Gentil, François. *The Retir'd Gard'ner*, p. 287. Translated from French by George London and Henry Wise. New York: Garland Publishing, 1982.

Gerritsen, Henk and Piet Oudolf. *Dream Plants for the Natural Garden*. Portland, Ore.: Timber Press, 2000.

Gildemeister, Heidi. *Mediterranean Gardening: A Waterwise Approach*, pp. 34, 37, 40, 42, 45, 46, 50, 52, 54–55, 56, 59–60. Palma de Mallorca: Editorial Moll, 1995. First U.S. edition, 2002. ISBN 84 273 0749 7.

Gildemeister, Heidi. *Gardening the Mediterranean Way*. New York: Harry N. Abrams, 2004.

Girardin, René-Louis de. *An Essay on Landscape*, pp. 1–2, 16–22, 35–38, 102–111 New York: Garland Publishing, Inc., 1982.

Girot, Christophe. "Accepting the Landscape." Written for this book, 2004.

Giustiniani, Vincenzo. "Instructions to a Builder and Gardener." In Melanie Simo, "Vincenzo Giustiniani: His Villa at Bassano di Sutri, near Rome, and His Instructions to a Builder and Gardener." Translation of Giustiniani from Italian by Peter Armour. *Journal of Garden History* 1, no. 3 (1981): 258-59, 265-69.

Goethe, Johann Wolgang von. *Goethe's Theory of Colors,* sections 758-59, 761, 764-66, 769-70, 773-83, 787-90, 796-97, 801-2. Translated from German by Charles Lock Eastlake. London: John Murray, 1840.

Gustafson, Kathryn. "Site and Design." Interview with Scott J. Tilden, August 25, 2004.

Hansen, Richard, and Friedrich Stahl. *Perennials and Their Garden Habitats,* pp. 38-40, 46-47. Translated from German by Richard Ward. Cambridge: Cambridge University Press, and Portland, Ore: Timber Press, 1993.

Harvey, John. *Mediaeval Gardens,* London: B.T. Batsford Ltd., 1981.

Hirschfeld, C.C.L. *The Theory of Garden Art,* pp. 156-59, 203-8. Edited and translated from German by Linda B. Parshall. Philadelphia: University of Pennsylvania Press, 2001.

Hobhouse, Penelope. *Color in Your Garden,* pp. 8-10, 23. Boston: Little, Brown, 1985.

Hobhouse, Penelope. *The History of Gardening.* London: Dorling Kindersley, 2002.

Home, Henry. *Gentleman Farmer. Being an attempt to improve agriculture, by subjecting it to the test of rational principles,* p. viii. Edinburgh: n.p., 1788.

Hunt, John Dixon, editor. *The Dutch Garden in the Seventeenth Century.* Washington, D.C.: Dumbarton Oaks, Trustees for Harvard University, 1990.

Ito, Teiji. "Introduction," *The Japanese Garden: An Approach to Nature,* p. 1. London and New Haven: Yale University Press, 1972.

Itten, Johannes. *Itten: The Elements of Color,* pp. 8, 18. New York: Van Nostrand Reinhold, 1970.

Jefferson, Thomas. "Letter from Jefferson to Charles Willson Peale, Poplar Forest, August 20, 1811." In T*homas Jefferson: The Garden and Farm Books,* edited by Robert C. Baron, p. 199. Golden, Colorado: Fulcrum, 1987.

Jekyll, Gertrude. *The Gardener's Essential Gertrude Jekyll,* pp. 65-70, 172-73, 179-82. Boston: David R. Godine, 1964.

Jellicoe, Geoffrey, et. al. *The Oxford Companion to Gardens.* Oxford: Oxford University Press, 1987.

Jensen, Jens. *Siftings,* pp. 40-43, 47, 53-55, 59. Baltimore: Johns Hopkins University Press, 1990.

Ji, Cheng. *The Craft of Gardens,* pp. 43-46, 51-52, 54, 96, 99-104. Translated from Chinese by Alison Hardie. London and New Haven: Yale University Press, 1988.

Johnston, Stewart R. *Scholar Gardens of China: A Study and Analysis of the Spatial Design of the Chinese Private Garden.* Cambridge: Cambridge University Press, 1991.

Kahn, Louis I. (see Wurman).

Kakuzo, Okakura. *The Book of Tea.* New York: Duffield, 1919.

Kalim of Kashan. "Mughal Gardens in Persian Poetry." Translated by Wheeler M. Thackston. In *Mughal Gardens: Sources, Places, Representations, and Prospects,* edited by James L. Wescoat Jr. and Joachim Wolschke-Bulmahn, p. 244. Washington, D.C.: Dumbarton Oaks, Trustees for Harvard University, 1996.

Kamboh, Muhammed Saleh. "Bahar-e-Sukhan." Translated from Arabic by Abdul Rehman. In "The Mughal Concept of Gardens: An Enquiry into Shah Jahani Sources," *The Mughal Garden: Interpretation, Conservation, and Implications,* edited by Mahmood Hussain, Abdul Rehman, and James L. Wescoat Jr., pp. 118-19. Rawalpindi, India: Ferozsons, 1996.

Keane, Marc P. *Japanese Garden Design,* pp. 118, 125, 131, 132, 136-43. Rutland, Vt.: Charles E. Tuttle, 1996.

Keswick, Maggie. *The Chinese Garden: History, Art, and Architecture.* Cambridge, Mass.: Harvard University Press, 2003.

Kiley, Dan, and Jane Amidon. *Dan Kiley: The Complete Works of America's Master Landscape Architect,* pp. 13-14, 54, 92, 136. Boston: Bulfinch Press, 1999.

Kuitert, Wybe. *Themes, Scenes, and Taste in the History of Japanese Garden Art.* Amsterdam: J. C. Gieben, 1988.

Langley, Batty. *New Principles of Gardening.* London: A. Bettesworth and J. Batley, 1728.

Lahawri, Abdul-Hamid. "Pâdishâhnâma." Translated by Wheeler M. Thackston. In *Mughal Gardens: Sources, Places, Representations, and Prospects,* edited by James L. Wescoat Jr. and Joachim Wolschke-Bulmahn, pp. 250-52, 257. Washington, D.C.: Dumbarton Oaks, Trustees for Harvard University, 1996.

Le Blond, Alexandre. "The Theory and Practice of Gardening" (1712). In Joseph Wood Krutch, *The Gardener's World,* pp. 134-35. New York: G. P. Putnam's Sons, 1959.

Le Dantec, Denise, and Jean Pierre Le Dantec, *Reading the French Garden: Story and History.* Cambridge, Mass.: MIT Press, 1990.

Lennox-Boyd, Arabella, and Caroline Clifton-Mogg. *Designing Gardens,* p. 13. London: Frances Lincoln, 2002.

Ligne de, Charles-Joseph. *Coup d'Oeil at Belœil and a Great Number of European Gardens,* pp. 111, 120-22, 125, 133, 180, 182-83. Translated from French by Basil Guy. Berkeley: University of California Press, 1991.

Lille, Abbé Jacques de. *The Garden or, The Art of Laying Out Grounds,* pp. 4-5, 7-10, 53-54. Dublin: Zachariah Jackson, 1791.

Liu, Dunzhen. *Classical Gardens of Suzhou,* pp. 45-48. Translated from Chinese by Chen Lixian. New York: McGraw-Hill, 1992.

Lloyd, Christopher. *The Well-Chosen Garden.* New York: Harper & Row, 1984.

Loudon, Jane Webb. *Gardening for Ladies and Companion to the Flower Garden,* edited by A. J. Downing. New York: Wiley & Putnam, 1848.

Ibn Luyun. "The Islamic Garden in Spain." Translated from Arabic by James Dickie. In *The Islamic Garden,* edited by E. B. MacDougall and Richard Ettinghausen, p. 94. Washington D.C.: Dumbarton Oaks, 1976.

McHarg, Ian L. *Design with Nature,* p. 71. Garden City, N.Y.: Doubleday & Company, 1971.

Maqqari, al-. *Analectes.* In D. Fairchild Ruggles, *Gardens, Landscape & Vision in the Places of Islamic Spain,* p. 50. University Park: Pennsylvania State University Press, 2000.

Martino, Steve. "Desert Gardens." *The Environmental Gardener, Plants & Gardens,* pp. 88-91. Brooklyn: Brooklyn Botanic Garden, 1992.

Mason, William. Selection from Stephen Bending, "William Mason's 'An Essay on the Arrangement of Flowers in Pleasure-Grounds,'" *Journal of Garden History* 9, no. 4 (1989): 219-20.

Masuno, Shunmyo. *Inside Japanese Gardens: From Basics to Planning, Management and Improvement.* Osaka: Commemorative Foundation for the International Garden and Greenery Exposition, 1990.

Masuno, Shunmyo. *Ten Landscapes.* Rockport, Mass.: Rockport Publishers, 1999.

Masuno, Shunmyo. Quoted in "Landscapes in the Spirit of Zen: A Collection of the Work of Shunmyo Masuno," *Process: Architecture* 7 (1995): 8-10.

Masuno, Shunmyo. Quoted in Kim Schuefftan, "Landscapes of the Spirit: The Gardens and Spaces of Shunmyo Masuno," *Japanese Things* (1996): 29.

McHarg, Ian L. *Design with Nature,* p. 71. Garden City, N.Y.: Doubleday, 1971.

Mollet, André. *The Garden of Pleasure,* pp. 1-2, 9-10. London: T.N. for John Martyn and Henry Herringman, 1670 (University Microfilms).

Moore, Charles W., William J. Mitchell, and William Turnbull Jr. *The Poetics of Gardens.* Cambridge, Mass.: MIT Press, 1988.

Morris, Edwin. *The Gardens of China: History, Art, and Meanings,* pp. 123-29. New York: Charles Scribner's Sons, 1983.

Morris, William. *Hopes and Fears for Art. Five Lectures by William Morris.* London: Longmans, Green, and Company, 1919.

Nakane, Kinsaku. *Kyoto Gardens,* pp. 109-11. Osaka: Hoikusha Publishing Company, 1965.

Nakane, Shiro. "The Structure in the Japanese Garden." Written for this book, 2004.

Nichols, Rose Standish. *English Pleasure Gardens.* Boston: David R. Godine, 2003.

Nitschke, Günter. *Japanese Gardens: Right Angles and Natural Form.* Cologne: Taschen, 1999.

Norberg-Schulz, Christian. *Towards a Phenomenology of Architecture.* New York: Rizzoli International Publications, 1979.

Nusrati (Gulshan-i'Ishq). "Rose Garden of Love," In Ali Akbar Husain, *Scent in the Islamic Garden: A Study of Deccani Urdu Literary Sources,* pp. 244-45, 247-48. London: Oxford University Press, 2000.

Olmsted, Frederick Law. Quoted in Charles Beveridge, *Frederick Law Olmsted: Designing the American Landscape,* p. 137. New York: Rizzoli International Publications, 1995.

Olmsted, Frederick Law. "Plan for a Small Homestead," *Garden and Forest.* New York: The Garden and Forest Publishing Company, May 2, 1888.

Oudolf, Piet, and Noël Kingsbury. *Designing with Plants,* pp. 16-18, 20, 22, 24, 26, 28. Portland, Ore: Timber Press, 1999.

Page, Russell. *The Education of a Gardener,* pp. 175-78, 181-82, 187. Harmondsworth, England: Penguin Books, 1962.

Palladio, Andrea. *The Four Books on Architecture,* p. 47. Translated from Italian by Isaac Ware. New York: Dover Publications, 1965.

Pliny the Younger. *The Letters of the Younger Pliny,* pp. 139-40, 142-44. Translated from Latin by Betty Radice. Harmondsworth, England: Penguin Books, 1969.

Po Chu-i. "The Pine Trees in the Courtyard." Translated from Chinese by Arthur Waley. In *Anthology of Chinese Literature: From Early Times to the Fourteenth Century,* edited by Cyril Birch, p. 52. New York: Grove Press, 1965.

Poe, Edgar Allan. "The Domain of Arnheim or the Landscape Garden" In *The Complete Tales and Poems of Edgar Allan Poe,* pp. 607, 612. New York: Vintage Books. 1975.

Pollio, Marcus Vitruvius. *Ten Books on Architecture,* translated by Morris Hickey Morgan, p. 13. New York: Dover Publications, 1960.

Pope, Alexander. "An Epistle to Lord Burlington." *The Genius of the Place: The English Landscape Garden 1620-1820,* edited by John Dixon Hunt and Peter Willis, p. 211. London: Paul Elek, 1975.

Pückler-Muscau, Prince von. *Hints on Landscape Gardening,* pp. 42-47. Translated by Bernhard Sickert, Boston: Houghton Mifflin, 1917.

Qian, Long. Quoted in Hope Danby, *The Garden of Perfect Brightness: The History of the Yüan Ming Yüan and of the Emperors who lived there,* p. 13. London: Williams and Norgate, 1950.

Qi Biaojia. Selection from "Qi Biaojia's 'Footnotes to Allegory Mountain.'" Translated from Chinese by Duncan Campbell. *Studies in the History of Gardens & Designed Landscapes* 19, no. 3/4 (1999): 246-47.

Quintinye, Jean-Baptiste de la. *The Compleat Gard'ner,* pp. 29-32, 35-36. Translated from French by John Evelyn. London: Matthew Gillyflower, 1693.

Rapin, René. *Of Gardens,* pp. 118-20, 123-25, 143. Translated from French by Mr. Gardiner. London: Bernard Lintot, 1728.

Repton, Humphry. *An Enquiry into the Changes of Taste in Landscape Gardening,* pp. 35-41. London: J. Taylor, 1806.

Repton, Humphry. *Fragments on the Theory and Practice of Landscape Gardening,* pp. 97-100. New York: Garland Publishing, 1982.

Robinson, William. *The English Flower Garden and Home Grounds,* pp. 103-5, 108-9. London: John Murray, 1900.

Robinson, William. *The Wild Garden.* London: Century Publishing, 1983.

Rodale, J. I. *Pay Dirt.* Emmaus, Pa.: Rodale Press, 1945.

Rogers, Elizabeth Barlow. *Landscape Design: A Cultural and Architectural History.* New York: Harry N. Abrams, 2001.

Rousseau, Jean-Jacques. *Julie, ou la nouvelle Heloïse,* p. 396. Translated from French by Philip Stewart and Jean Vaché. Volume 6 of The Collected Writings of Rousseau. Hanover, N.H.: University Press of New England, 1997.

Rousseau, Jean-Jacques. *Reveries of the Solitary Walker,* p. 115, Translated from French by Peter France. Harmondsworth, England: Penguin Books, 1979.

Ruggles, Fairchild D. *Gardens, Landscape & Vision in the Places of Islamic Spain.* University Park, Pa: Pennsylvania State University Press, 2000.

Ruskin, John. *The Poetry of Architecture: Cottage, Villa, Etc.,* p. 185. New York: John Wiley & Sons, 1873.

Sackville-West, Vita. *In Your Garden Again.* London, England: Michael Joseph, 1953.

Sackville-West, Vita. *Joy of Gardening,* pp. 33-36. New York: Harper & Brothers, 1958.

Sackville-West, Vita. *More for Your Garden,* pp. 69-70. London: Michael Joseph, 1955.

Salazar, Cervantes de. Quoted in "Concept of the Garden in Pre-Hispanic Mexico" by Patrizia Granziera. *Garden History, The Journal of the Garden History Society* 29, no. 2 (Winter 2001): 188.

Shen, Fu. *Six Records of a Floating Life.* Translated from Chinese by Leonard Pratt and Chiang Su-hui. Harmondsworth, England: Penguin Books, 1983.

Shepherd, J.C., and G.A. Jellicoe. *Italian Gardens of the Renaissance.* New York: Princeton Architectural Press, 1993.

Shigemori, Mirei. *Gardens of Japan,* pp. 63-66. Tokyo: Nissha, 1949.

Sima Guang. "The Garden of Solitary Delight," *The Craft of Gardens,* pp. 123-24. Translated from Chinese by Alison Hardie. London and New Haven: Yale University Press, 1988.

Sitwell, George. *On the Making of Gardens.* Boston: David R. Godine, 2003.

Spence, Joseph. "Letter to Rev. Mr. Wheeler." In *The Genius of Place: The English Landscape Garden 1620-1820,* edited by John Dixon Hunt and Peter Willis, pp. 268-70. London: Paul Elek, 1975.

Steele, Fletcher. *Gardens and People: A Book about the Art of Harmony Between Man and his Land,* pp. 34-36, 72-75. Boston: Houghton Mifflin, 1964.

Strabo, Walafrid. Verses 19-22. In *Hortulus.* Translated from Latin by Richard Stanton Lambert. Wembley Hill: Stanton Press, 1923.

Sweden, James van. *Gardening with Nature: How James van Sweden and Wolfgang Oehme Plant Slopes, Meadows, Outdoor Rooms, and Garden Screens,* pp. 25-27, 160-61. New York: Random House, 1997.

Sweden, James van, and Tom Christopher. *Architecture in the Garden.* New York: Random House, 2003.

Tachibana no Toshitsuna. *Sakuteiki: Visions of the Japanese Garden,* pp. 157-58, 175-89. Translated from Japanese by Jiro Takei and Marc P. Keane. Boston: Tuttle Publishing, 2001.

Tange, Kenzo and Walter Gropius. *Katsura: Tradition and Creation in Japanese Architecture,* p. 34. London and New Haven: Yale University Press, 1960.

Thackston, Wheeler M., editor and translator. *The Baburnama: Memoirs of Babur, Prince, and Emperor.* New York: Oxford University Press, 1996.

Thomas, Graham Stuart. "Old Roses in the Garden," *The Old Shrub Roses,* pp. 44-47. London: J. M. Dent & Sons, 1978.

Thomas, Graham Stuart. *Cuttings from my Garden Notebooks.* Sagaponack, N.Y.: Sagapress, Inc., 1997.

Turner, Roger. *Capability Brown and the Eighteenth-Century English Landscape.* New York: Rizzoli International Publications, 1985.

Udemans, Godefridus. *"Geestelijck Roer van't Coopmans Schip."* In "The Dutch Garden in the Seventeenth Century," *Dumbarton Oaks Colloquium on the History of Landscape Architecture* XII, edited by John Dixon Hunt. Washington, D.C.: Dumbarton Oaks, Trustees for Harvard University, 1990.

Verey, Rosemary. *Good Planting,* pp. 120, 122, 127-28, 131-32, 134. New York: Barnes & Noble Books, 2001.

Virgil. *Eclogues, Georgics, Aeneid -6.* Translated from Latin by H. R. Fairclough. Cambridge, Mass.: Harvard University Press, 1994.

Walker, Peter. "Minimalism in the Garden." Written for this book, 2004.

Walker, Peter, and Melanie Simo. *Invisible Gardens: The Search for Modernism in the American Landscape.* Cambridge, Mass.: MIT Press, 1998.

Walpole, Horace. *The History of the Modern Taste in Gardening,* p. 58. New York: Ursus Press, 1995.

Wang, Shizhen. Quoted in Kenneth J. Hammond, "Wang Shizhen's Yan Shan Garden Essays: Narrating a Literati Landscape," *Studies in the History of Gardens & Designed Landscapes* 19, no. 3/4 (Autumn/Winter 1999): 285.

Warner, Charles Dudley. *My Summer in a Garden,* p. 14. New York: Modern Library, 2002.

Watelet, Claude-Henri. "The Garden of Mr. Watelet Near Paris. A Letter to a Friend." Translated from French by Samuel Danon. In C. C. L. Hirschfeld, *The Theory of Garden Art,* pp. 87-92. Philadelphia: University of Pennsylvania Press, 2001.

Wharton, Edith. *Italian Villas and Their Gardens,* pp. 5-12. New York: Da Capo Press, 1976.

Wilber, Donald Newton. *Persian Gardens and Garden Pavilions.* Washington, D.C.: Dumbarton Oaks, Trustees for Harvard University, 1979.

Woolridge, John. *Systema Horti-Culturae: or The Art of Gardening.* In *The Genius of Place: The English Landscape Garden 1620-1820,* edited by John Dixon Hunt and Peter Willis, p. 89. London: Paul Elek, 1975.

Wurman, Richard Saul, and Eugene Feldman, eds. *Notebooks and Drawings of Louis I. Kahn.* Philadelphia: Falcon Press, 1962.

Xiao, Jiucheng. Quoted in "The Confucian Role of Names in Traditional Chinese Gardens" by John Markham. *Studies in the History of Gardens & Designed Landscapes* 18, no. 3 (Autumn 1998): 189.

Yao, He. Quoted in "The Confucian Role of Names in Traditional Chinese Gardens" by John Markham. *Studies in the History of Gardens & Designed Landscapes* 18, no. 3 (Autumn 1998): 189.

Zheng Yuanxun. Quoted in "The Confucian Role of Names in Traditional Chinese Gardens" by John Markham. *Studies in the History of Gardens & Designed Landscapes* 18, no. 3 (Autumn 1998): 188.

Zoen. *Secret Teachings in the Art of Japanese Gardens: Design Principles Aesthetic Values,* paragraphs 1, 2, 10, 13, 17, 18, 18, 20, 21, 22. Translated from Japanese by David A. Slawson. Tokyo: Kodansha International, 1987.

EDITOR

Barbara Burn

DESIGN

HvAD Henk van Assen and Amanda Bowers

PRODUCTION MANAGER

Jane Searle

Library of Congress Cataloging-in-Publication Data

The glory of gardens : 2,000 years of writings on garden design / edited by Scott J. Tilden.

    p.   cm.

ISBN 0-8109-5541-5 (hardcover)

1. Gardens. 2. Gardens–Design. I. Tilden, Scott J.

SB455.G56 2005

712—dc22

           2005024442

Printed and bound in China

10 9 8 7 6 5 4 3 2 1

HNA ■■□□□

harry n. abrams, inc.

a subsidiary of La Martinière Groupe

115 West 18th Street

New York, NY 10011

www.hnabooks.com

The editor and publishers wish to thank the following for permission to use copyright material from:

Brooklyn Botanic Garden for excerpts from "Desert Gardens" by Steve Martino, *The Environmental Gardener,* copyright © Steve Martino 1992.

Cambridge University Press for excerpts from *Perennials and Their Garden Habitats,* copyright © Richard Hansen and Friedrich Stahl 1993.

Fernando Caruncho for excerpts from his interview, which appeared in "Dialogue with a Gardener," *Mirrors of Paradise: The Gardens of Fernando Caruncho,* by Guy Cooper and Gordon Taylor 2000.

Curtis Brown Group, Ltd. for excerpts from *In Your Garden* and *More for Your Garden,* copyright © 1951 and 1955 by the Estate of Vita Sackville-West.

Heidi Gildemeister for excerpts from *Mediterranean Gardening: A Waterwise Approach,* copyright © Heidi Gildemeister 1995.

Basil Guy for excerpts from *Coup d'Œil at Beloeil and a Great Number of European Gardens* by Prince Charles-Joseph de Ligne, translated and edited by Basil Guy, copyright © Basil Guy 1991.

Dumbarton Oaks for excerpts from "The Islamic Garden in Spain" by James Dickie in *The Islamic Garden,* edited by Elisabeth MacDougall and Richard Ettinghausen, copyright © Dumbarton Oaks, Trustees for Harvard University 1976.

Houghton Mifflin Company for excerpts from *Gardens and People,* copyright © Fletcher Steele 1954.

Houghton Mifflin Company for excerpts from *Notes from Madoo: Making a Garden in the Hamptons,* copyright © Robert Dash 2000.

Kodansha International Ltd. for excerpts from *Secret Teachings in the Art of Japanese Gardens* by David A. Slawson, copyright © Kodansha International Ltd. 1987.

Frances Lincoln Ltd. for excerpts from *The Graham Stuart Thomas Rose Book,* copyright ©The Estate of Graham Stuart Thomas 2004.

Frances Lincoln Ltd. for excerpts from *Colour in Your Garden,* copyright © Penelope Hobhouse 1985.

Frances Lincoln Ltd. for excerpts from *Good Planting,* copyright © Rosemary Verey 1990.

Little, Brown & Company for excerpts from *Dan Kiley: The Complete Works of America's Master Landscape Architect* by James Amidon and Dan Kiley, copyright © The Office of Dan Kiley 1999.

McGraw-Hill Companies for excerpts from *Chinese Classical Gardens of Suzhou* by Liu Dunzhen, copyright © McGraw-Hill, Inc. 1993.

The MIT Press for excerpts from *Leon Battista Alberti/On the Art of Building in Ten Books,* translated by Joseph Rykwert, Neil Leach, and Robert Tavernor, copyright © Joseph Rykwert and Robert Tavernor 1988.

Henry Francis du Pont Winterthur Museum for excerpts from *The Winterthur Garden: Henry Francis du Pont's Romance with the Land* by Denise Magnani, et al., copyright © Henry Francis du Pont Winterthur Museum 1995.

Oxford University Press for excerpts from *Scent in the Islamic Garden: A Study of Deccani Urdu Literary Sources* by Ali Akbar Husain, copyright © Oxford University Press, Pakistan, 2000.

Random House, Inc. for excerpts from *Gardening with Nature* by James van Sweden, copyright © Oehme, van Sweden and Associates, Inc. 1997.

Abdul Rehman for excerpts from his translation of "Bahar-e-Sukhan" by Muhammed Saleh Kamboh, which appeared in *The Mughal Garden: Interpretation, Conservation, and Implications,* edited by James L. Wescoat, Jr. 1996.

Taylor & Francis for excerpts from "Qi Biaojia's 'Footnotes to Allegory Mountain'" by Duncan Campbell, *Studies in the History of Gardens & Designed Landscapes,* copyright © Taylor & Francis 1999.

Taylor & Francis for excerpts from "Tradition & Transformation: The Pleasure Garden in Piero de'Crescenzi's Liber Ruralium Commodorum" by Johanna Bauman, *Studies in the History of Gardens & Designed Landscapes,* copyright © Taylor & Francis 2002.

Taylor & Francis for excerpts from "Vincenzo Giustiniani: his villa at Bassano di Sutri, near Rome, and his Instructions to a Builder and Gardener," *Journal of Garden History,* copyright © Taylor & Francis 1981.

W. M. Thackston for excerpts from his translation of the poem "Padishahnama" by Abdul-Hamid Lahawri, which appeared in *Mughal Gardens: Sources, Places, Representations, and Prospects,* edited by James L. Wescoat, Jr. 1996.

Timber Press for excerpts from *Designing with Plants,* copyright © Piet Oudolf and Noël Kingsbury 1999.

Timber Press for excerpts from *The American Woodland Garden: Capturing the Spirit of the Deciduous Forest,* copyright © Rick Darke 2002.

Charles E. Tuttle Company, Inc., for excerpts from *Japanese Garden Design* by Marc P. Keane, copyright © Charles E. Tuttle Publishing Company, Inc. 1996.

Tuttle Publishing, an imprint of Periplus Editions (HK) Ltd., for excerpts from *Sakuteiki: Visions of the Japanese Garden,* translated by Jiro Takei and Marc P. Keane, copyright © Jiro Takei and Marc P. Keane 2001.

University of Pennsylvania Press for excerpts from *Theory of Garden Art* by C. C. L. Hirschfeld, edited and translated by Linda B. Parshall, copyright © University of Pennsylvania Press 2001.

Yale University Press for excerpts from *The Craft of Gardens/ Ji Cheng,* translated by Alison Hardie, copyright © Alison Hardie 1988.

Zokeisha Publications, Ltd., for excerpts from *Katsura: Tradition and Creation in Japanese Architecture* by Walter Gropius and Kenzo Tange, copyright © Zokeisha Publications, Ltd. 1960.

Every effort has been made to trace the copyright holders, but if any have been inadvertently overlooked, the publishers will be pleased to make the necessary arrangements at the first opportunity.